Praise for *E*

"In this excellent collection of essays, biologist Steven L. Peck has interwoven his unique and thoughtful insights on the complex intersection of science and his personal commitment to faith. As a first-rate scientist who thinks intensely about the meaning and rigor of scientific inquiry, and as an exceptionally gifted writer, he shares with readers the value of science from a powerful perspective in captivating prose."

> —DANIEL J. FAIRBANKS
> Dean of Science and Health
> Utah Valley University
> Author of *Everyone Is African, Evolving,* and *Relics of Eden* and coauthor of *Ending the Mendel-Fisher Controversy*

"With the meticulousness of a scientist who has spent years in the laboratory and in the field honing his skill, Peck has dissected his religion—his most precious and most deeply held beliefs—with the incisive blade of evidence-based logic. He displays his work here as a true entomologist would: in a beautifully arrayed display of his most exquisite words, artfully chosen to share with the world. Whether you're a scientist, a faithful member of the LDS faith, neither, or both, your mind will be enlightened and your faith strengthened by *Evolving Faith: Wanderings of a Mormon Biologist.*"

> —ANDREA PRATT REDISKE
> MS, Microbiology
> Doctoral student in Science Education
> University of Central Florida

"Wrap up in one Latter-day Saint someone with professional-level training and publications in physics, philosophy, theology, mathematics, ecology, and evolutionary biology—not to mention fictional writing—and you've got Steven L. Peck. No other LDS author has possessed the broad vision Peck uses to explore basic dimensions in the debates about science and religion. Beyond any others, Peck outlines insightful philosophical and theological paths toward a productive synthesis.

His writing is engaging, his thinking incisive, and his suggestions provocative. This book of collected essays is a groundbreaking resource for serious students of LDS theology in relation to the rapidly expanding advances of modern science."

—DUANE E. JEFFERY
Emeritus Professor of Biology
Brigham Young University

"Peck's writing and storytelling is entertaining and compelling. His approach of utilizing faith as part of rational pursuits is strong but not alienating. This accessible collection of essays reflects the hand of a bright scientist and a devoted person of faith."

—JANI RADEBAUGH
Associate Professor of Geological Sciences
Brigham Young University

"In his latest work, biologist Steven Peck's own famously polymath brain is itself under the microscope, and what a fascinating specimen it is! We see an eclectic collection of approaches—scientific, theoretical, theological, and personal—combined in an unmistakably loving way, offering a model for how religious believers can flourish in a science-driven world many fear is increasingly hostile to faith."

—CYNTHIA BAILEY LEE
Computer Science Department lecturer
Stanford University

EVOLVING FAITH

WANDERINGS OF A MORMON BIOLOGIST

STEVEN L. PECK

NEAL A. MAXWELL
INSTITUTE *for*
RELIGIOUS SCHOLARSHIP

Brigham Young University
Provo, Utah

To the Waters family—they have blessed my own in so many ways

To all in the village I seemed, no doubt,
To go this way and that way, aimlessly.
But here by the river you can see at twilight
The soft-winged bats fly zig-zag here and there—
They must fly so to catch their food.
And if you have ever lost your way at night,
In the deep wood near Miller's Ford,
And dodged this way and now that,
Wherever the light of the Milky Way shone through,
Trying to find the path,
You should understand I sought the way
With earnest zeal, and all my wanderings
Were wanderings in the quest.

"William Goode" (no. 220)
Edgar Lee Masters (1868–1950)
Spoon River Anthology, 1916

Permissions. No portion of this book may be reproduced by any means or process without the formal written consent of the publisher. Direct all permissions requests to: Permissions Manager, Neal A. Maxwell Institute for Religious Scholarship, Brigham Young University, Provo, UT 84602.

Library of Congress Cataloging-in-Publication Data

Peck, Steven L., 1957- author.
Evolving faith : wanderings of a Mormon biologist / Steven L. Peck.
    pages cm
ISBN 978-0-8425-2944-0 (trade paper : alk. paper) — ISBN 978-0-8425-2945-7 (e pub) — ISBN 978-0-8425-2946-4 (kindle)
1. Religion and science. 2. Church of Jesus Christ of Latter-day Saints—Doctrines. I. Title.
BL240.3.P435 2015
261.5'5 — dc23   2015031365

Cover design: Ben Dougal
Book design: Andrew Heiss

"The Red Wheelbarrow," by William Carlos Williams, from *The Collected Poems: Volume I, 1909-1939*, copyright © 1938 by New Directions Publishing Corp. Reprinted by permission of New Directions Publishing Corp.

∞ The paper used in this publication meets the minimum requirements of the American National Standard for Information Sciences—Permanence of Paper for Printed Library Materials. ANSI Z39.48-1992.

Printed in the United States of America

maxwellinstitute.byu.edu

Contents

Foreword

AFTER JOB AND HIS FRIENDS HAVE EXPENDED their energy talking through possible meanings of Job's losses—not the least of which is the possible absence of God in the righteous man's life—the Lord finally comes and speaks to him. What is surprising is how little the Lord's instructions initially seem to pertain directly to Job's suffering. The Lord instead wishes to ask Job a few questions about what he knows about the earth and the universe. He asks, "Hast thou walked in the search of the depth? . . . Hast thou perceived the breadth of the earth? declare if thou knowest it all" (Job 38:16, 18). Does he know anything about the tides, the sea, the fishes, the atmosphere, the rain, the sky-roaming fowl? Does he know anything about the wild goats, the leviathan, the behemoth? Job remains silent and listens. He comes to understand that he belongs in a far more complex, wondrous, and strange universe than he had imagined and that the Lord—although chiefly concerned with his children—also has myriad creations on this planet and throughout the vast universe that require his attention and love. The Lord is the kind of divine sovereign who "searcheth after every green thing" (39:8).

Seeking to understand life, the universe, and everything (to borrow a phrase from Douglas Adams) is an infinite, impossible, and yet indispensable human task that seems to mimic the divine mind. And the story of Job suggests that although it might diminish us to have to pay attention to the world around us, ultimately the wonder that such attention inspires is healing and redemptive. Joseph Smith's revealed account of Moses helps us to understand why awe—the kind of awe we experience when we contemplate the miracle of the oceans, of the galaxies, or even just the miracle of photosynthesis in a plant—would be healing. When the Lord shared the immensity of his creations with Moses, it left him momentarily speechless and stunned. Moses collapsed, presumably overwhelmed by what he had seen, and concluded, "For this cause I know that man is nothing, which thing I never had supposed" (Moses 1:10). Given his deep sense of nothingness, we might expect Moses to capitulate to the apparently mighty Satan. Instead, Moses's profound humility seems to give him renewed determination to resist his temptations. His experience of awe does not crush him entirely because he understands that God knows and loves him, that he is created in God's image, and that he has the human privilege to learn and appreciate the rest of God's creations. Awareness of the love that pervades the universe is precisely what allows Moses to experience awe instead of shame or despair. Instead of lamenting that he is not unique as he had supposed, he rejoices in his newly discovered membership in a vast community of life. The prerequisites for such healing awe include sufficient curiosity and humility. Theologian William Brown was persuaded, after a careful study of the Bible's various meditations on the creation, that perhaps what makes us exceptional in the creation isn't so much our capacity for knowledge but our capacity for awe, leading him to wonder if we shouldn't rename ourselves from *homo sapiens* (knowing man) to *homo admirans* (wondering man).[1]

Steve Peck is a wondering man, and in your hands are the distilled results of years of his wondering. He is brilliant—a "knowing man" to be sure, well-informed about a lot of things. He reads promiscuously and widely, rarely settling on just one field or topic. To call him an entomologist, which is his area of specialization, does not do his mind justice. He relishes the chance to explore the most far-reaching implications of science, but he also devours philosophy and many other genres of literature. On campus at Brigham Young University he is as comfortable with a group of scientists as he is with a group of poets. He may very well be the most balanced intellect between the sciences and the humanities that BYU has ever seen. And his publication record suggests he is more than a dilettante. His publications as a novelist, poet, essayist, philosopher, and scientist often move across traditional disciplines and boundaries. His fiction, for example, has appeared in one of the top science journals in the world, *Nature*, and his science has appeared in the leading science fiction journal, *Analog*.[2] His entomological research is well known and well regarded in his field, but he has also published in leading philosophy journals.

When I first got to know Steve years ago, I was drawn to his smarts. I knew I could learn a lot from him. He and I decided to team teach a class on religion and the environment, and it was an unforgettable semester.

We had brilliant students, and Steve's mind was a burning fire of ideas. But more than his impressive knowledge, what stood out to me was his exceptional and exuberant capacity for awe and wonder. In the best sense, Steve Peck is still a child—excitable, incurably curious, constitutionally humble, passionate, earnest, eager, even giddy when he comes upon a new insight. He is good company, as you will discover in this collection, because every conversation with Steve feels like you are standing on the precipice of discovery.

Unlike some children, however, he listens, he is willing to change his mind, and he has the maturity to keep the process of inquiry free, fun, and exploratory. Broad and hungry reading allows him to catch more glimpses of what different fields of knowledge can't see, how they might complement each other, and what might lie beyond what we presently understand. Because of his appetite for learning, you won't find much in the way of definitive dogma in this book. Steve is serious about thinking, but he doesn't take himself too seriously. He is a speculator. In the financial sense of the word, this means that he is willing to wage his bets on hidden value, to take higher risks for higher yield. *No sense in sitting on what we already know,* he seems to say. *What would be the point of that?* That's because for Steve knowledge is to be invested in questions that we wonder about and things we would like to understand better. If nothing else, his practice of creative thinking helps to protect himself against staid, stale, or borrowed thinking.

Unlike high-risk speculators, however, Steve is not willing to trade on the knowledge he has already gained, especially sacred knowledge. Indeed, it is the sacred that provides the down payment on his responsible speculation. What interests him is a growth of understanding regarding what he already knows. It is one thing to have truth. It is another thing altogether to understand truth. Understanding requires asking questions, teasing out possibilities, recognizing and wondering about what we don't know. Without a sense of mystery surrounding what we know, we stand little chance of learning more. As William Brown puts it, "'Mystery' . . . is being grasped by something larger than ourselves, ever compelling us to stretch, rather than limit, the horizons of our experience."[3]

Speculate has another connotation besides the financial, one that suggests the value of our climbing to lofty heights so as to look into the distance before us. To neglect the power of our own imagination or to act as though mental work plays no role in how well or how poorly we understand truth is to falsely pretend that truth is merely information. Steve understands that knowledge is not a *thing* but a *relationship*—particularly between a loving and revelatory God, a fascinating and complex world, and our utterly unique personalities and imaginations. As such, knowledge needs *us* to move around and shift perspective from time to time.

The fate of science in the twenty-first century provides an important reminder that knowledge is only as valuable as we make it. Indeed, collectively we humans now know far more than Job about the leviathan, the tides, the atmosphere, the wild goats, and even the cosmos itself—more than ever before in the history of humankind. But it is fair to wonder why this knowledge doesn't inform our day-to-day lives more than it does. We must ask why with all of this knowledge we are failing so profoundly in our God-given responsibility to care for the creation. Where previous generations could claim that the horizons of knowledge were simply too limited to facilitate responsible stewardship, our only excuse now seems to be a kind of willful ignorance. And what a pity when our scientific knowledge has been so hard-earned. Indeed, it took humanity the better part of its history to begin comprehending just a portion of what Job and Moses witnessed. Scientific knowledge has come slow and not without struggle by limited human beings. A number of significant revolutions of thought have been resisted because they seemed to threaten our fundamental beliefs: the Copernican revolution unsettled our notion that this earth was the center of the universe, the Huttonian revolution exploded our timeline of the earth's age, the Darwinian revolution challenged our assumptions about the origins and development of biological life, and Hubble's law shattered our confidence in a static and relatively circumscribed universe.

In each case, religion and science have appeared at first to be at odds only to then benefit from the work of creative and faithful thinkers who, like Steve, have helped them to settle into a more mutually enriched relationship. This book is merely a sampling of the paths of knowledge and faith Steve has wandered; it is offered with hope that others will be inspired to confidently seek greater light and knowledge. Of course, there are always doubters all around, and there are individual thinkers who take more liberty than is merited—either by scientific understanding or by revelation—to declare what they think they know about such matters as, for example, proof for the existence or nonexistence of God or for the age of the earth. We would do well to remember the timeless wisdom often attributed to Galileo: "The Bible tells us how to go to Heaven, not how Heaven goes."[4] Empirical knowledge and spiritual knowledge, he insists, involve two different epistemologies: "I do not feel obliged to believe that the same God who has endowed us with senses, reason and intellect has intended us to forego their use and by some other means to give us knowledge which we can attain by them."[5] Galileo's was the era when theology was the queen of the sciences, believed to hold a proper understanding of every matter, moral *and* empirical. Galileo taught us the value of a temporary suspension of disbelief when considering empirical information that appears to contradict religion.[6] He taught the value of letting science and religion speak their respective languages. As philosopher of science Michel Serres tells us, science speaks in the indicative tense while religion speaks in the imperative.[7] It is a difference between learning *what is* and learning *what we ought to do*. No need, then, to see them as oppositional.

In theory and in doctrine, even if not always in practice, Mormonism welcomes science. *Evolving Faith* joins a rich but often underappreciated tradition of the Latter-day Saint embrace of science. Brigham Young encouraged such thinking when he said, "Teach [students] in their childhood the names and properties of every flower and plant. . . . When they are old enough, place within their reach the advantages of a scientific education. Let them study the formations of the earth, the organization of the human system, and other sciences. . . . It is the duty of the Latter-day Saints, according to revelations, to give their children the best educations that can be procured, both from the books of the world and the revelations of the Lord."[8]

When they are well understood, scientific truths, although not essential to our salvation, are essential for improving life—human and nonhuman—and for appreciating and protecting the grandeur of the gift of creation. Only a narrow and penurious appetite for truth would dismiss science simply for being "secular" knowledge. Let us not forget Brigham Young's teaching that *all truth* belongs to Mormonism no matter its source, or the famous Mormon scientist Henry Eyring's suggestion that we have nothing to fear because "in this Church you don't have to believe anything that isn't true."[9] It is the aim of the restoration to make all knowledge sacred. In the meantime, when things seem mysterious or hard to reconcile, our community needs curious minds, broad interdisciplinary thinking, and bold creativity. What a shame it would be to guide ourselves by the light of the restoration, all the while assuming that *our current understanding* of the restoration is sufficient, that it needs no adjustments or improvements. What a shame it would be to assume that this grandest of settings for our small and beautiful lives on this stunning blue ball of a planet doesn't merit our greatest reverence, curiosity, and most careful stewardship.

Nothing in this book suggests that the understanding of contemporary science provides us with the equivalent of God's knowledge. Indeed, Steve is staunchly critical, and justifiably so, of scientistic overreach. Despite the advances in human knowledge, the Lord's interrogations of Job apply to us today because there is still plenty to wonder about, as these essays make clear. But we must confess that at least part of the reason we could still use a good lecture from the Lord about the creation has to do with our utter neglect of the science we already have. Collectively we might be in possession of a great deal of information, but do we take individual responsibility to understand science? How much do we know—individually—about the planets, about the fishes of the sea, about how the earth regulates the climate, or about how life generates life? Indeed, Steve is just as adamant that we believers too often dismiss science for its contingent and partial understanding of things, that we too frequently condemn it for what appear to be contradictions with revelation or received tradition. What a waste when we could instead be doing the hard and fun work of speculating and asking questions and perhaps gaining new insights! If the restoration is ongoing as President Dieter F. Uchtdorf has taught,[10] then at least one way we can keep ourselves open to new revelations is to follow Steve Peck's example and learn as much as we can and then—carefully, speculatively, and *faithfully*—wonder.

—George B. Handley
Brigham Young University

Notes

1. William P. Brown, *The Seven Pillars of Creation: The Bible, Science, and the Ecology of Wonder* (New York: Oxford University Press, 2010), 4.

2. Steven L. Peck, "Démodé," *Nature Physics* 10 (January 2014): 80, http://www.nature.com/nphys/journal/v10/n1/full/nphys2860.html; and "Five Wagers on What Intelligent Life Elsewhere in the Universe Will Be Like," *Analog: Science Fiction and Fact*, March 2015, http://www.analogsf.com/2015_03/index.shtml.

3. Brown, *Seven Pillars of Creation*, 5.

4. The original quote, which Galileo attributed to an "eminent ecclesiastic," states, "The intention of the Holy Ghost is to teach us how one goes to heaven. [N]ot how heaven goes." Galileo attributed biblical authorship to the Holy Ghost and used the descriptors interchangeably throughout the letter. See Galileo Galilei, "Letter to the

Grand Duchess Christina of Tuscany, 1615," http://legacy.fordham.edu/halsall/mod
/galileo-tuscany.asp.

5. Galilei, "Letter to the Grand Duchess."

6. For a fuller account of Galileo's experiences, see Ronald Numbers, ed., *Galileo Goes to Jail and Other Myths about Science and Religion* (Cambridge, MA: Harvard University Press, 2009), 68–79.

7. Michel Serres, *The Natural Contract*, trans. Elizabeth MacArthur and William Paulson (Ann Arbor: University of Michigan Press, 1995), p. 81.

8. *Journal of Discourses*, 17:45.

9. Henry Eyring, "My Father's Formula," *Ensign*, October 1978, https://www.lds.org/ensign/1978/10/my-fathers-formula.

10. Dieter F. Uchtdorf, "Are You Sleeping through the Restoration?," April 2014 general conference, https://www.lds.org/general-conference/2014/04/are-you-sleeping-through-the-restoration.

Acknowledgments

This book and the essays it contains would not have been possible without the love and support of my wife, Lori Awbrey Peck; my four boys, Timothy, Christopher, Jaron, and Nathan; and my daughter, Emily. Watching them grow up and serve missions, marry amazing people, and give me grandkids has been meaningful beyond words. I owe them much of who I am. I'm especially grateful to the Maxwell Institute and Brigham Young University for supporting this project. My blogging community at ByCommonConsent.com has been a welcome source for generating ideas and a fount of meaningful interaction. I'm also grateful for the academic journal editors who have taken my work seriously by having it peer-reviewed, edited, and published, thereby creating greater opportunities for interaction within the field of science and faith.

In particular, I owe a debt of gratitude to the Maxwell Institute's Blair Hodges. His encouragement, editing, insights, observations, suggestions, and ideas have made this a better work.

Introduction

> I want to say to my friends that we believe in all good. If you can find a truth in heaven, earth or hell, it belongs to our doctrine. We believe it; it is ours; we claim it.
>
> —Brigham Young[1]

I GREW UP NEAR THE BOWLING ALLEY on the south end of town in a three-bedroom ranch-style brick home in Moab, an old mining and cattle town situated in southern Utah between Arches and Canyonlands National Parks. From its humble beginnings Moab has evolved into a tourist mecca in which mountain bike shops line its central main street and upscale restaurants cater to a robust tourist economy. But when I was growing up, it was a dying holdover from the heyday of uranium mining launched as a manifestation of McCarthy-era communist fears—a time when nuclear weapons were frantically being stockpiled to ensure the mutual self-destruction of our Cold War enemies should they attack. By the time my father had taken a job there, the commie threat was no longer pressing and the town was a dried-out little patch of desert where you might stop for supplies on the way to anywhere else. A little outpost with few long-term prospects for anyone.

But I was a kid. Concerns about the Cold War and stagnant economies distantly passed me by like the thunder that rumbles in Moab's nearby La Sals—remote mountains rising from the desert floor on the southeast horizon. Often in late summer you can spot towering dark cumulonimbus thunderheads ringing these imperial laccoliths. You sense something powerful and dark happening in the distance, but only rarely does the precious water from these storms fleck the hot dry canyons carved into the heart of the Colorado Plateau. Growing up, I never noticed that the people living there were struggling. To me it was a magical place. My family had a large garden and kept pigs and chickens, a dog and cat, and we even had a few fruit trees. I bunked with my four brothers in one room, while my sister enjoyed a room of her own (we thought she was spoiled). It seemed to me we were as rich as Croesus. In retrospect, our apparently extravagant living was actually the modest product of my dad's single income as a social worker. Yet, as far as I could tell, we had everything we needed and could do anything we wanted under the dry blue sky.

We had the whole of the Canyonlands to explore. The hills that surround Moab rise steeply from the valley floor, and beyond them were endless canyons, caves, and roads waiting for wandering youthful adventurers. My friends and I would regularly sling a sleeping bag over a shoulder and ramble into the cold desert without a map or compass and walk until dark. Then we'd throw our bedrolls onto the sand and call it a camp. In the morning we would continue wending our way up unexplored canyons. From time to time we found Anasazi petroglyphs scratched into the desert patina of rock walls, varnished by long action of wind and rain. Sometimes we stumbled upon abandoned mines, perhaps with a box of TNT still sitting near the entrance (we usually left those dangers alone because everyone knew that dynamite became unstable as it aged).

On these excursions our imaginations were fired with tales of alien abductions, Anasazi ghosts, and visits to distant stars. We were avid readers—Ray Bradbury, Ursula Le Guin, Kurt Vonnegut, and other writers of speculative fiction permeated every aspect of our lives. My friends and I relished and communally shared these books. When we weren't exploring the canyons, we were reading, and when we weren't reading, we were writing. We hoped one day to follow our heroes and become writers. We wrote stories and poems and shared them among ourselves for no other reason than the joy of writing and bringing delight to each other. (Sometimes my writing even got me out of trouble, like that time in seventh grade when I constructed a long narrative poem about weasels that caused my fiercest bully and most dangerous nemesis to tell me, wet-eyed and sniffling, "Peck, that's the best thing you've ever done.")

Now I'm an evolutionary ecologist at Brigham Young University. Mostly I've studied the ecology of flies (don't roll your eyes; they are cooler than you think!), first fruit flies in the Pacific isles, and more recently tsetse flies in West Africa—one of the most deadly creatures on the planet, believe it or not.[2] I've also dabbled in the philosophy of science, and I've written about how we can learn more about ecologies using various methods like computer simulations and gaming. I also teach a class in the history and philosophy of biology. All of these things have been amazingly rewarding, but my greatest love of all is still writing. Over the years I've been delighted to combine this love of writing (a love that far exceeds my talent) with my passion for science and faith. Writing, nature, and a love of wild places—these things have informed pretty much everything I have since done.

As with everything else in my life, my love of nature and wild places has deeply informed my religious faith. I've turned to writing as a way to both explore and express my perspectives on God and this magnificent creation of which we're all a part. I've written about my wanderings through the strange and exciting canyons of science and faith in a number of fictional books, stories, and poems and in countless blog posts.[3] I've also published a number of scholarly oriented articles and essays on a variety of issues pertaining to science and faith—particularly that of my own religious tradition, the Church of Jesus Christ of Latter-day Saints. For this present volume I've gathered together a number of essays to introduce Latter-day Saints to some of the interesting vistas, nooks, and crannies that I've explored in the canyons of science and faith. This book is divided into two sections. Part I includes essays that were published in peer-reviewed academic journals or presented at academic conferences. I have made a number of minor adjustments and updates to these works in preparation for this collection. Part II includes essays that are more personal or that were presented in less-scholarly venues or published online at blogs like *By Common Consent* and my personal blog, *The Mormon Organon*. Several essays could fit in either section. As with science and faith, the essays do not divide into the two parts as neatly as I would like, yet the resulting bit of overlap may reinforce an overall unity in theme and content.

Part I begins with an essay describing what science is, how it works, and why it is not a threat to faith when properly understood. "Embracing Science, Resisting Literalism, and Shifting Paradigms" explains that science is simply a set of agreed-upon processes used to make sense of the world. Viewing the world through a scientific lens does have challenges—it requires making adjustments and accommodating new ways of thinking. It requires deeper engagement with our scriptures and a willingness to revisit some of the literalistic interpretations we've inherited. However, such reframing can offer rich rewards that facilitate a more active and developed faith.

Chapter 2, "Randomness, Contingency, and Faith: Is There a Science of Subjectivity?," was originally published in one of the premier academic journals exploring faith and science issues.[4] I directly criticize the "scientism" propounded by many of the so-called new atheists. (Scientism is the idea that science will eventually explain everything there is to know.) I argue that subjective truths (like knowledge of God) constitute a valid form of knowing, although they are not objectively verifiable. I demonstrate that subjective experiments may lead to a more complete understanding of the universe.

The third essay is the result of one of the biggest intellectual adjustments I've ever made. I remember on my mission in Arkansas telling a man we were teaching that he had to quit believing in evolution if he wanted to join the church. I believed this with all my heart. I'd been taught in seminary that evolution and the gospel were completely incompatible. Nothing I'd read in books like *Mormon Doctrine* or heard from my mission president suggested otherwise. When I arrived at BYU as an undergraduate, I was shocked to find that evolution was being taught as one of the most important scientific findings of the last two hundred years and that Darwin was being held up as important as Newton and Einstein. My naive views had to undergo some radical reconstruction to accommodate my faith with the scientific truths I was presented with, but in the end I was thrilled to discover, as Elder Richard G. Scott has explained, that the "scientific approach" and the "revealed truth approach" are not opposites, but rather are two mutually reinforcing "ways to find truth."[5] I take this seriously. In "Crawling Out of the Primordial Soup: A Step toward the Emergence of an LDS Theology Compatible with Organic Evolution," I explore how learning about evolution can be an important part of understanding how perspectives of modern science and faith can strengthen and inform each other.[6] Obviously it isn't always easy to reconcile the claims of science and faith. We should expect to be left with many interesting puzzles to resolve. This essay, while speculative, explores possible ways to reconcile some of the tensions between evolutionary science and the LDS faith. It is important to remember that none of these possibilities must be thought of as official positions of the church, but rather as ideas that church members might faithfully entertain and further develop.

The fourth chapter confronts one of the most perplexing and wondrous aspects of the universe: our conscious minds. Often there is a temptation to give slight attention to what science and philosophy are saying about this topic because LDS doctrine teaches that our nature is dual, in that our physical, mortal bodies are enlivened by a spirit, or "intelligence." However, for several years I taught an honors class at BYU exploring what contemporary philosophers and scientists were saying about consciousness. It opened new horizons and introduced some challenges about the nature of consciousness that puzzle even Latter-day Saints. I explore how Mormon beliefs compare and contrast with contemporary scientific and philosophical views about human consciousness in "The Current Philosophy of Consciousness Landscape: Where Does LDS Thought Fit?"[7]

How does novelty enter into the world? Are the regularities of the universe structured such that novelty and newness can emerge spontaneously? I approach such questions in my fifth essay, "Life as Emergent Agential Systems: Tendencies without Teleology in an Open Universe."[8] Although Latter-day Saints were not the original target audience for this piece, I think they will be intrigued by the ideas presented here.[9]

The same goes for chapter 6, "Death and the Ecological Crisis." It was originally written for a non-LDS audience, but it is deeply informed by my personal understanding of a number of sometimes-overlooked gospel principles. Our scriptures instruct us to receive the gifts of creation with gratitude and thanksgiving (e.g., Psalm 136:1, 25; 1 Timothy 4:4; D&C 59:13-19; 89:11-12)—attitudes that I see disappearing in a busy society where most people are disconnected from the processing of food. The recognition that an actual creature lies behind our neatly packaged meats is often completely forgotten. In this essay I reflect on these attitudes and their implications for our place in and engagement with nature.[10]

In 2004 BYU hosted an important conference entitled "Stewardship and the Creation: LDS Perspectives on the Environment." Over 300 people from all over the world participated, and conference organizers edited a volume of the proceedings that was published by BYU's Religious Studies Center. Leading off part II is "An Ecologist's View of Latter-day Saint Culture and the Environment," my contribution to the conference and the resulting volume.[11] Here I explain how LDS principles impose on us a requirement to actively care for God's creation. I wanted to reach a broad audience in this piece in order to let people know that LDS theology is rich with ideas that prompt us to be engaged in stewardship of Earth's resources.

In a similar vein, the eighth essay, "Reverencing Creation,"[12] is a meditation on how we are to relate to this wonderful home we've been given. And viewing Earth as our home is the right perspective. The *eco-* in my field of ecology has its root in the Greek word for house. Throughout many of these essays, I argue that evolution is the best way to view the history of biological life on our planet, but it is important to remember that we shouldn't allow any of these methodological concerns about the *how* of creation make us lose sight of the *who* of creation. If we acknowledge that our earth is a divine creation for which we have been given stewardship, we ought to pay special attention to the normative demands imposed by God to care for what he has so providentially provided. In this essay I argue that reverence is the best way to approach our relationship to the earth.

"Grace vis-à-vis Violence" is a very personal exploration of how both grace and violence have structured and played out in my own life,[13] while the tenth essay extends the discussion into stranger realms. In 2002, while visiting Vietnam to collect butterflies for environmental indicators of change, I was infected with a species of soil bacteria that crawled up my optic nerve and set up residence in my brain. For over a week, I experienced severe visual and auditory hallucinations. I entered a harrowing alternate reality as my diseased brain fought off a deadly infection. It may seem like a work of fiction, but "My Madness"[14] is an all-too-true account of my horrific experience as doctors frantically sought to save my life. The essay serves as a stark reminder of, first, the impact that our embodied nature has on our everyday experience of the world and, second, the fact that even in this advanced era we face many unsolved questions scientifically and religiously.

The eleventh piece takes a light-hearted approach to the serious issue of scriptural literalism. Readers who interpret the Old Testament narrative of Noah in an overly literal fashion often try to make sense of a universal flood by focusing on questions like how big the ark would have to be in order to fit all the animals of the earth. But there is much more at stake biologically than mere boat size, and even harder questions that must be answered if literalists are to persuasively uphold the literal historical reality of a worldwide flood. "Noah's Lament" is a short, hopefully not-too-irreverent story told with tongue planted firmly in cheek showing what it would mean if the literalist reading is correct.[15]

Evolving Faith's final essay, "Crossing Boundaries and Sacred Spaces," takes a look at something I've been concerned about for some time now as an ecologist: how boundaries define ecologies and affect the creatures that live in different habitats. Do we believers cross similar boundaries when moving between the secular and the sacred?[16]

As you can tell from my brief overview, this book is not a systematic reconciliation of the claims and methods of science with religious faith. Instead, I offer my various writings as food for thought in order to invite other Latter-day Saints to faithfully explore the canyons of science and faith as I have done. Questioning is an important element of lifelong religious faith, as Dieter F. Uchtdorf, a member of the LDS Church's First Presidency, explained:

> Brothers and sisters, as good as our previous experience may be, if we stop asking questions, stop thinking, stop pondering, we can thwart the revelations of the Spirit. Remember, it was the questions young Joseph asked that opened the door for the restoration of all things. We can block the growth and knowledge our Heavenly Father intends for us. How often has the Holy Spirit tried to tell us something we needed to know but couldn't get past the massive iron gate of what we thought we already knew?[17]

I offer this book with hope that it might help us move past some of the iron gates we have erected. Certainly some of the meditations and wanderings included here will become outdated as scientists—as they always do—update and refine current scientific findings. Soon enough they will view the world from even grander vistas than the one on which I currently stand. Yet, what I hope endures from this collection is the perspective that one can embrace both good science and the truths of the gospel without compromising either one. Both science and faith are important and valid lenses through which we come to understand the world and our place in it. While each essay in this book stands alone, together they represent my own evolving approach to dealing with questions of science and faith.

Notes

1. "Truth and Error," *Journal of Discourses*, 13:335.
2. See "BYU professor helping to eradicate fatal sleeping sickness," BYU News, July 17, 2014, http://news.byu.edu/archive14-jul-tsetsefly.aspx.
3. See the appendix for a selected list of publications to date.
4. Steven L. Peck, "Randomness, Contingency, and Faith: Is There a Science of Subjectivity?," *Zygon: Journal of Religion and Science* 38 (March 2003): 5–24. This essay was

also featured in a volume containing the best papers on science and religion published in the last hundred years. See Sara Fletcher Harding and Nancy Morvillo, eds., *Religion and Science*, Critical Concepts in Religious Studies (London: Routledge, 2010).

5. See Richard G. Scott, "Truth: The Foundation of Correct Decisions," October 2007 general conference, www.lds.org/general-conference/2007/10/truth-the-foundation-of-correct-decisions.

6. Steven L. Peck, "Crawling Out of the Primordial Soup: A Step toward the Emergence of an LDS Theology Compatible with Organic Evolution," *Dialogue: A Journal of Mormon Thought* 43 (2010): 1–36.

7. Steven L. Peck, "The Current Philosophy of Consciousness Landscape: Where Does LDS Thought Fit?," *Dialogue: A Journal of Mormon Thought* 38 (2005): 36–64.

8. Steven L. Peck, "Life as Emergent Agential Systems: Tendencies without Teleology in an Open Universe," *Zygon: Journal of Religion and Science* 48 (December 2013): 984–1000.

9. This essay was originally presented at a theology conference entitled "What Is Life? Theology, Science, and Philosophy," held in Krakow, Poland, in June 2011. This event was hosted by Nottingham University's Centre of Theology and Philosophy and cosponsored by Brigham Young University's Richard L. Evans Chair of Religious Understanding.

10. Steven L. Peck, "Death and the Ecological Crisis," *Agriculture and Human Values* 27/1 (2010): 105–9.

11. Steven L. Peck, "An Ecologist's View of Latter-day Saint Culture and the Environment," in *Stewardship and the Creation: LDS Perspectives on the Environment*, ed. George B. Handley, Terry B. Ball, and Steven L. Peck (Provo, UT: Religious Studies Center, Brigham Young University, 2006).

12. Steven L. Peck, "Reverencing Creation," *Sunstone* 167 (June 2012): 8–11. For a richer exploration of these ideas, see George B. Handley, "The Environmental Ethics of Mormon Belief," *BYU Studies* 40/2 (2001): 187–211.

13. Steven L. Peck (as SteveP), "Grace vis-à-vis Violence," *By Common Consent* (blog), April 20, 2009, http://bycommonconsent.com/2009/04/20/grace-vis-a-vis-violence/.

14. Steven L. Peck, "My Madness," *Dialogue: A Journal of Mormon Thought* 41/2 (Summer 2008): 57–69. The essay was also discussed on BYU Radio's *Thinking Aloud* program with host Marcus Smith on February 20, 2012, http://www.classical89.org/thinkingaloud/archive/episode/?id=2/20/2012.

15. Steven L. Peck (as SteveP), "Noah's Lament," *By Common Consent* (blog), May 25, 2009, http://bycommonconsent.com/2009/05/25/noahs-lament-update/.

16. Modified from Steven L. Peck (as SteveP), "Boundary Issues in Sacred Spaces: Ecotone Analogies. Part I: Preliminaries," *By Common Consent* (blog), June 4, 2009, http://bycommonconsent.com/2009/06/04/boundary-issues-in-sacred-spaces-ecotone-analogies-part-i-preliminaries/ and "Boundary Issues in Sacred Spaces: Ecotone Analogies. Part II: Transitions," *By Common Consent* (blog), June 7, 2009, http://bycommonconsent.com/2009/06/07/boundary-issues-in-sacred-spaces-ecotone-analogies-part-ii-transitions/.

17. Dieter F. Uchtdorf, "Acting on the Truths of the Gospel of Jesus Christ," February 2012 Worldwide Leadership Training address, https://www.lds.org/broadcasts/article/worldwide-leadership-training/2012/01/acting-on-the-truths-of-the-gospel-of-jesus-christ?lang=eng.

PART
ONE

1

Embracing Science, Resisting Literalism, and Shifting Paradigms

ARE SCIENCE AND RELIGION COMPATIBLE? The ongoing wars between science and religion are legendary, and among the faithful you will discover a surprising number who harbor deep suspicions about science.[1] This is understandable. Some prominent scientists have been vocal in their scorn for religion and its adherents, leaving the impression that science itself is against religion. This is unfortunate because it is not true. Those who use science to attack religious perspectives are engaging in a blatant misuse of science. But they are not the only ones contributing to this unnecessary war. Religion is sometimes used inappropriately to dismiss science as a legitimate way of knowing. I have found that both science and religion can make vital contributions to the ways we understand the universe in its fullness. The essays collected in this book represent my ongoing efforts to transcend the ongoing war between science and religion, but before we get into the nitty-gritty details, we need to have a good foundation of what science is and how it works. Having a clear picture of science will help us fittingly weigh its claims (especially for those who think it can answer all questions of human interest) as well as help those who hold it in suspicion to celebrate its magisterial accomplishments.

So what exactly is science? A schoolkid's definition (let's call it the "SKD") might go something like this:

1. Find or create a hypothesis—a prediction or explanation of something.

2. Make sure the hypothesis is falsifiable—that it could actually be proved wrong.

3. Test it against reality. If it fails, discard it; if it doesn't, publish it.

4. Rinse and repeat. There is some truth in the SKD in the same way that being a good tennis player means being able to hit the ball really hard while keeping your knees bent and your eye on the ball. That description of good tennis playing gets some things right, but there is much that could be taken away and much more that could be added to reach a richer and more accurate description.

The funny thing about the SKD is that it can be used as a weapon to imbue one's personal ideas with the aura of science—and by *aura* I mean the credentialing and authority that come with the label *science*—without an understanding of how science generally works or how it is practiced or why it is so powerful in explicating the world. For instance, consider some people who argue that evolution is a false theory. Their tactical approach is to discredit scientific work by pointing out that certain scientists have failed in one or more of the SKD steps and therefore are not practicing true science.[2]

If the SKD is incomplete, we must ask again: What is science? For the sake of argument here, I'm going to act as if science is a unified concept by saying things like "Science is such and such" and "Science does not permit such and such," but as you'll see, I will subvert this stance later to show that science is neither unified nor without limitations. (But bear with me—science does mean *something*.) Science's upfront and non-negotiable stance is known as methodological materialism. This means that science generally assumes there are no hidden forces affecting the processes being investigated. Scientific descriptions posit no influence from God, angels, or demons. No magic. No miracles. This does not mean that scientists cannot or do not believe in God or miracles. It also does not mean that science claims that nothing that does not fit its materialist claims is worth knowing. No, science does not even claim that it will reveal all truth; in fact, it really cannot get much purchase on lots of things we make value claims about, including art, ethics, religion, and so on. Science does not even claim to get at the ultimate root of things (this despite misguided attempts by people like Richard Dawkins who claim it can discover all truth). In short, science is not a perfect method that speaks to all truths of every conceivable kind.

Some people seem to be afraid of methodological materialism. But you shouldn't be. After all, you are already very familiar with it. Methodological materialism is what you expect from your car mechanic, who naturally assumes that whatever is causing the clunking noise in your DeSoto is a mechanical problem with a particular material cause requiring a particular fix based purely on the physical realities about the ways cars are put together. If your mechanic said, "It looks like malicious fairies have given your engine a curse that causes dark fluxuals from the netherial world of Kandoonianus," you would likely get a new mechanic. I'm not saying that there definitely cannot be a curse from said fairies, but you know that's not the way to bet, and you expect, based on your experience with the world, that the best way to approach car repair is from the perspective of methodological materialism. Your assumption about mechanics is science's best move too for exactly the same sorts of reasons. Your mechanic may be an atheist, Buddhist, or Mormon, but any such status is irrelevant regarding expertise in repairing your car. The mechanic assumes it's a mechanical problem and moves on from there, regardless of any spiritual commitments he or she might have.

To sum up so far, and this should be strongly emphasized: Methodological materialism *is not* a threat to spirituality or belief in the existence of God. Methodological materialism *is* a good scientific assumption for confronting the physical world.

Practically speaking, science does the best things it can do to predict and explain the workings of the world using tools that have proved effective in the past. Agreed, this is sort of a minimalist description, but let's roll with it now and unpack what some of those effective tools are. In addition, let's look at stances or postures and attitudes that science takes.

Some Tools of Science

Experimentation

Hold as much as you can constant. Simplify the world as much as you can. Then manipulate something. If you have controlled everything else, then the relationship between the effect and the cause must be, well, *causal*. A great deal of effort has gone into making experimental tools reliable. Taking measurements, handling the data, randomizing things so your own biases don't get in the way and you can average out other effects you aren't interested in, statistical analysis, recording of data—all great tools. It turns out that it's easier to falsify rather than to confirm things, so you usually want to aim for that. Hence the SKD as described above is not a bad abstraction and simplification of some really complex stuff.

Observation

As much as we would like to do experiments, the world is too big and complex to allow this all the time. Take astronomy, for example. Fitting galaxies into the laboratory beaker has proved fairly hard. Ecological systems too, or geology or emergent behavior—all very tricky. When the parts do not sum to the whole and the whole influences the parts, everything you want to do with science gets even more tricky. You still want to measure and play around a little. Correlate phenomena. Hypothesize on what you think will happen if other things happen. You want to carefully gather data, categorize, systematize, organize, analyze. You want to propose explanations of what you see. All very important in science. Notice that the SKD has little or nothing to say about this part of the scientific process.

Modeling

If you believe in a world that is causal, you ought to be able to mathematize things. Math is a formal way of writing down quantitative descriptions of how some things are thought to influence other things. Sometimes a good causal theory can be written down with a few strokes of a pen—like Einstein did with $E = mc^2$. Then using that math, predict things. If you are good at predicting, it's a good sign you've got a good model. What more could you ask for from a model? Things have gotten more complicated with computers, and the range of phenomena you can describe has skyrocketed. Most importantly, modeling brings together experimentation and observation in helpful ways. Models, of course, are abstractions of idealized worlds and should never be taken for reality, but they are very useful for testing whether you understand how the world works. They have both explanatory and predictive power when they work right, which are two of science's highest values.

These three things constitute the main tools of science. So given these tools, what else defines and constrains science, thus making it so powerful for explaining the workings of the world?

A stance of openness to revision and holding results as tentative

Science is very humble. It has to change its mind sometimes. Conclusions are tentative. New facts, new analyses, and new interpretations sometimes force a confrontation with old facts, old analyses, and old interpretations. Science thrives on this. It holds all its claims open to scrutiny and exploration. Not to change them willy-nilly, mind you. No, science is more than a list of suggested ideas to hold on to this month. Its claims have been put into the furnace for testing, heated, and then sledgehammered to see if the claims will crack. When they don't, we gain confidence that we are onto something. We always know we might find a hotter furnace or a bigger hammer, so science is ready to change. But it does not bow to claims that it might be melted or cracked. It is a process whose proof is in the pudding—but always ready for a revised recipe.

Peer review and publication

Science is not a democracy. Not all voices get a say. Your voice has to pass muster. Your claims have to be examined. Your analysis, your interpretation, has to be scrutinized by experts. It has to fit into the context of other work that has been done. Science is a crowded field, and only the best, most well-tested ideas get through the gauntlet. Then when something is published, it is still open to the scientific community for further scrutiny. This is a bloody process. The claims continue to be prodded, attacked, poked, replicated, and bothered until weaknesses are exposed or until people start to think there is something here worth looking at. If it isn't published in the peer-reviewed literature, it's not science because science is ultimately a group activity. Hence the power of claims about things like anthropogenic climate change in which the peer-reviewed literature is united despite the protestations of the air hammers of the Internet. Peer review is crucial to the practice of good science. If scientific findings are not subjected to it, it's not science.

Research programs

Science has a lot of work to do. It is within individual disciplines and specific research programs that best practices are established through tradition, trial and error, lab experience, repeatability, instrumentation, training, consensus—finding what works and what doesn't. New technologies come and go. They are weighed against former methods. Winners and losers are identified. Collaborations are formed and dissolved. Students who are trained and credentialed in academic programs go on to introduce new ideas and challenge old ones by bringing their creative genius into the work. They help change and improve things—not in some absolute way, but in practical ways.

So that is a basic description of science. As you can tell by now, it is not the clean method of the cartoonish SKD. It is a Darwinian process in which ideas, theories, and hypotheses are thrown into a struggle for existence. Fitness is defined by how well particular claims account for and predict the world's processes. Only the best claims survive and to go on to reproduce. If something new comes along, it has to fight in the arena and survive to fight another day. And science is imperfect—it is practiced by regular humans with all the weaknesses, shortcomings, and misalignments we all share. But a strong structure is in place to create a dynamic exchange of ideas in order to mitigate individual shortcomings. This is why no other method has come as close to explaining so many concrete things about the world. Science works, and that is its highest recommendation.[3]

Avoiding the Temptation of Literalism

We understand some things only from within, subjectively. Indeed, it is within this domain that the scriptures open to us new and more profound realities. Science and other objective-leaning disciplines aim at revealing the details, the facts, the laws of our universe. Science has been highly successful at elucidating the objective world in which we are embedded and is our best method for establishing correspondence between our understanding and this world. However, there are certain truths that are revealed only in subjectivity. There is the richness of experience, the feelings of individual existence that simply cannot be captured in science. It is so deeply entangled that the methods of science do not lend themselves to discovering the depth of this experience, nor do they claim to. At the same time, we know that our physicality is tied to the history of the universe. We are part of a long process in which our chemical, material body has emerged from a long and slow physical-historical process, all rooted in natural unfoldings.

Through this process, structures have evolved that allow for a sensual connection to the physical world. We are physical creatures with the ability to reason, perceive, understand temporal and spatial relation-ships, and in general interact with a world outside and also with other individuals so situated. This occurs in the mind. We know from our own experience that these realities exist. We have experienced them in prayer, meditation, or in other moments of connection to these deeper realities.

We do not arrive at these truths by weighing independent evidence; we have not been persuaded by a statistical analysis, nor have we come to these insights only because we have been convinced by logical argu-ment. Significant p-values did not provide quantitative support for these realities. No, it is through direct experience that we learn of them. There are truths in the subjectivity of experience that cannot be captured in any other way, as I discuss in another chapter. This is not the whole story, however. In my experience, many of these experiences that have revealed subjective truths have come to me while reading. The scriptures have provided a pathway that connects me to the Spirit, thus revealing to my mind experiential truths that have provided much more than addi-tional static facts about the world. Such experiences have added meaning, depth, and richness to my world.

When it comes to thinking about science and religion, what interests me is how completely integrated my spiritual experiences are with the physical aspects of my mind. They are not separate from the normal workings of my brain. My rationality, my senses, and my memory are not turned off or suppressed. In fact, my conscious experience is completely integrated with these spiritual experiences. The process seems to engage mind, body, and spirit. The text of the scriptures pulls me into new realities.

I offer these prefatory remarks in order to talk about literalism, a way of interpreting scripture that runs the risk of robbing the scriptures of their intended effect. I think reading certain scriptures in an overly literal fashion can impede our access to the depth that the scriptures actually offer. I don't think the scriptures exist to give us information about the scientific nature of the universe. While there are elements of this, we can be rewarded by thinking about the historical contexts for the emergence of scriptures in the world. The purpose of scripture is to connect us to deeper, more important realities, about which science can offer no insight. It may be that I personally have a more mystical bent, but to me I've never looked at the scriptures as a history book or a manual of scientific practice. The scriptures facilitate contemplation of the more profound aspects of the universe, enabling us to experience the influence of the Spirit of God and opening grander and more prescient truths about the meaning of existence and our place in the universe. These truths have little to do with the mechanical workings of the universe—they relate only to the spiritual realities that open to us a relationship with God and his other children on a higher level than the surface realities obtained by objectively inclined science.

This is why reading the scriptures as a scientific text can do violence to their purpose. They are designed to connect us subjectively, consciously, and spiritually to richer truths and meaning. The tools of science described above can hardly be brought to bear on these ancient texts. To use the scriptures to discover objective facts about the physical world and its history is to tear them way from what they are there to ground. Literalism is like giving a child a calculus book as a step stool to reach a washbasin. In so doing, much is lost that lies with the proper use of the book. Certainly children need step stools, but that particular use misses the true potential the book has to offer.

Moreover, using the scriptures as a scientific guidebook does harm to science. Such use misrepresents how truths about the world are best discovered and clarified. Elder Dallin H. Oaks touched on this point in an address given at the Harvard Law School:

> We seek after knowledge, but we do so in a special way because we believe there are two dimensions of knowledge, material and spiritual. We seek knowledge in the material dimension by scientific inquiry and in the spiritual dimension by revelation. In the interest of time I will say no more of the material dimension except to affirm the obvious truth that thousands of Latter-day Saints perform brilliantly in the material world without denying—and, indeed, by using—the parallel truths and methods of the spiritual world.[4]

Elder Oaks clearly affirms that knowledge of the material world is best discovered by science. Other truths come from revelation. I believe that the scriptures provide one of our most important sources of revelation. The scriptures are sacred. They allow us to touch the deepest truths available. To use them to read the surface of physical things (a purpose for which they are not intended and do not lend themselves) is a mistake that leads us away from where science is strong and should be used (as Elder Oaks points out) and, worse, wrenches the scriptures away from the beauty and truth they have to offer.

New Faithful Paradigms Emerge

As we gain a better understanding of our sacred scriptures and as we learn not to misapply their teachings in the realm of science, we can open ourselves up to many great revelations that God has given to us, truths deeply embedded in the very universe itself. As I try to demonstrate in other essays found in this collection, learning more about things like evolution can give us a greater appreciation for God's creation and the plan of salvation. As an evolutionary ecologist, I've spent a lot of time thinking about evolution, including the resistance to it I've detected in some of my faithful students. I've been thinking about the fear that some people feel as they face the prospects that a new scientific age is bringing to an end their way of understanding the universe and their place and the place of God in it. The simple creationism of a Harry Potter–like God that was appropriate to believers in the seventeenth century (and that we borrowed from the Greeks)[5] is giving way to more complex conceptions. Revelations given to Joseph Smith can help us approach newer scientific outlooks with gospel-informed perspectives. Latter-day Saints have much to contribute to the robust and ongoing conversation among believers of many traditions regarding the relationship between science and religion. Entering this conversation may require adjustments, however, in ways we deal with the natural world and its history. I confess that in the past I've not been sympathetic enough to the difficulties experienced by people who struggle to reframe their worldview in order to improve their understanding of scientific perspectives while keeping their faith intact. My goal is to help such people overcome their reluctance to understanding evolution as a scientific perspective that doesn't necessarily conflict with the gospel. I recently read a book that helped me empathize with people who are shaken when their perspective of the world changes, when they must reframe their beliefs in the face of large cultural shifts. The book tells the story of a Crow visionary named Plenty Coups, a remarkable person who survived the complete loss of his cultural perspective.[6]

Plenty Coups's life straddled the division between the traditional Crow way of life and the takeover of all Indian affairs by the United States government. He was raised in a culture in which everything was couched in terms of his people's continual war with the Sioux. Young children were raised with the idea that being a warrior and "counting coup" (a way of letting your enemy know that it was you, a Crow, who was the one killing him by touching him with a stick before striking him down) were among the highest goods, that to triumph in battle was the aim of a well-lived life. Women, for their part, prepared food for the people, but they worked especially hard to nourish the warriors. Plenty Coups's world began to collapse within a few short years as the buffalo disappeared and white settlers took control over more and more land. The Crow joined the US government in its fight with the Sioux, and in the end the Crow were the only tribe that was allowed to settle on its original tribal lands. Of course, the other tribes saw this as a betrayal, but to the Crow, they had simply allied themselves with a powerful people with whom they had no real quarrel, while the Sioux had been their mortal enemy for over two centuries.

Suddenly everything the Crow had lived for changed. The buffalo and the beaver they depended on had been hunted to nothing. The other tribes who had fought against the United States had been divided up onto various reservations and their cultures scattered and destroyed, and in fact made illegal. Many of the native peoples did not know how to live in the new world imposed on them. Everything Plenty Coups and his people had believed in had become meaningless. In fact, Plenty Coups said that after the people of the United States had taken control of their lives, "nothing happened."

What Plenty Coups meant by *nothing* goes beyond the fact that his way of life had become mean*ingless*. The Crow were even more lost than that because they had even lost the context where meaninglessness or meaning could be conceptualized. The ground for meaning itself had been destroyed. That's why "nothing happened"—nothing could happen; all categories had been wiped out. Plenty Coups, however, provided a unique way to help his people reinterpret their old ways in a new context. At the same time, even though he went on to lead his nation in learning to farm, and even though he promoted education among his tribe members and became a representative of Native rights in Washington, DC, Plenty Coups still felt as though "nothing happened."

For people who must adjust to a world where evolution is a reality they must grapple with rather than dismiss, things are not so bad compared to the wrenching cultural dislocations faced by Plenty Coups and his people. Still, there are considerable adjustments that are necessary in order to view the world through both scientific and religious lenses. But when we learn to see the world through both lenses, much depth is added to our perspective. Plenty Coups's experience suggests that the way to handle this adjustment is through courage in the face of risk.

He argues that we are finite beings and as such are always face-to-face with the fact of our finitude and our abject and absolute vulnerability to forces beyond our control—including the risk that new information and new understanding might present. The apostle Paul was speaking of this finitude when he said we go through life seeing "through a glass, darkly" (1 Corinthians 13:12), or as a scientist might say, our microscope lens is cloudy. It requires courage to face boldly the reality that we are always at risk and that there are things in life that we cannot control or perhaps fully comprehend. But notice that the difference between Plenty Coups and many other American Indian leaders was that he saw clearly that the buffalo and beaver were indeed gone. He saw that the European settlers were unconquerable, while other leaders kept a false hope alive that they could drive the Europeans out—or that an Indian messiah would arise to free them or that by doing the Ghost Dance they could bring spiritual help from the other side to defeat the settlers. Plenty Coups's story shows that by not facing the reality of the situation, by focusing on winning or beating the white settlers, the other chiefs did not save their people.

Facing the reality of a religious world that includes the evolution of humans is hard for some people. And it has been hard for me to recognize the pain that others face in adjusting to these new realities. But as Plenty Coups showed, facing realities is the best way. To face these new risks of reinterpreting our deepest understandings of fundamental things requires courage.

In the essays that follow, I hope you will keep an open mind. The three elements I've discussed in this chapter—having a correct understanding of science, avoiding the dangers of literalism, and navigating difficult paradigm shifts while maintaining faith and hope—foster a richer understanding of our world. My hope is that through these essays readers will sense that there is no reason to abandon either their faith or their desire to understand the world through science. To the contrary, as we have been exhorted in modern scripture, God expects us to seek further light and knowledge "by study and also by faith" (D&C 88:118). This will take intellectual flexibility because science is an ongoing activity, much like the restoration of the gospel. And we can share the knowledge we gain too:

> Teach ye diligently and my grace shall attend you, that you may be instructed more perfectly in theory, in principle, in doctrine, in the law of the gospel, in all things that pertain unto the kingdom of God, that are expedient for you to

understand; of things both in heaven and in the earth, and under the earth; . . . that ye may be prepared in all things when I
shall send you again to magnify the calling whereunto I have
called you, and the mission with which I have commissioned
you. (D&C 88:78–80)

Notes

1. See, for example, Ian G. Barbour, *When Science Meets Religion: Enemies, Strangers, or Partners?* (New York: HarperCollins, 2000).

2. Note: Whenever someone puts *true* in front of *science* let it serve as a warning that you are likely about to be introduced to something that is not science.

3. For a specific account of what I'm describing, see Ludwik Fleck, *Genesis and Development of a Scientific Fact*, ed. Thaddeus J. Trenn and Robert K. Merton (Chicago: University of Chicago Press, 1979). Fleck details how his research team improved the method for diagnosing syphilis. As dry as that sounds, it reads like a fascinating detective novel. More important for us, it provides a concrete understanding of how science works in the nitty-gritty world as opposed to the neat SKD description. Fleck's research was filled with false starts, flashes of creativity and speculation, backtracking, teamwork, collaboration, trial and error, abandoned trajectories, instrumentation problems, the rethinking of conceptual foundations, the need for background education, the use of inference as well as induction and deduction, and the messiness that goes into real science. In fact, Fleck quips, "If a research experiment were well defined, it would be altogether unnecessary to perform it" (p. 86).

4. See Dallin H. Oaks, "Fundamental Premises of Our Faith," February 26, 2010, http://www.mormonnewsroom.org/article/fundamental-premises-of-our-faith-talk-given-by-elder-dallin-h-oaks-at-harvard-law-school.

5. See, for example, Gerhard May, *Creatio Ex Nihilo: The Doctrine of 'Creation out of Nothing' in Early Christian Thought*, trans. A. S. Worrall (London: T&T Clark, 2004).

6. Jonathan Lear, *Radical Hope: Ethics in the Face of Cultural Devastation* (Cambridge, MA: Harvard University Press, 2006).

2

Randomness, Contingency, and Faith: Is There a Science of Subjectivity?

THE LAST TWO DECADES HAVE SEEN a flurry of books and papers on the compatibility of evolutionary biology and religion.[1] As a religious evolutionary biologist, I find this both refreshing and reassuring. Despite the ongoing and healthy dialogue between those who believe in God and those who do not, there seems to be a misunderstanding on both sides of the debate over the implications of contingency and randomness for the religious believer. In particular, some have argued that the contingency and stochasticity of evolutionary processes suggest that the universe is without purpose or design.[2] While I appreciate the appeal of these arguments, I disagree that randomness and contingency imply an empty and ontologically meaningless universe. Furthermore, the metaphysics behind their arguments has too frequently been ignored.[3] As an evolutionary biologist, I have spent most of my research in climbing, as Dawkins calls them, "Mount Improbables" in computer simulations of evolutionary processes, and I find the argument that this stochastic and contingent universe necessarily implies no design or purpose uncompelling and flawed.[4]

As I invoke the word *design*, I am concerned that you will cast me in the pit with the creationists (including the so-called intelligent design creationist movements). I do not want that. If you read my publications or had a discussion with me, I suspect you would easily place me with any other group of evolutionary biologists. However, I do believe that the universe has a purpose, but also that it was not brought about suddenly or with constant interventions by God. If you were to ask me about the age of Earth, the evolution of Earth's biota (including human beings), or anything else dealing with evolution, you would find my opinions typically to be mainstream science. While I question particulars, as do all evolutionary biologists, for some aspects of evolution (e.g., what are the modes and rates of sympatric speciation?), I accept without hesitation that evolution has occurred and continues to occur. It is the unifying principle of biology and explains the myriad structures we see today in Earth's biota. I am committed to the scientific agenda in understanding our universe. I do believe, however, that we were created ultimately by a God who delights in freedom, richness, and beauty and that the universe was fashioned in such a way that we were an inevitable part of its processes.

A common thread of misunderstanding runs through materialist literature on the nature of faith and the power of subjective truth. Materialists insist that science, especially evolutionary science, has dispelled religion by explaining its existence as an artifact of intelligence evolution (perhaps arising by giving an advantage in hunting or securing mates, or by functioning as an invasive meme that has been exceptionally successful in spreading in our big-brained species of ape).[5]

I sense that most materialists do not understand religion. To them, people of faith seem to have decided to believe something for arbitrary and indefeasible reasons—perhaps they were raised that way, or the Bible says so and because of its historical holiness they believe it, or they have decided there is a God and they are going to believe it whether there is evidence for it or not. Stephen Jay Gould saw religion merely as an ethical system and had no qualms about allowing a place for religion as long as its practitioners stuck to their "magisterium" and as long as religion stayed only in the realm of providing an ethical framework for human behavior.[6] But he clearly felt that there is no basis for religion ultimately, that it is nothing more than a useful strategy designed by evolution to help us survive as social creatures. Michael Shermer holds that such beliefs are "weird," that thoughtful persons ought to be able to escape the evolutionary heritage of superstition we have inherited, and that Science (with a capital S) is the answer to the world's problems.[7] Recently, Varadaraja V. Raman defined faith as "accepting without questioning, and sometimes in spite of apparent logical inconsistency."[8]

While I am sure there are some people who believe in God for irrational reasons, I find that most people of faith enjoy an inwardness that provides a profound sense of worth and reality. Faith is not without reason. Faith is certainly not belief without questioning (although it inappropriately can be). It is not without basis. But that basis is found in subjectivity.

Subjectivity is a creature of such mystery that science has largely left it alone[9] or called it nonexistent.[10] As B. Alan Wallace has written,

> *Strictly speaking, at present there is no scientific evidence even for the existence of consciousness.* All the direct evidence we have consists of nonscientific, first-person accounts of being conscious. The root of the problem is more than a temporary inadequacy of the technology. It is rather that modern science does not even have a theoretical framework with which to conduct experimental research.[11]

Materialist arguments, in particular those of Daniel Dennett and Richard Dawkins, have disallowed any place for God in the universe. They argue that, given the laws of physics, chance and contingency are the best explanation for understanding the world. However, if their personal metaphysics are flawed, their ultimate conclusions are likely to be as well. The materialists have also largely ignored subjectivity or dismissed it as irrelevant. I believe this introduces flaws in their perceptions that weaken their arguments against God. In this essay I explore the nature of these flaws by examining several questions in three areas: (1) How does personal metaphysics affect one's ability to do science? To explore this question I look at Alfred Russel Wallace's attempt to rationalize nineteenth-century spiritualism. (2) Are the materialist arguments about contingency used to dismiss the importance of our place in the universe valid? (3) What are the implications of subjectivity on belief and science? Are there truths that cannot be reached through science? Are there subjective truths? If so, is there a science of subjectivity? These areas of inquiry may seem diverse, but they are united by their questioning materialists' claims that science is the ultimate arbiter of truth. Examining these three areas will give an apposite look at why materialism fails.

Metaphysics and Science

Alfred Russel Wallace—when objectivity fails

Perhaps one of the most intriguing characters to have created a unique metaphysics that combines elements of science and an alternative worldview was Alfred Russel Wallace. Wallace, independently of Darwin, articulated the mechanism driving evolution: natural selection. On March 9, 1858, Wallace mailed Darwin his paper "On the Tendency of Varieties to Depart Indefinitely from the Original Type." The paper, based on Wallace's observations and ruminations on species diversity and origin during his travels in the Malay Archipelago, was written while Wallace was sick with malaria on Ternate Island. Darwin, who had been working independently on the mechanism of species change, was horrified to discover that he might lose priority. His friends Sir Charles Lyell and Sir Joseph Hooker, two of the most prominent scientists of the nineteenth century, urged Darwin to quickly draft a paper based on his notes and thinking about species origin. Both papers were read by Darwin at the July 1, 1858, meeting of the Linnean Society while Wallace was on the other side of the world collecting beetles, birds, and other animals for British collectors.[12]

Wallace never showed any envy or ill feelings for Darwin's priority in establishing the principal mechanism in understanding how species change through natural selection.[13] Wallace became active in publishing some of the most clear and lucid arguments for the theory of evolution.[14] He was one of the preeminent scientists of his day. His books on his explorations and collections from the Amazon rain forest and his adventures among the islands of the South Pacific Malay region brought him acclaim from both popular readers and scientific peers. He published hundreds of scientific articles and books, many of which are considered landmarks in natural history. Today he is acknowledged as codiscoverer of the theory of evolution through natural selection as well as the father of biogeography, the study of species distribution and patterns. Wallace was never one to temper his opinions or engage in periphrasis to avoid the harsh judgment of his peers, and he boldly took up some unpopular causes, such as nationalizing land ownership for more equitable land distribution among all classes of society. He was an active socialist and antimilitarist and was avidly concerned with the health and welfare of the poor. Such causes tended to distance him from the landed gentry, from whom most of the scientists, such as Darwin, came. One of the most peccant ideas that Wallace embraced was that of spiritualism.

In the late 1800s, spiritualism was sweeping both England and America. Séances, Ouija boards, fortune-telling, consulting with spirits of the departed, and searching for criminals by using divining rods were all part of the mainstream cultural currency. The existence of fairies was discussed, explored, and espoused by all segments of society; the bizarre and paranormal were embraced widely in the middle and upper classes. In darkened rooms, participants gathered to hear otherworldly beings knock mysteriously, speak through one of those assembled, or raise the table around which the curious had gathered. Sometimes strange objects or even people could be seen floating without support through the air.

Wallace was introduced to spiritualism through its connection with hypnotism (or mesmerism, as it was called) and phrenology, which he began to dabble in when he was a young man working as a teacher. As he became more scientifically mature, he began to disparage the reluctance with which many of the scientific elite embraced new ideas, for example, his and Darwin's theory of evolution.

His interest in spiritualism first flowered during his travels in the Malay Archipelago and extended as spiritualism swept the Americas and Britain. At first he was quite cynical and approached the matter with skepticism and doubt. However, the more he looked and the more often he experienced the claims being made by the spiritualism practitioners directly, the more convinced he became:

> I was so thorough and confirmed a materialist that I could not at that time find a place in my mind for the conception of spiritual existence, or for any other agencies in the universe than matter and force. Facts, however, are stubborn things. My curiosity was at first excited by some slight but inexplicable phenomena occurring in a friend's family, and my desire for knowledge and love of truth forced me to continue the inquiry. The facts became more and more assured, more and more varied, more and more removed from anything that modern science taught or modern philosophy speculated on. The facts beat me. They compelled me to accept them *as facts* long before I could accept the spiritual explanation of them; there was at that time "no place in my fabric of thought into which it could be fitted." By slow degrees a place was made; but it was made, not by any preconceived or theoretical opinions, but by the continuous action of fact after fact, which could not be got rid of in any other way.[15]

Wallace, to the embarrassment of his associates in science, including Darwin, became an avid defender of spiritualism. But his defense was as logically rigorous and well documented as his defense of evolution had been. He harnessed the same mind that had independently solved one of the greatest puzzles of the Enlightenment—the origin of species—in order to investigate and substantiate spiritualism. It is intriguing to follow his defense. In *Miracles and Modern Spiritualism*, he begins by castigating David Hume and other philosophers and scientists for dismissing miracles without exploring the facts themselves, stating that "few if any have thoroughly and honestly investigated the nature and amount of the evidence that those events really happened."[16] He then gives an impressive list of miracles attested by multiple credible witnesses, including learned men of science (no women are mentioned) such as Augustus De Morgen and Robert Hare, prominent physicians of the day, clergymen, and authors such as William Thackeray and Anthony Trollope. After defending miracles, animal magnetism, and clairvoyance, he turns to spiritualism. To Wallace, spiritualism was not part of a larger belief in an organized religion or even in the existence of God. The activities he witnessed implied only that "intelligent beings may exist around and among us, unperceived during our whole lives, and yet capable under certain conditions of making their presence known by acting on matter."[17] So spiritualism was another scientific phenomenon to be investigated using the best tools of his discipline: observation, hypothesis generation, hypothesis testing, and inference. His first observation of spiritualist phenomena had a profound effect on him:

> It was in the summer of 1865 that I first witnessed any of the phenomena of what is called Spiritualism, in the house of a friend—a sceptic, a man of science, and a lawyer, with none but members of his own family present. . . . [I] sat with my friend, his wife, and two daughters, at a large loo table, by daylight. In about half-an-hour some faint motions were perceived, and some faint taps heard. They gradually increased; the taps became very distinct, and the table moved considerably, obliging us to all shift our chairs. Then a curious vibratory motion of the table commenced, almost like the shivering of a living animal. I could feel it up to my elbows. These phenomena were variously repeated for two hours. On trying afterwards, we found the table could not be voluntarily moved in the same manner without a great exertion of force, and we could discover no possible way of producing the taps when our hands were upon the table.[18]

Observation was not enough for the skeptical Wallace. He continued his investigation by conducting scientific experiments on the phenomena:

> On other occasions we tried the experiment of each person in succession leaving the table, and found that the phenomena continued the same as before, both taps and table movement. Once I requested one after another to leave the table; the phenomena continued, but as the number of sitters diminished with decreasing vigor, and just after the last person had drawn back leaving me alone at the table, there were two dull taps or blows, as with a fist on the pillar or foot of the table, the vibration of which I could feel as well as hear. No one present but myself could have made these, and I certainly did not make them.[19]

He continued to analyze the curvature and direction of the table movement and the inability to duplicate the sound of the taps by various methods and objects, and to form and reject explanations other than the presence of otherworldly beings. He was convinced not because he wanted to believe or because he found meaning in what he believed but because he could find no other explanation for the facts at hand. As he continued to describe what led him to this belief, we find him examining tables, chairs, and other objects that had levitated, started vibrating, or behaved in some anomalous fashion, looking for strings or other sources of deception. He looked under floating tables in a brightly lit room trying to understand what was happening and was compelled by his observations to believe in intelligences, on a spectral plane not our own, as the only rational explanation for what he saw.

So here we have a profound intellect, using the best analytic methods of his day, saying he could not reject the hypotheses of spirits who spent their time moving tables and tapping simply for the benefit of people assembled to experience such things.

What do we do with Wallace? This is a question his contemporaries also asked themselves. What do we do with a scientist who believes in spiritualism and claims it is science that brought him to this belief? Wallace's claim in the book is a strong one. It is well documented with numerous examples, observations, and experiments. If the book had been written about evolution or biogeography, it would have been heralded as some of the finest thinking of the nineteenth century. But no—it was about spiritualism, and the galling thing is that he used the same methods to explore this topic as he did to explore evolution. Few scientists today have ever heard of Wallace's book on spiritualism, let alone read it. Most of the evolution texts that mention Wallace focus on his contribution to the study of evolution, but his later life turned out to be a scientific embarrassment and is swept under the rug.

Why do we believe Wallace when he writes about evolution yet ignore him when he turns to spiritualism? Part of the reason is the context in which we receive his writings today. Spiritualism is now out of fashion, hoaxes have been exposed, and there is no longer a social context for the idea of spiritualism. The experiments, while repeatable in Wallace's day, are no longer repeatable, and thus they fail one of the hallmarks of the scientific method. But they *were* repeatable then! When one reads Wallace's works, one is struck by how he acted with complete warrant in exploring spiritualism scientifically. As Thomas S. Kuhn later demonstrated as usually operating in science,[20] Wallace's thought was conditioned on the social constructs of his day.

Perhaps his belief in spiritualism can be explained, in part, by his being actively deceived. Charlatans were manipulating the data, something one would not expect from data gathered from the natural world. For example, Charles Williams, a well-known medium who had performed séances in the presence of Darwin and the writer George Eliot, was exposed by George Romanes as a fake.[21] Wallace was a trusting individual who took at face value those he supposed were other seekers of the truth. The scientific method cannot work in an environment where the objects of experiment are being manipulated dishonestly. But Wallace knew this and was looking for ways he could have been deceived. He just could not find them.

Scientific materialists point out that Wallace's metaphysics made him vulnerable to the misapplication of science. Under materialist metaphysics, Wallace would not have asked the question about unobservable entities peopling the universe. Darwin, the quintessential materialist, did not lose his focus on such distasteful subjects and is universally revered as evolutionary theory's founding father. Conversely, Wallace is nearly forgotten and drifts in and out of obscurity as a scientific oddball. But what is important here is that metaphysics matters. While materialists might think that this is a vindication of their worldview, it more appropriately shows that worldview cannot be divorced from science. Wallace's study of spiritualism demonstrates that science as a method is at the mercy of its assumptions. Wallace failed to discover an objective reality not because his science was poor but because his metaphysical assumptions were flawed.

What are the effects of the materialists' own metaphysics? B. Alan Wallace has pointed out that two fundamental assumptions of the materialist agenda—that only the physical world exists and that science will uncover all truths about this world—are empirically unknowable and assumed without reflection or questioning.[22] Since Alfred Russel Wallace's time, the materialist program is the de facto worldview that shapes science today. Materialists' metaphysical assumptions are not questioned and have become the central dogma for scientific investigations. It is becoming clear, however, that this religious zeal for materialism has its own dangers. What is being lost by the unrecognized materialist assumptions? Can we take the materialist assumptions and unreflexively go on our way because we have seen major successes in the world of science? Can we dismiss, as they do, any possible influence of factors from nontypical physical sources? Is the idea of God soon to follow the knocking ghosts of Wallace's day under scientific materialism's relentless onslaught, or are materialists ignoring aspects of reality not available under their methodology and agenda? If you assume that the universe contains only x, when it in fact contains both x and y, then, like Wallace, your metaphysical assumptions are going to trip you. Even if y is not needed at the level of most scientific investigations (in the same way that Newtonian physics works quite well despite its nescience of relativity or quantum mechanics), at some level aspects of reality are being missed if one assumes only x.

Evolution's Role in Structuring Belief: Science and Religion

Kierkegaard—science as an approximation

Søren Kierkegaard wrote that our picture of an objective reality is always only an approximation: we can get nearer and nearer to lining up our inner model of the universe with some objective reality, but it is always a model.[23] Today we have a better understanding of the way that a model of reality works within the brain, and we know how our individual model of reality is constructed from a combination of sensory input and neural architecture. I argue that this model is quite good. It contains enough accuracy to navigate through an objective reality with some sense of continuation and meaning. From an evolutionary perspective, the model must at least be good enough at this navigation to survive. Assuming that George Berkeley's strong idealism is incorrect, organisms that ignore this objective reality (whatever its form) do not survive long. For example, simple rules like "Do not jump off high cliffs" or "Run when being chased by a sabertooth tiger" are handy ways to use this correspondence between inner map and outer reality. Having good models is essential to an organism's survival. For example, for a plant, moving toward the light is a good way to connect the inner map with the objective reality. One school of thought contends that an objective reality is always unknowable. Perhaps in some ultimate sense this is true, but we need to know enough about this hidden reality to survive. That our species is still here suggests that our map is at least correct in a few particulars. Natural selection is a good screen for filtering useful inner maps of an underlying objective reality from nonuseful maps.

Science as a Wrightian adaptive landscape

Sewall Wright proposed that the process of evolution could be viewed as an adaptive landscape.[24] Though its particulars have been challenged, this has been a fruitful model for understanding evolution, speciation, and rates and modes of evolution. For example, if we plot two dimensions of gene combinations on the x and y axes of a Cartesian coordinate system, and on the third dimension (z) plot fitness levels, we get a hilly landscape where the hills represent increased fitness and the valleys represent places of decreased fitness. A population of a given species will move up the landscape to a local peak through natural selection. When the population reaches a peak, it is stuck there until the environment changes or new mutations send it to a new peak (most of the literature on adaptive topologies is concerned with getting off these local peaks to more global maximums). It is a challenging problem that may require that the metaphor itself be scrapped and more elaborate adaptive landscapes be considered.[25]

Wright's adaptive landscapes do provide, however, an interesting metaphor for the philosophy of science, in line with that of others, such as David Hull, who consider science itself an evolutionary process.[26] Karl Popper's ideas of science, such as the notion that science proceeds by rejecting null hypotheses, may be viewed as a selection process, in which finding increasingly fit hypotheses to explain given phenomena is the goal. The fitness function can be thought of as the hypothesis's success in matching its explanatory power with some underlying reality, so that science itself is under a process similar to natural selection. Science, in this metaphor, climbs this fitness function defined by the distance between its description of reality and the underlying (and always unavailable) universe. But what does this adaptive landscape of scientific theories look like? Is there an analogy to the rugged adaptive landscapes seen in biological systems? Because of their complexity, the landscapes found in biological systems seem to display what is known as correlated ruggedness. The landscape is covered with numerous peaks and valleys, almost like a fakir's bed of nails. If science itself can be seen to be moving over an even more complex adaptive landscape—again, its fitness function defined by its closeness to some underlying reality—then we may expect that the same problems that occur in biological systems occur with science: getting stuck on local peaks and missing global optimums. (The idea that valleys may be myths and that peaks may be more scientific explanations of cause and effect may offer some connection to the postmodern literary theory of deconstruction, in which our science grows out of particular myths or worldviews.) The analogy is not perfect, but it is interesting to speculate that science might not be able to escape these local maximums, which in turn would cause us to miss greater truths, defined by models with an even closer match to the global reality. Following a conjecture that Gödel's proof[27] applies to science[28] (assuming that the scientific method can be mapped to some system of predicate logic) would suggest that there are scientific truths (or theorems) that cannot be proved within science. Scientific materialism can never find even all scientific truths!

Science is an imperfect mechanism for discovering truth. It is powerful in the same sense that evolution is powerful—that is, the most well-adapted theories are those that are most useful in describing the universe. Science is nonetheless imperfect in that it may tend to get stuck at local fitness peaks, suggesting that some scientific truths may never be reached by science. So what other sources of truth are available to us? Is religion one? Gould argues that religion can only offer relational ethical advice—tied not to some ultimate truth but to convention—and provides an allowable system with which to frame these ethical rules.[29] I am not comfortable with that role for my personal faith. If it is not grounded in some universal truths, such as that a being exists that loves and is concerned about me, I'd rather scrap the whole thing and join the materialists and embrace whatever ethical system *is* based in truth (granted that deep reality may still be ultimately unknowable, even from my religious perspective). So, given the limits of science, the question arises: Has materialism dealt a deathblow to religion? Does Mount Improbable's gentle slope obliterate the idea of a personally approachable god?

Simulation and evolutionary ecology: Hidden purpose, masked design

It has been argued that our existence, indeed all of Earth's biota, is the result of randomness and contingency. Gould and others have argued that, were the clock of Earth's history wound back to the Precambrian, with different outcomes from chance events we might have an entirely different set of life forms on the planet today.[30] They argue that our existence as the human species has been contingent on thousands of small random events that have changed the course of evolution. That may be so, but these are not scientific statements. They are not testable. It is strange how quickly talk about ultimate origins seems to abandon science, all in the name of science. For example, to explain away the anthropomorphic principle that the universe seems perfectly designed for carbon-based life forms, skeptics posit infinite universes. We happened to evolve in one that supported carbon-based life. This is an intriguing possibility but certainly not a scientific hypothesis, because it is not testable. It is another just-so story of possible explanations of origins, as is the anthropomorphic principle. For different reasons both are accepted or postulated as articles of faith.

Dennett and Dawkins have both argued that chance and contingency point to an ultimately purposeless and meaningless universe.[31] My perspective as an evolutionary theorist suggests a different possibility. In my research I explore adaptive landscapes to understand how evolution happens.[32] In my models evolution is represented by rugged landscapes, much like a mountain range with scattered high peaks and low valleys. Each rise in elevation represents an increase in the average fitness of the population. A population on the landscape is driven uphill by selection. Dawkins has done an excellent job of describing these landscapes in *Climbing Mount Improbable*. It is a blind process in which a rich diversity of computer entities can be developed by climbing these adaptive landscapes. He claims that this is proof against religion and that blind processes can lead to amazing complexity with Darwinian processes only. I agree, except on one point: in every artificial example Dawkins uses, someone has set up the landscape.

In Dawkins's computer simulations, as in mine, there is always a landscape that defines which outcomes are possible and even which ones are likely. In my own simulations, I have observed that once I set up the landscape there are random, yet inevitable, events that I know will occur with a given probability. In my simulations, in the "Mount Improbable" that my computer creatures climb, some peaks are higher than others. Once one climbs a hill, it is difficult to go back down, but there is a finite probability that the creatures will escape these local peaks. Somewhere in the landscape is a peak that is higher than any other. However, given certain search algorithms and only Darwinian rules for reaching the peak, if I let the simulation run long enough and under specified conditions, reaching the highest peak is inevitable. Although the process is stochastic, it is a function of the underlying search algorithm. The time until the highest peak is reached is a random variable, and it may take a long time, but reaching it at some time happens with a probability equal to 1 (meaning that the event is certain to happen).

Consider a population of organisms living on my adaptive landscape. To those creatures on the surface, it would appear that reaching that peak occurred entirely through random processes. The algorithm would be invisible to the inhabitants of my landscape. Like the materialists, they would proclaim that they live in a random universe where chance and contingency rule. If they were wise, however, they might ask, "Who placed the adaptive peaks and valleys there?" "They just exist," claim the materialist creatures on my landscape. They do not need the "giant programmer in the sky" hypothesis to explain it. It just exists, and reaching the highest peak was just a matter of chance and evolution. They could postulate (given the ruggedness of the landscape) that any number of peaks could have been reached and that there was no reason that this particular one should be the one they ended on. Yet the members of that population sitting on my landscape speculating that all was unpredictable because it was random would be wrong. I had set it up from the beginning to reach that particular peak. It did not require my intervention in the process. I just let it run its course, and although I could not have guessed the exact time the peak would be reached, I could calculate an expected time and variance and get a pretty good idea when it would occur.

Dawkins uses similar devices in his *Climbing Mount Improbable* to argue for a random universe, but in every example he gives, he has set up a mountain to climb, just as I have. These mountains are the laws of the universe.

Where do the mountains or laws come from in our universe? For example, there is a large consensus that it is likely that life in the universe is common. Given the existence of billions of galaxies, it seems that a system like ours is bound to exist elsewhere. Is our universe constructed in such a way that certain mountains will inevitably be climbed? Is the design of the universe such that intelligent life is an eventual given? Is our evolution an inevitable outcome of the way the universe is constructed? We cannot answer these questions from inside this system. So postulating multiple universes or ones driven by mindless randomness is even less subject to experimentation than Wallace's wall-knocking, table-lifting spirits.

Today great strides are being made in understanding how evolution structured the biodiversity of our planet. Because I believe that life evolved according to the rules and laws of our universe, I can join the effort to understand how evolution proceeds with the same scientific methods and procedures that my colleagues use. However, I also believe that science is not the only way to obtain truth. Science is not ultimate. Its greatest failures come in the area of understanding subjectivity.

Subjectivity as a way of knowing

Kierkegaard recognized that how we experience this underlying map subjectively is all that really matters to the individual. "Subjectivity is truth," he argued.[33] This raises the questions, Are there subjective truths? Are there truths available only subjectively? If so, what is the nature of these truths, and are they amenable to some sort of subjective scientific method?

Of course there are subjective truths, or at least there is one subjective truth. René Descartes identified it long ago with *cogito ergo sum*, or "I think, therefore I am." We are aware of our own consciousness, and in fact it is the only one to which we have access. Some have dismissed consciousness as an illusion.[34] Others have postulated a dualist position that the mind and brain are separate things.[35] Some suggest that explaining consciousness is beyond the power of the human mind.[36] Despite a plethora of ideas that attempt to explain it, consciousness remains a mystery (notwithstanding such provocative titles as Dennett's *Consciousness Explained*).[37] It has been called an emergent property or supervenience,[38] but these terms convey little about causal mechanisms. Something happens, but no one is sure what specific factors in the brain bring consciousness about.

Subjective truths

Kierkegaard chides speculative philosophers, such as Hegel, because their theories and systems are not grounded in a subjective matrix:

> If a dancer could leap very high, we would admire him. But if he tried to give the impression that he could fly, let laughter single him out for suitable punishment; even though it might be true that he could leap as high as any dancer ever had done. Leaping is the accomplishment of a being essentially earthly, one who respects the earth's gravitational force, since the leaping is only momentary. But flying carries a suggestion of being emancipated from telluric conditions, a privilege reserved for winged creatures, and perhaps also shared by the inhabitants of the moon—and there perhaps the System will first find its true readers.[39]

We might so accuse hardline materialists who similarly suggest that there is no consciousness and that it is all an illusion. (Whose, I wonder, if no one's there?) My subjective consciousness is my only reality. Kierkegaard posited that objective scientific or historical certainty can only be approximated. It might get closer and closer to a presupposed objective reality, but there would always be incomplete facts, impossible observations, and other omissions that would prohibit a complete description of the phenomenon. Therefore, our subjective grasp of certainty could never reach beyond approximation.

> Kierkegaard points out that certainty is an illusion as long as it is based on observations or knowledge outside the one subjective truth that we can be certain about: our own existence. To Kierkegaard, this was the only truth that mattered, hence the title of the section of the *Concluding Unscientific Postscript*: "Subjectivity Is Truth." He goes on to define truth: "An objective uncertainty held fast in an appropriation-process of the most passionate inwardness is the truth."[40] Truth is not something floating out there in the universe; truth is a condition of existence that can be appropriated only within the subjective capabilities of the individual.

This idea that all our knowledge really derives from personal subjectivity is developed further by B. Alan Wallace:

> When encountering a scientist's findings—even if we are scientists—most of us don't know that her empirical data are sound, rather we tend to take them on faith. Otherwise, the only way to know they are sound is to create a comparable laboratory of our own (we can't use hers, or if the data can be replicated only in hers, and in no other laboratory, they are suspect), replicate the experiment, and see whether our findings corroborate hers. Likewise, we don't know that the mathematical analysis of her data is sound unless we apply our own analysis and thereby confirm her results. Likewise, we don't know that her theoretical interpretation of the quantitative results is sound unless we apply our own knowledge of the theory to corroborate hers. In other words, her findings— which on the surface seem to be public and third-person—are *known* by us to be valid if and only if we pursue the same research ourselves. That is, all "third-person" or collaborative research really consists of multiple first persons doing their own research and trusting the work of their collaborators.[41]

So faith is not merely an attribute of religious praxis; it is a necessary ingredient for moving science forward. We trust that the assumptions, experiments, analyses, and conclusions of our colleagues are accurate and are done in the same way we would do them if we were doing the experiments. This process describes Karl Popper's "World 3," the accumulation of knowledge, represented by the papers, books, and other forms of discourse done according to appropriate procedures dictated by the scientific method.[42]

Faith, then, is an element of all subjective acquisition of knowledge. To Kierkegaard, faith and truth are inseparable:

> The truth is precisely the venture which chooses an objective uncertainty with the passion of the infinite. I contemplate the order of nature in the hope of finding God, and I see omnipotence and wisdom; but I also see much else that disturbs my mind and excites anxiety. The sum of all this is an objective uncertainty. But it is for this very reason that the

inwardness becomes as intense as it is, for it embraces this objective uncertainty with the entire passion of the infinite. In the case of a mathematical proposition the objectivity is given, but for this reason the truth of such a proposition is also an indifferent truth.

But the above definition of truth is an equivalent expression for faith. Without risk there is no faith. Faith is precisely the contradiction between the infinite passion of the individual's inwardness and the objective uncertainty.[43]

Here is expressed Kierkegaard's famous leap. Faith begins with a recognition that there exists uncertainty of any knowledge (except mathematical, which has no existential value, Kierkegaard posits). Deciding that something is true always involves a certain level of uncertainty.

This is where scientific materialism fails. By denying a subjective component to the appropriation of truth, and by not recognizing the role of faith in the appropriation of truth, the materialist outlook is philosophically flawed—reminiscent of Kierkegaard's dancers described earlier. The assumptions, as summarized by Wallace, are (1) "The physical world is the only reality" and (2) "The universe originates wholly from impersonal natural forces; it is devoid of any intrinsic moral order or values."[44] These assumptions are all accepted without question or reflection, when in fact there exist no empirical observations that support or verify these assertions. Because materialists are blind to the form of dogmatism that they have embraced, they are left denying the most fundamental existential truth we can appropriate: our own subjectivity.

The nature of subjective truths

I do not mean to suggest that there is no difference between objective and subjective truths. Objective truths, the kind we seek through the scientific method, are those that we suppose would be discovered by anyone using the same instruments, methods, and analysis that we have used. In doing science we detail what we did to perform the experiment—in essence, giving a recipe for what we hope guides others in a repeatable sequence of actions that lead to the same data that we obtained. These are what we call objective truths, despite, as I have pointed out, their ultimately subjective nature. These are truths that we hope map an objective reality—one that would exist whether we were here or not.

Nevertheless, are there purely subjective truths available only to the individual? My experience of subjectivity is forever unavailable to any other existing individual: the fundamental me that experiences life's rich qualia, the person framed by my quantitative mental states, the combination of processes that combine to make up that entity is unique and individually mine. That at least is a subjective truth that is singularly available to me alone.

If there is one such truth, are there others? Are there subjective truths that have no counterpart in the objective world but may be a part of a world hidden from the objective world? What would be the nature of such subjective truths? One point must be made here: the subjective truths I am looking for are universal truths available only subjectively—not some sort of personal truth, or something that is true just for me, but rather universal truths that explore a universe hidden from the measurable universe with which science seeks to grapple.

My faith in God is what I believe to be one such subjective universal truth. When I pray, when I am reading and pondering the scriptures, I feel God's presence subjectively. How I experience and interact with this subjective experience is ineffable, personal, and real. Just as when I experience the color red while looking at the fire hydrant outside my window, my subjective experience with God is vibrant and undeniable within the context of my mind when it is experienced. This subjective experience convinces me that there is a God. This does not mean I am unaware that my mind might be sending me signals generated from within my brain alone, but just as I reject Berkeley's idealism because the preponderance of evidence seems to me to support an independent objective world, my subjective experience with God suggests that something outside myself is causing the perception of a relationship with God. I do recognize the possibility that these feelings and sensations could be nothing more than an evolved strategy for coping with a big brain, perhaps necessary for the higher level of cognitive power human beings enjoy.[45] I find it harder to believe that God is not there than that God exists.

Still, how do we weigh subjective experience? Is there a science of subjectivity? I think there is. I remember hearing of an interview with an atheist scientist (I have forgotten the name of this scientist) who claimed that you might as well believe that there is a teapot circling the planet Pluto as believe that there is a god interacting with the affairs of the universe. Both are outside of science's ability to detect. One can posit any such nonevidential nonsense, but clearly the burden of proof lies with the proposer, and thus far there has been little evidence to support the god hypotheses. Perhaps.

The teapot analogy shows some of the problems of getting behind subjective truths—assuming they exist. For example, what if the teapot speaks to me? Of course, such a claim would be taken as nothing more than madness, but if I offer a formula by which anyone can speak to the teapot, "Do the following: stand on your head, blink three times, and say didy-didy-da-da," and when people follow my recipe the teapot speaks to them, then there is some supporting evidence for . . . what? Only one thing—I am not alone in my madness. Myriad things could be going on: a teapot that circles Pluto that actually talks to people, or a repeatable brain malfunction caused by too much blood rushing to the head of an upside-down person chanting nonsense, or a maniacal government experiment located in a deep silo in northern Colorado that monitors brain wave activity and sends messages that the brain can pick up when it detects the formula being followed. The second and third are at least susceptible to scientific tests, but the hypothesis about the teapot is again untestable. Suppose, then, that our exhaustive search for alternative explanations falls short. At what point do we begin to accept the hypothesis that there is a talking teapot? As the number of people who try the subjective experiment continues to grow (all agreeing that when you follow the recipe the teapot speaks to you), can you ever accept that there is a talking teapot? Do we apply Sherlock Holmes's famous dictum—When you have eliminated the impossible, whatever remains must be the truth, no matter how improbable—and assume that there is indeed a talking teapot? It seems that no matter how many people subjectively experience a talking teapot, without additional warrant we cannot accept that a talking teapot orbits Pluto, because it does not fit with what we know about the rest of the universe. We need something else. We need that warrant. The only place we have seen consciousness before is in complex biological beings. Teapots are not complex enough to be talking with us. Therefore, despite the number of reported cases of a talking teapot, we cannot accept it as true. It makes no sense in light of the other facts we know about the universe.

Suppose the teapot itself supplies that warrant. Does that change things? Suppose it tells those receiving the messages that it was once an ordinary teapot until one day a group of aliens abducted it from Earth and filled it with advanced neurotechnology that gave it senescence. Then they equipped it with a transmitter of a new and unknown technology, allowing it to communicate with biological brains, and set it circling Pluto. While still far-fetched, this does seem to place the claim of a teapot communicating to earthling brains in the realm of objects and processes that could conceivably exist in the universe.

A subjective truth, then, has to fit into what we have learned about the objective nature of the universe. Subjective truths should not contradict objective truths. Still, if there are subjective truths, then they lie completely outside the scientific method. Yet, again, the fact that consciousness exists demonstrates that there is at least one subjective truth that seems irrefutable—our own consciousness. That, at least, for each individual is undeniable (except for those hardline materialists who *have* managed to deny its existence), and yet ever unavailable to the thousands of other individual consciousnesses that surround it. What I experience as my relationship with God is ever outside your purview. You can never know what I feel as a conscious being. You may check my brain states while I claim to be experiencing God. You may correlate behavioral responses to my claims of experiences with God. Yet the qualia of God are experienced only at the subjective level. From such subjective experiments as prayer, feeling after God, and letting God guide my life, I have gathered subjective evidence that God is there and individually interested in me. While it is impossible for you to experience the things that contribute to my belief (try to describe, using words, the taste of a lemon to someone who has never experienced something sour), I can recommend the process to you and see if you come to the same conclusion. So faith is not a matter of belief despite evidence or lack of evidence; faith is the subjective experiment of coming to find nonscientifically available subjective truths. Just as we suspect that others have consciousness despite the complete lack of any objective measure, we may assume that subjective truths are universal but can be appropriated only by the individual. Objectively they are invisible, like other people's individual consciousness.

Conclusion

I am not convinced that materialists hold the intellectual high ground in their dismissal of religion. I have found great value in the methods of science in exploring the visible universe. Once we move beyond my belief in God, and the materialists' rejection thereof, we find that our practice of science is the same. We publish in the same journals, speak at the same conferences, and read the same books. In the realm of the subjective experience of the universe, however, we disagree profoundly.

Notes

1. A few examples include Richard Dawkins, *Climbing Mount Improbable* (New York: W. W. Norton, 1996); Stephen Jay Gould, *Rocks of Ages: Science and Religion in the Fullness of Life* (New York: Ballantine, 1999); Kenneth R. Miller, *Finding Darwin's God: A Scientist's Search for Common Ground between God and Evolution* (New York: Cliff Street Books, 1999); Holmes Rolston III, *Genes, Genesis, and God: Values and Their Origins in Natural and Human History* (Cambridge: Cambridge University Press, 1999); Gregory R. Peterson, "Whose Evolution? Which Theology?," *Zygon: Journal of Religion and Science* 35 (June 2000): 221-32; Robert Pollack, *The Faith of Biology and the Biology of Faith: Order, Meaning, and Free Will in Modern Medical Science* (New York: Columbia University Press, 2000); Michael Shermer, *Why People Believe Weird Things: Pseudoscience, Superstition, and Other Confusions of Our Time* (New York: W. H. Freeman, 1997); Larry Arnhart, "The Truth, Goodness, and Beauty of Darwinism," *Zygon: Journal of Religion and Science* 36 (March 2001): 77-92; Michael Ruse, *Can a Darwinian Be a Christian? The Relationship between Science and Religion* (Cambridge: Cambridge University Press, 2001).

2. Daniel C. Dennett, *Darwin's Dangerous Idea: Evolution and the Meanings of Life* (New York: Simon and Schuster, 1996); and Dawkins, *Climbing Mount Improbable*.

3. B. Alan Wallace, *The Taboo of Subjectivity: Toward a New Science of Consciousness* (New York: Oxford University Press, 2000).

4. Dawkins, *Climbing Mount Improbable*.

5. In addition to Dawkins, *Climbing Mount Improbable*, and Dennett, *Darwin's Dangerous Idea*, see Susan Blackmore, *The Meme Machine* (Oxford: Oxford University Press, 1999).

6. Gould, *Rocks of Ages*.

7. Shermer, *Why People Believe Weird Things*; and Shermer, *How We Believe: The Search for God in an Age of Science* (New York: W. H. Freeman, 2000).

8. Varadaraja V. Raman, "Science and Religion: Some Demarcation Criteria," *Zygon: Journal of Religion and Science* 36 (September 2001): 549.

9. Wallace, *Taboo of Subjectivity*.

10. Daniel C. Dennett, *Consciousness Explained* (New York: Little, Brown, 1992); and Blackmore, *Meme Machine*.

11. Wallace, *Taboo of Subjectivity*, 3.

12. Following Harry Clements, *Alfred Russel Wallace: Biologist and Social Reformer* (London: Hutchinson, 1983).

13. Arnold C. Brackman, *A Delicate Arrangement: The Strange Case of Charles Darwin and Alfred Russel Wallace* (New York: Times Books, 1980).

14. Alfred Russel Wallace, *Darwinism: An Exposition of the Theory of Natural Selection with Some of Its Applications* (London: Macmillan, 1889).

15. Alfred Russel Wallace, *Miracles and Modern Spiritualism*, 3rd ed. (London: George Redway, [1874] 1896), vii.

16. Wallace, *Miracles and Modern Spiritualism*, 38.

17. Wallace, *Miracles and Modern Spiritualism*, 43.

18. Wallace, *Miracles and Modern Spiritualism*, 132.

19. Wallace, *Miracles and Modern Spiritualism*, 133.

20. Thomas S. Kuhn, *The Structure of Scientific Revolutions* (Chicago: University of Chicago Press, 2012).

21. Janet Browne, *The Power of Place: Charles Darwin* (New York: Knopf, 2002).

22. Wallace, *Taboo of Subjectivity*, 37-39.

23. Søren Kierkegaard, *Concluding Unscientific Postscript to Philosophical Fragments* (Princeton, NJ: Princeton University Press, 1846).

24. Sewall Wright, *Evolution and the Genetics of Populations, Volume 4: Variability within and among Natural Populations* (Chicago: University of Chicago Press, 1978).

25. Sergey Gavrilets, "A Dynamical Theory of Speciation on Holey Adaptive Landscapes," *American Naturalist* 154 (1999): 1-22.

26. David L. Hull, *Science as a Process: An Evolutionary Account of the Social and Conceptual Development of Science* (Chicago: University of Chicago Press, 1988).

27. Gödel's theorem proved that within any axiomatic system in mathematics there are true theorems that cannot be proved within that system.

28. As does David J. Chalmers in his book *The Conscious Mind* (Oxford: Oxford University Press, 1996).

29. See Gould, *Rocks of Ages*.

30. Stephen Jay Gould, *Wonderful Life: The Burgess Shale and the Nature of History* (New York: Norton, 1990).

31. Dawkins, *Climbing Mount Improbable*; and Dennett, *Darwin's Dangerous Idea*.

32. Steven L. Peck, Stephen P. Ellner, and Fred Gould, "A Spatially Explicit Stochastic Model Demonstrates the Feasibility of Wright's Shifting Balance Theory," *Evolution* 52 (1998): 1834-39; and "Varying Migration and Deme Size and the Feasibility of the Shifting Balance," *Evolution* 54 (2000): 324-27.

33. Kierkegaard, *Concluding Unscientific Postscript*, 187.

34. Dennett argues such in *Darwin's Dangerous Idea*.

35. Karl Popper and J. C. Eccles, *The Self and Its Brain* (New York: Routledge, 1977); and Chalmers, *Conscious Mind*.

36. Colin McGinn, *The Mysterious Flame: Conscious Minds in a Material World* (New York: Basic Books, 1999); and Joseph Levine, *Purple Haze* (Oxford: Oxford University Press, 2001).

37. Dennett, *Consciousness Explained* (New York: Little, Brown, 1992).

38. Philip Clayton, "Neuroscience, the Person, and God: An Emergentist Account," *Zygon: Journal of Religion and Science* 35 (September 2000): 613-52.

39. Kierkegaard, *Concluding Unscientific Postscript*, 112-13.

40. Kierkegaard, *Concluding Unscientific Postscript*, 182.

41. Wallace, *Taboo of Subjectivity*, 184.

42. Karl Popper, "Knowledge: Subjective versus Objective," in *Popper Selections*, ed. D. Miller (Princeton, NJ: Princeton University Press, 1985), 58-77.

43. Kierkegaard, *Concluding Unscientific Postscript*, 182.

44. Wallace, *Taboo of Subjectivity*, 161.

45. There has been much talk of the possibility of there being a God module in the brain. Its existence or nonexistence is irrelevant to the question of God's existence. Most of the evolved structures of our brain are used to process outside signals such as light, sound, and olfactory chemicals. If part of my brain is used to experience God, whether it is processing real signals or not is still an open question. On the God module, see Carol Rausch Albright, "The 'God Module' and the Complexifying Brain," *Zygon: Journal of Religion and Science* 35 (December 2000): 735-44; Andrew Newberg, Eugene d'Aquili, and Vince Rause, *Why God Won't Go Away: Brain Science and the Biology of Belief* (New York: Ballantine, 2001); and Michael Spezio, "Understanding Biology in Religious Experience: The Biogenetic Structuralist Approach of Eugene d'Aquili and Andrew Newberg," *Zygon: Journal of Religion and Science* 36 (September 2001): 477-84.

3

Crawling Out of the Primordial Soup: A Step toward the Emergence of an LDS Theology Compatible with Organic Evolution

EVOLUTION IS A MESSY PROCESS. In his provocatively titled essay "Narnia's Aslan, Earth's Darwin, and Heaven's God," evangelical Christian Wesley J. Wildman details some of the waste and brutality of natural selection that are inevitable accompaniments of evolution. He then poses a stark challenge: "Surely such a loving, personal Deity would have created in another way, a way that involved less trial and error, fewer false starts, fewer mindless species extinctions, fewer pointless cruelties, and less reliance on predation to sort out the fit from the unfit." By way of conclusion he issues the far-from-rhetorical question: "What sort of God could, would, and did create the world through evolution?"[1] Wildman's question suggests that evolution has striking implications for theology—including, I would add, LDS theology.

And in fact, what might it mean that God "used" evolution to create life's diversity? Was this a choice for God among other alternatives? Do Wildman's pessimistic conclusions hold for Mormonism? Does evolution imply a noninterventionist Deity? Are there more optimistic views possible, some of which may actually suggest that evolution enhances and expands our view of God? Are adjustments necessary to our key doctrines of the creation, fall, and atonement to accommodate an evolutionary perspective? And why should we make this accommodation? What is lost and what is gained if our faith community fully and without compromise embraces evolution? There *are* deep and unavoidable theological implications for incorporating into our theology the belief that natural selection structured the way life evolved on our planet.

I would like to sketch some of these implications. By this I mean rough out some of the potential problems and perplexities that will need to be sorted through in embracing a fully compatible perspective between evolution through natural selection and the LDS faith. In this conspectus, I hope to gesture to possible solutions to the perplexities that merging evolution and theology may bring to LDS thought. There are many sticking points, and I mean only to make a beginning and to seed conversation. I make no claims that the results are either complete or thorough, but I hope that making such a start will be useful.

Another potential difficulty is that some of the proposed solutions to the identified problems cannot be sorted out except through further revelation. Since Latter-day Saints fully anticipate the bestowal of further light and knowledge, the current incompleteness should neither surprise nor disturb. Ruminations such as these might serve as a catalyst for the kinds of questions that must be asked before revelation can be given. In scriptural and LDS history, questions are well known to have opened every major revelation from the first vision of Joseph Smith to the 1978 revelation on priesthood ordination for all worthy males. Questions such as those orbiting a reconciliation of evolution and LDS faith are difficult and will sometimes remain without answers, yet that does not mean we should not ask them. Elie Wiesel captures this need nicely in a conversation with a friend:

> "Man comes closer to God through the questions he asks Him, he liked to say. Therein lies true dialogue. Man asks and God replies. But we don't understand His replies. We cannot understand them. Because they dwell in the depths of our souls and remain there until we die. The real answers, Eliezer, you will find only within yourself."
>
> "And why do you pray, Moishe?" I asked him.
>
> "I pray to the God within me for the strength to ask Him the real questions."[2]

For the purposes of this chapter, I will assume that evolution through natural selection is a true description of how life arose on this planet and that life on Earth has emerged through a completely Darwinian process (throughout this chapter, *Darwinian* refers to evolution through natural

selection). Much has been written on the nature of the evidence supporting these claims, including the evidence found in the fossil record, comparative anatomy, geological stratigraphic analysis, DNA molecular studies, the physics of radiometric data, and so on, and I will not here debate
the nature of the evidence nor the conclusions drawn from inferences
made from that evidence. Here I accept them as accurate according to
current understandings in contemporary evolutionary science. The LDS
tradition also has a rich history of attempts at legitimizing and reconciling evolutionary science with the faith and tracing views of evolution
within Mormonism, historically and contemporaneously.[3] This project is
different in that I assume from the outset that evolution through natural
selection has been established as true (and I use that word very deliber-
ately) and that there is a legitimate, faithful response both to doctrine
and to our best understanding of how life on Earth unfolds.

Because evolution through natural selection is thought to be a universal principle[4] or physical algorithm,[5] let me briefly give the necessary
ingredients for its operation and tease apart why natural selection creates
tension for LDS theology.

Evolution by natural selection requires three elements: (1) variation in
traits, including a source of novel variation; (2) selection on trait differences
based on the environment in which relevant entities are embedded; and
(3) offspring able to inherit trait differences from their parents. Often a
fourth element, embedded in the above conditions, is made explicit: (4) time.

If these conditions are in place, natural selection will enhance how
well the object fits local environmental circumstances. This adaptation
will occur whether those entities are chemicals, organisms, or digital
computer programs. Within the philosophy of biology, this phenomenon
is referred to as an a priori principle rather than a cause. The task, then, of
the empirical scientist is to show that a particular kind of entity is just the
sort of thing to which these four principles apply. I will focus on the evolution of organisms on Earth because it is our best and clearest example.

These principles have theological implications. First, note that this
process is competitive. Some of those organisms are selected at the expense of others. There are winners and losers. Second, the variation is
random with respect to what will be successful and unsuccessful. The organisms are confronted with both the requirements for survival and the
local environment in which they find themselves. These factors create a
direction in selection: toward better fit with that environment. Evolution
is then determined by which traits succeed in a given local environment

and which do not. There is no grand overall direction toward which it moves, no master plan that it fulfills. The evolutionary process is blind variation in traits being chosen at a specific location and time that results in some organisms being more successful than others in the local environment in which they are reproducing.

Third, these competitive bouts are played out in units of energy. Over time these energy exchanges create a positive feedback loop. The organisms that are able to capture the most energy and employ it for successful survival are most likely to replace other entities in the next generation by entities with traits like their own. Two basic strategies have been especially useful in survival: (1) using chemical changes induced by the energy of sunlight or heat to create energy in more usable forms to maintain the organism's structure and function, and (2) stealing this energy from those who create it or from others who have stolen it. Most plants are good examples of the first strategy; cattle and puma are examples of the second.

Empirical observations on how evolution has played out to date on Earth depict a process that is enormously creative, patulous (spreading widely from a center), complex, and diverse. All of these characteristics increase through time as the history of life on Earth unfolds. This increase, scientists believe, occurs because evolving organisms tend to transform their environment. These modifications change the selective regime in which organisms are embedded, and these changes cause even more complexity. This pattern of increased environmental complexity is called niche construction in evolutionary biology.[6] For example, when life forms moved from Earth's early oceans to land, plants opened new niches. These vegetative incursions created new habitats as plants competed for limited resources and diversified over time to capture those limited resources. Next, insects began exploiting these plants, which further changed the environment, allowing a greater diversification of habitats. Amphibians then exploited both of these new feeding opportunities, followed in turn by reptiles, then birds, and then mammals. Each of these waves of diversity opened new niches and habitats, creating further occasions for exploiting the competitive interactions of organisms and increasing habitat diversity, organism complexity, and the amount of creativity in the universe.

This narrative is the standard, empirically based, scientific explanation of every example of structured life on Earth. God enters this story (or fails to do so) with no necessary explanatory power. God has long been used as an explanation for otherwise puzzling aspects of life on Earth and its abundant and obviously designed features. For example,

Xenophon's Socrates pointed out in the fourth century BC that nature's numerous designed aspects suggest a designer: "Again, the incisors of all creatures are adapted for cutting, the molars for receiving food from them and grinding it. And again, the mouth through which the food they want goes in, is set near the eyes and nostrils; but since what goes out is unpleasant, the ducts through which it passes are turned away and removed as far as possible from the organs of sense. With such signs of forethought in these arrangements, can you doubt whether they are the works of chance or design?" Aristodemus, Socrates's interlocutor, answers: "No, of course not. When I regard them in this light they do look very like the handiwork of a wise and loving creator."[7]

The argument that design implies an outside designer runs very deep, from antiquity up into the modern period. William Paley developed its most carefully articulated expression in his *Natural Theology* (1802). In it he famously argues that, were you to find a watch on the beach, you would never attempt to claim that it had been produced by natural processes. Its very existence implies a watchmaker.[8] Darwin had read Paley thoroughly and understood that any explanation of the origin of life on Earth must include an explanation of design. Evolution by natural selection does so. Despite unscientific attempts to deny this achievement—for example, by the Discovery Institute's cleverly conceived intelligent design movement[9]—most scientists agree that evolution provides a sufficient explanation of design. In fact, the Darwinian conclusion that design is not evidence of a designer has been one of evolution theory's most threatening aspects.

What are the implications of design-without-a-designer for theology? More specifically, what are its implications for LDS thought and philosophy? To explore this question in detail, I want to draw on distinctions in theological outlooks made by Niels Gregersen, University of Copenhagen professor of theology.[10] He identifies five theological responses to the idea of "emergence" that serve elegantly to partition the space of responses to evolution. Emergence is the idea that properties of a complex system may arise that are unpredictable or unanticipated from a reductive description of lower-level processes. Emergent properties are generally explainable by the lower-level processes but rely on complex, local interactions. A classic example is a snowflake, the existence of which would have been hard to predict just from the properties of freezing water, but which is explicable in terms of those properties.

I find these five responses useful for exploring evolution theologically because, in part, evolution and emergence are twin concepts that play in, about, and through each other in integrated ways and are part and parcel of the complexity that needs a theological response. These responses are equally useful in illuminating aspects of LDS theology.

Gregersen's Five Theological Responses

The five perspectives or responses are (1) flat religious naturalism, (2) evolving theistic naturalism, (3) atemporal theism, (4) temporal theism, and (5) eschatological theism. I will consider each perspective in turn; but interestingly, all are possible responses in LDS thought, although admittedly sometimes with a bit of twisting and hammering. Before beginning, however, a couple of clarifications are necessary to draw attention to certain aspects of LDS theology that will need special consideration as we assess the possibility of Darwin-compatible Mormon theism. Moreover, none of these models embrace a cheap fundamentalist creationism, by which I mean a view in which creation consists of sudden legerdemain-like wand waving. All five perspectives try to explain emergence in terms of the full complexity of the evolutionary story as detailed in the observable physical record and currently accepted as standard by scientists.

A difficulty that will make this project of bringing together evolution and LDS theology tough slogging is that, within LDS thinking, what we mean by a "physical universe" is often muddled. Mormonism displays a kind of expansive physicalism suggesting that the universe in toto is a farrago of matter of one kind or another (D&C 131:7), that part of it ("spirit matter") remains undetectable by our perceptual apparatuses and instrumentation, while we have phenomenological or manipulative access to only the less "fine" or less "pure" part. This materiality includes Gods, spirits, intelligences, and so on, and may exist in extraspatial or temporal dimensions (or both); but it does, presumably, still follow laws of some kind. All matter is subject to God's manipulation, thanks to his greater knowledge and influence. This theological description imposes a kind of dualism in which some aspects of the universe are available to us and others are not. Because we lack reliable epistemic access to the "spirit matter" part of this world, this concept must remain outside our scientific theories and practices, even though it may play a role in a deeper physical reality.[11]

Second, in Mormon thought God is embodied. It is not completely clear what this means,[12] but it implies that at least in some sense God has a biology. What such a biology might entail, however, is quite speculative, but at least two key doctrines are contingent on the concept: (1) the literal physical son-father relationship of Christ to God the Father, and (2) the human capacity for a bodily theosis,[13] which recapitulates God's developmental process, if not completely in scope, at least in such a way that it can be considered human beings' movement toward becoming godlike.[14] I am clearly riding roughshod over some controversial ideas about which much ink has been spilled and in which more nuance and refinement could be considered; but among average church members whom I know, the claim "As man is, God once was. As God is, man may become" would be considered neither surprising nor controversial.

1. Flat religious naturalism

In Gregersen's partitioning of religious space by emergence, the first category is flat religious naturalism. In this view, the natural world is all there is—nothing beyond the physical reality accessible to current and future science. This view, though denying anything supernatural, leaves open the possibility that other substances might be discovered. For example, dark matter would be fully acceptable in flat naturalism because it can be inferred through human observation at galactic scales. But the idea that God might use supernatural means or substances (including a soul or Descartes's *res cogitans*) to accomplish his goals or purposes is dismissed.

While this perspective might seem to be the basic grounding of a strict materialism, it still acknowledges the sacred nature of the universe.[15] An encounter with God is therefore not one of personal relationship, transcendence, or immanence, but rather one of mystery. God in this view is just nature and its processes, and the proper response is awe. Nature is, in fact, divine. This view resonates well with certain forms of Buddhism and other forms of nontheistic religion.

While at first glance it seems unlikely that Mormonism could be situated along this axis, Mormonism does in some sense embrace a mystery about fundamental questions that have occupied post-Plotinean Western religions. These questions focus on God's nature, attributes, and powers. For example, in this view, the laws that frame and structure the matter from which all things, including God, are constituted are not created by God but are self-existent with him. Matter, intelligence, and the laws that govern their interaction would be self-existent and uncreated—with some resulting confusion in the way Mormons talk about God. For example, some speak as if God created the laws of the universe and buy into anthropic arguments about God's fine-tuning the universe as the lawgiver, then fall into talking about God using natural, albeit possibly higher, laws to organize the universe from unorganized matter.[16]

Theologically, Mormonism offers the following intriguing revelation on matter:

> There is no such thing as immaterial matter. All spirit is matter, but it is more fine or pure, and can only be discerned by purer eyes; we cannot see it; but when our bodies are purified we shall see that it is all matter. (D&C 131:7-8)

If we carry this statement a little further, matter could be broadly conceived to include God, spirits, and intelligence as part of the "finer" or "purer" matter thought to make up the extended universe. In this context, flat religious naturalism might be conceivable in the LDS faith, as it has few answers to questions about why the universe exists as it does and embraces the idea that its constituent substances are eternal. This matter includes the intelligences that eventually became God by taking on his mantle. Therefore, mystery and awe at this scale may be the only appropriate response.

2. Evolving theistic naturalism

Evolving theistic naturalism is the perspective that God has emerged from the natural world and is a quality of nature itself. Nature has moved forward in increasing complexity, and part of this complexity is God. Just as consciousness emerges from neural complexity in materialist explanations of consciousness, God emerges from the complexity of the entire universe. Obviously, in this view God is not prior to the universe, nor does he act as its creator in the traditional sense.

Mormonism does not accommodate this view very well. Seeing God as *just* an emergent property of the natural universe does not seem to fit within the spectrum of proposed LDS theologies.

3. Atemporal theism

This view is the classic post-Plotinean view of God that includes the divine attributes of omnipresence, omnipotence, and omniscience. According to this view, God exists outside of time, is the rational ground of all being, and has created the universe and its laws, fine-tuning it for human life. Atemporal theism assumes that God is "outside of" time and that, in some sense, the past, present, and future are all "present" before God. An implication of this view is that God cannot be affected by the world, thus emphasizing his transcendence. This view is compatible both with evolution and with creationism, which posits that the world was created suddenly in all its complexity. This view of God seems to impose a strict determinism on the final teleological goal of the creation (which, again from God's perspective, occurs as a simultaneous "now"). God, in this view, is unchangeable. Human freedom may be possible, but such assertions are often incoherent since God knows what we will choose and sees our exact future resulting from those choices.

Mormon belief systems seem varied (or generally confused) on this point. Blake Ostler, in a theological study, makes the point that Joseph Smith's doctrines, developed in Nauvoo, Illinois (1839–44), do not allow this view of God, but it is not uncommon to find discourse that assumes this view.[17]

Yet because of the Plotineanization by conservative Christianizing influences, Mormonism has maintained a relationship with this view.

4. Temporal theism

Taking the form of process theology, the theological possibilities of temporal theism have received a friendly reception among many Mormon thinkers.[18] In this view God has a core identity that makes him God but influences, and is influenced by, temporal changes. In addition, the future is open. While it may be possible that God understands and can "see" all logical possibilities, those potentialities are realized only in some actual futures. Furthermore, those futures' realizations depend on the actions of free agents, which may include fundamental particles and their associations.

This viewpoint seems most open to theistic Darwinism by providing an opening for God to be part of the unfolding universe. This view continues to be the most promising way to harmonize the two fields and is the perspective largely embraced by Catholic scholars Pierre Teilhard de Chardin and John Haught (discussed below).

5. Eschatological theism

The last model Gregersen explores is eschatological theism. In this perspective, emergent features in the world do not depend strictly on the past. The future is often determined by contingent events in the present that could have been otherwise had God not intervened. New futures hinge on small events that turn out to be major turning points (recall the proverb "For want of a nail the kingdom was lost"). Eschatological theism denies that future emergent events result exclusively from the operation of natural law; rather, God "pulls" the future into existence through such bifurcation and contingent points in history to achieve the ends that he is interested in bringing about. Thus he exercises influence on these events. As this argument goes, the future cannot be strictly determined through an analysis of the present state of things, and a future state can be understood only retrospectively by looking into the past. It is eschatological in the sense that God's purposes and aims can be understood only in retrospect: "The point here," explains Gregersen, "is that potentialities do not simply reside in the past configurations of matter; they result from interplay between creaturely potencies and the coming into being of the divine possibilities offered to the world. Accordingly, the past and the present must be seen in light of the future, rather than the future being explained out of the past or the present."[19]

This view is strongly interventionist. Contingent events in the past that were brought together were among the possibilities present at the time of the contingent event. This reading of the past, then, looks very similar to declaring that what happened was just God's will. So in practical terms, it is not clear how this point of view offers any advantage over looking at things from the viewpoint of atemporal theism. In both, God is clearly teleologically drawing things toward a future that he has determined.

However, from the LDS viewpoint that prophecy is an important part of how the world works, eschatological theism may be useful in showing how the specific prophecies found in the scriptures are brought to pass by God's intent—that they were pulled into the future by divine action.

All five of these viewpoints assume compatibility between theology and evolution. But Gregersen's perspectives are very general, and it will be useful to look at some specific responses from philosophers and theologians to problems of teleology and design.

Theological Responses to Evolution

Since the moment Darwin's *On the Origin of Species* appeared in 1859, theologians have responded with attempts at both dismissal and reconciliation.[20] The latter have taken the form of everything from complete acceptance—simple variations on the theme of "That's just the way God did it!"—to deeper, more nuanced attempts at bringing the two ways of knowing together.

To get a sense of how LDS thinking may respond to the introduction of evolution into its theological concepts, it is useful to look at how other Christian groups have responded to the challenge.[21] Most efforts by Catholic and Protestant theologians have focused on three aspects, all of which are also relevant to LDS responses to evolution: (1) teleology and divine purpose, with humans being an important goal toward which the universe is directed; (2) design and its implications about God's attributes; and (3) the presence of natural evil. All three topics orbit the question of how and to what extent God acts in the world. I discuss the third topic, natural evil, separately from the first two as part of the section titled "Mormon Evolutionary Theology" below.

Teleology and divine purpose

One of the most troubling aspects in reconciling Darwinism with the idea of a personal God is its relentless lack of direction—its purposelessness on macroevolutionary scales.[22] Laypersons often interpret this lack of a "goal" as supporting the claim that evolution is a random process, but that is not quite right. Within a local environment, by random variation inheritable traits (traits that occur through the genetic code) are selected disproportionally in such a way that those traits that provide the organism with some advantage in that environment tend to survive at higher rates. These traits are passed on to the next generation more frequently. So while there is no final goal toward which evolution tends, it is driven by selection within local environments. Nonetheless, it is correct to say that, over long time periods, evolution is not aiming at any particular direction or purpose.

One of the first philosophers to explore how certain features found in living organisms could arise evolutionarily without teleology was

French philosopher Henri Bergson (1859-1941). He saw evolution moving toward intelligence, instinct, and complexity. Bergson couched this form of evolution in terms of an élan vital, a life force that pushed life (and its precursor elements prior to life) forward in time, resulting in differentiation over a span of time in which the past is "gathered into a present."[23]

Michael Vaughan, in presenting Bergson's work, explains this process as "the organized being's ability to organize the re-emergence of creative change through the structures that it creates."[24] This force is not seen as something "extra"—such as the vitalism[25] that Enlightenment thinkers posited to explain life—but is an inherent property of matter and assemblages of matter. Evolutionary change is seen as inventive and creative. Vaughan adds:

> The truth is that adaptation explains the sinuosities of the movement of evolution, but not its general directions, still less the movement itself. The road that leads to the town is obliged to follow the ups and downs of the hills; it adapts itself to the accidents of the ground; but the accidents of the ground are not the cause of the road, nor have they given it its direction. At every moment they furnish it with what is indispensable, namely, the soil on which it lies; but if we consider the whole of the road, instead of each of its parts, the accidents of the ground appear only as impediments or causes of delay, for the road aims simply at the town and would fain be a straight line. Just so as regards the evolution of life and the circumstances through which it passes—with this difference, that evolution does not mark out a solitary route, *that it takes directions without aiming at ends, and that it remains inventive even in its adaptations.*
>
> But, if the evolution of life is something other than a series of adaptations to accidental circumstances, so also it is not the realization of a plan. A plan is given in advance. It is represented, or at least representable, before its realization. The complete execution of it may be put off to a distant future, or even indefinitely; but the idea is none the less formidable at the present time, in terms actually given. If, on the contrary, evolution is a creation unceasingly renewed, it creates, as it goes on, not only the forms of life, but the ideas that will enable the intellect to understand it, the terms which will serve

to express it. That is to say that *its future overflows its present, and can not be sketched out therein in an idea.*[26]

Bergson thus opens the door for a theological response (although he was not a theist as such) that allows for direction in evolution without teleology, but that nonetheless moves to places of potential theological interest such as intelligence, complexity, and even consciousness.

Design and God's implied attributes

One of the first theologians to attempt to address these concerns was Jesuit paleontologist Pierre Teilhard de Chardin (1881-1955). His engagement with evolution was personally costly since his church put considerable institutional pressure on him for his insistence on a theological engagement with evolution. He saw the universe as moving toward greater and greater "seeing" and described humans as the highest expression of this ability. Each human being stands as one who can "see" himself or herself in reflexive self-awareness. Therefore, the highest expression of life is found in this subjective experience. He breaks the history of the universe into "Pre-Life," "Life," and "Thought," the last of which he calls "the Noosphere." The emergence of consciousness characterizes the evolutionary stage of the Noosphere. It is important to keep in mind that this capacity for thought emerges from the universe through the progression of a flat ontology. Speaking of the universe, he wrote: "It is beginning to seem that there is definitely *more* in the molecule than the atom, *more* in the cell than in the molecule, *more* in the society than in the individual, and *more* in mathematical construction than in the calculations and theorems. We are now inclined to admit that at each further degree of combination *something* which is irreducible to isolated elements *emerges* in a new order."[27]

In Teilhard de Chardin's view, design is inherent in the evolutionary processes, which tend inexorably toward greater and greater complexity until consciousness arrives and finds its highest expression in humans. He also embraces a strong eschatology, which he calls the Omega Point. At this point, which occurs at the end of time, the universe preserves all that has happened, including all persons and their consciousness. In the final end of the universe, a universal consciousness will emerge. This consciousness is not God, but rather the final intent and purpose of God's creation. Teilhard de Chardin also recognizes the hard questions that arise through the brutality and wastefulness of the evolutionary process. He makes no effort or claims to understand these negative aspects but notes that such "evil" resembles "nothing so much as the way of the Cross."[28]

While his attempt to reconcile these disparate fields has not endured as a solution to the problem of an evolutionary theology, his efforts were significant in raising questions about how to fully embrace both evolution and theology in inventive and imaginative ways.

Since Teilhard de Chardin's effort, many theological efforts by both Catholics and Protestants have been situated in temporal theism. An especially promising area seems to be the process theology movement.[29] In this panentheistic view, God is more than, but also present in, all matter. As mentioned earlier, current efforts to reconcile evolution and religion have found this a productive area of shared space.

Catholic theologian John Haught argues that, in this process theology view, God is present "deeply" in creation and influences evolutionary processes in ways that are not manipulations of matter in an interventionist sense. Rather, God is deeply present in the fabric of the universe in ways that are indistinguishable to science or other forms of human observation.[30] God's purposes unfold because they are deeply present in the created world; they appear to emerge in the universe's overall movements and processes, moving forward in creative and unexpected ways. Haught sees creation in terms of "promise" rather than "design." He argues that science can fully study the universe's ontology and that its observations will be valid and informative, but that God is working on a different level. His purposes will unfold as the universe unfolds, not only as an ordering and organizing influence but also as a source of novelty:

> Theologically speaking, process theology suggests that we should logically foresee rather than be surprised, that God's creation is not driven coercively, that it is widely experimental, and that it unfolds over the course of a considerable amount of time. To those who object that process theology is hereby illegitimately redefining the idea of God's power in order to contrive a fit with neo-Darwinian theory, the reply is simply that no other conception of power is more consistent with the quite orthodox religious belief that God is infinite love.[31]

Haught therefore sees creation, not as a one-time event, but as an ongoing process in which God is continuously present. This unfolding is not interventionist. God is not prodding creation when it gets off track. Rather, his presence permeates all aspects of the universe.

Anglican theologian and scientist Arthur Peacocke writes similarly that his own naturalistic theology "is also based on an evolutionary perspective of the cosmological and biological sciences. This view entails an understanding of creation by God as a continuous activity, so that dynamic models and metaphors of divine creation and creativity become necessary. The work of God as Creator is regarded as manifest all the time in those very natural processes that are unveiled by the sciences in all their regularities."[32]

It is important to point out that although these views are naturalistic in that they do not accept miraculous interventions or divine guidance, they also embrace such basic Christian ideas and values as grace, incarnation, atonement, and resurrection, albeit with significant reinterpretations. For example, Karl Peters, professor emeritus of philosophy and religion at Rollins College, after describing a particularly meaningful interaction with his family, terms it a manifestation of grace in his life: "Reflecting on this event as a classical empiricist with a non-personal model of God as the creative process, I can see how the various elements that I have described—the family relationships, the beautiful weekend, the choir music, the setting of the service, the way it was conducted, my past experiences, my understanding of God as present when love is present—all came together serendipitously as an event of grace. I can think of the event as an example of serendipitous creativity—of God as the creative process—at work in my life."[33]

In addition to responses from process theologians, classic Trinitarian Christians have also responded to developing formal Christologies that embrace evolution through natural selection as creation. Celia Deane-Drummond, chair of theology and the biological sciences at the University of Chester in Great Britain, describes the work of creation as a "theo-drama" in which the freedom of creation emerges through actor-agents. These "actors" interact freely with one another, expressing individual choices and responses. She sees God's relationship with all of creation as an encounter. God, incarnated as Christ, enters the stage and becomes part of the play, an act that thereby affects the unfolding drama for all creation. Atonement and redemption are universal in scope, and humans have the greatest freedom to participate with Christ in redemption through his atonement. Her perspective specifically incorporates ecological concerns into the drama, with humans being required to care for and assist Christ with the redemption of all creation. Her work is a profound reconfiguring of Christ and his mission in a Darwinian framework that may have relevance to Mormons, as may her view of a universal atonement.[34] She describes her task thus: "This is also how I have sought to present the challenge of relating Christology and evolution: Namely, it is a challenge that insists on retaining hope for the future but also probes our own identity as evolved human persons living in an evolved world."[35]

Theologies continue to engage fruitfully and meaningfully with evolutionary biology. This ongoing conversation is important because evolution by natural selection continues to play an important role in understanding the development of life on Earth in ways that impinge directly on the idea of creation. The theologies of many religions play a role in this conversation. For example, in a 1996 statement on evolution to the Pontifical Academy of Sciences, Pope John Paul II said: "New knowledge has led to the recognition of the theory of evolution as more than a hypothesis. It is indeed remarkable that this theory has been progressively accepted by researchers, following a series of discoveries in various fields of knowledge. The convergence, neither sought nor fabricated, of the results of work that was conducted independently is in itself a significant argument in favor of this theory."[36]

These examples show that evolution is being taken seriously as a subject for theological discourse outside Mormonism. All of these theological responses, however, usually assume classic Nicene conceptions of Deity. It is clear that process theology has been influential in framing a response to evolution. However, the LDS view of God is much different, and Catholic and process responses may not transfer adequately to Mormonism. For example, both Teilhard de Chardin and Haught assume God's omnipresence within all that exists (and beyond). While LDS thinkers would agree that God's influence is everywhere, his actual presence is constrained by his possession of a physical body. Also, these theologians assume the Trinitarian nature of God in a different way than Mormons do. Third, these responses differ from Mormon thought in their assumption that God is the author of the laws of the universe and that creation occurred ex nihilo. These differences have strong implications for the way that a Mormon theology of evolution must be constructed.

However, other aspects translate well from Catholic and process rapprochements between religion and evolution. The concept that God is affected by his creation and that agents have agency and thereby influence the direction in which the future unfolds are ideas that line up nicely (with some adaptation) into Mormon ideas, to which we now turn.

Mormon Evolutionary Theology

Before offering a few of my own speculations, it is important to point out that Latter-day Saints have held a variety of positions on the subject of evolution over the years. Such variety is a reminder that Latter-day Saints have long had a variety of options to consider.[37] One of the first Mormons to argue for an evolutionary-inclusive LDS theology was W. H. Chamberlin. Chamberlin was part of the 1911 controversy at Brigham Young University when several scholars were dismissed because they were promoting evolution and modern biblical criticism.[38] In evolution, Chamberlin saw evidence for God's immanence in the world. In a paper to students published in BYU's newspaper, *White and Blue*, on February 14, 1911, he argued that evolution can never conflict with religion because they deal with different planes of influence and interest.[39] He clarified the immanence that he saw in nature in a *Deseret News* article a month later on March 10:

> Without penetrating beneath the surface of the vast ocean of life and experience science has been able to perform its well-known service for mankind. The mighty deep itself suggests the magnitude of the blessing for man that will come from the religious man's identification of the power in and through Nature, creating and sustaining it with the Spirit of God and in his successful efforts to discover and conform to the laws that condition life in harmony with the Divine nature and will.[40]

However, Chamberlin's notion of immanence must be understood with reference to his approach to the material world. He embraced the idea of "spiritual realism"—a reaction to the naturalism of evolutionary thinker Herbert Spencer and the positivistic worldview embraced by the Vienna Circle and a growing number of European contemporaries.[41] Spiritual realism was a form of idealism that described all of existence as flowing from "a society of minds." In that sense it was "spiritual" and dependent on mind. W. H. Chamberlin's brother and biographer, Ralph Chamberlin, described it thus: "The Philosophy of Spiritual Realism holds that reality is spiritual. Mind is inherent in all Nature in the form of innumerable spiritual agents or selves, which are free causes."[42] W. H. Chamberlin posited that all "efficient" (meaning direct) causes reflected the reality of final causes arising in minds. He did not dispute the existence of an inorganic world prior to the appearance of life in the universe. However, the outflowing of existence from mind provides evidence for panpsychism (the idea that all matter has some kind of awareness). Ralph Chamberlin, explaining his brother's thought, said, "Matter is not inanimate, in the sense of inert, 'but an expression of activity,'" and continued, "The elements may be interpreted as uniform methods or expressions of an underlying activity and viewed as 'analogous to the habits as we know them in ourselves.'"[43]

Ralph Chamberlin further argued that the evolution of the entire universe, even prior to the development of life, was very similar to the way that an embryo develops, with many processes moving simultaneously toward the final goal of an individual organism: "Just as the developing embryo of the sea-urchin, or of any section of it, varies as a whole, and can be understood only as a reciprocally related set of movements working toward an end, giving the impression of being guided by a hidden pattern, so inorganic nature, prior to the organic evolution, varied in such a way as strongly to suggest a similar control."[44] He commented that life on Earth, viewed retrospectively, seemed to have followed a similar route to the ends toward which the universe is heading, as seen today in extant organisms. Quoting W. H., Ralph Chamberlin explained:

> In relation to our interests or needs, minds are the sole support of our experience of any and all objects of Nature, of their temporal and spatial relations, and especially of the causal interconnections which we discover as maintaining among the objects of Nature, and which we describe as the laws or uniformities of Nature. The minds that form that phase of life called environment embrace *a priori*, as living premises embrace a conclusion, the matter and energy by this environment. What man calls Nature is a symbol of the presence of mind.[45]

My reading of Chamberlin's thought is that the conditions in which God and a society of minds find themselves as individuals include both ourselves and all of matter that is spiritual (this is backwards from the way that most Mormons would construct the nature of matter, i.e., spirit *is* matter, rather than the other way around). In Chamberlin's antimaterialist view, God is conceived as the highest entity, the most knowledgeable and powerful, in a society of minds. Like us, he is a "thou" who, through this society, brings into being the world we see around us. That world is conditioned completely by the society of minds and their goals. As Ralph Chamberlin describes it, "The world is an active, living whole, an organic system of a higher order, a product and expression of a society of minds."[46]

Evolution here is seen as part of God's purposes being brought forth by this society of minds. Two aspects are important for my argument. First, this approach is deeply idealistic in the sense that there is no material world, only a spiritual world of mind. Second, it is deeply teleological. While it has echoes of Bergson's work with a universe unfolding in ways that are creative, Chamberlin appears to see God's work moving forward in a way reminiscent of Haught's evolution in which the evolutionary process is inextricably embedded in the universe, except that he explains this depth as "mind" moving the evolutionary process forward.

While Chamberlin's work is friendly to evolution and Darwinism, it is so at the expense of a physical world, an approach that creates problems from a modern scientific perspective. In addition, it is much too teleological for modern scientific views of how evolution proceeds, which have now moved away from teleological explanations. However, on the positive side, this perspective also moves away from the hermeneutic of suspicion in which early LDS thought held much of evolutionary theory.

John A. Widtsoe, a chemist and apostle, although sympathetic to ideas from biological evolution as he understood it, did not engage Darwinism directly. He merely noted in his book *Rational Theology* that "the exact process whereby man was placed upon the Earth was not known with certainty, nor is it vital to a clear understanding of the plan of salvation."[47] B. H. Roberts, the most theologically minded member of the Council of the Seventy, was friendly to evolutionary ideas but discounted the contemporaneous scientific version of Darwinism in favor of *panspermia*, meaning that organisms of various kinds lived elsewhere and moved to Earth by unspecified means. Through a vitalistic life force, they developed to their present state. After rejecting three types of evolution, which he called materialistic, agonistic, and theistic, he noted:

> The development theory of this chapter and work recognizes and starts with the eternity of life—the life force; and the

eternity of some life forms, and the possibilities of these forms, perhaps in embryonic status, or in their simplest forms (save as to man) are transplanted to newly created worlds there to be developed each to its highest possibilities, by propagation, and yet within and under the great law of life of Genesis 1, viz., each "after," and within, "its kind" (Gen 1:11-12, 21, 24-25).[48]

The battle among Joseph Fielding Smith, James E. Talmage, and B. H. Roberts is well documented and need not be repeated here.[49] In short, when contemporary Christian creationism was introduced into Mormonism through Joseph Fielding Smith's reading of Seventh-day Adventist writer and PhD geologist George McCready Price's work,[50] engagement between Mormon theology and evolutionary theory slowed to a standstill. Evolutionary theology has been slow to make headway in mainstream Mormon thought, in part, perhaps, because of the controversy that emerged from this encounter and Smith's subsequent forceful (if not canonical) expression of his personal opinions.[51]

But it may be time to take some steps in this direction again. Creationist responses to the theory of evolution, which may have been understandable in the first half of the twentieth century, are becoming less and less tenable. I feel that it is important to begin to articulate an informed LDS theology that is friendlier to our current understanding of biological evolution.

A couple of points should be kept in mind. These are not statements of my belief. Rather, I offer them as toy models—ideas that we can play with to test their utility and durability. The problem of "unconceived alternatives" that has been articulated for science[52] carries even more weight in theological speculation, where a firm grasp of transcendental realities can be largely inaccessible or unavailable. This condition is especially true when both revelation and scriptures are underdetermined on the subject of how the creation actually happened. Currently, evidence from the natural world and its scientific interpretation are the only "revelation" we have for understanding that process. The scriptures can be read in literalistic ways that are unsympathetic to evolutionary views, for example, or sympathetically if read more metaphorically. Even so, we may have enough information on "the three pillars of eternity" (the creation, fall, and atonement) to start working toward some coherence in appraising the evidence of the natural world, especially since their associated controversies have been articulated in rather unbalanced and scientifically uninformed ways.[53]

What do we gain by taking Darwinian evolution seriously in LDS thought? First, we make available a conceptual space where, at a minimum, LDS theology does not oppose the most important theories of today's science. I recognize the fluid status of scientific thought and its strengths and weaknesses, but it appears that evolution, at least, will continue to be extremely influential in understanding how life developed on Earth. It is very unlikely that anything will replace evolution through natural selection as broadly conceived in the foreseeable future.

Second, evolution adds an interesting and informative dimension to several key doctrines. I will offer some tentative steps on how evolution may inform and be made compatible with Mormon theology. I repeat that these explorations serve as pump priming for more complete development. I also suggest where these ideas may be problematic or need further sorting out.

I want to speculate on reconciling the intersection between Mormon theology and Darwinian evolution in four areas—natural evil, design, embodiment, and teleology—and then speculate (wildly) on how these can be reconciled.

1. Natural evil

The first major theological question raised by evolution involves the existence of natural evil. Several authors have opined that LDS views have solved the classic problem of evil. Arguments for this assertion range from the naive stance that God is not culpable for the evils of the world because Adam and Eve chose to disobey to more nuanced views. One of them is David Paulsen's contention that Joseph Smith rescues the theodicy problem. His theology suggests a God who is subject to certain natural laws: "Elsewhere Joseph taught that there are also 'laws of eternal and self-existent principles—normative structures of some kind, I take it, that constitute things as they (eternally) are. What are possible instances of such laws or principles?'"[54] He argues that Joseph Smith gives three conditions under which God does not or cannot prevent evils: (1) unpreventable absolutely, (2) preventable by God but not absolutely, and (3) not preventable without preventing some greater good or causing some greater evil.[55]

If God did use such a method as natural selection, it would make sense that this method was the natural law that Paulsen describes as necessary—necessary because natural selection is a horrifying process, as Wildman's essay referenced above reminds us. It is hard to imagine that evolution by natural selection is a reasonable choice for creation if other methods were available. Phillip Kitcher, philosophy professor at Columbia University, writes of the problem that evolution poses to theology:

> Many people have been troubled by human suffering, and that of other sentient creatures, and have wondered how those pains are compatible with the designs of an all-powerful and loving God. Darwin's account of the history of life greatly enlarges the scale on which suffering takes place. Through millions of years, billions of animals experience vast amounts of pain, supposedly so that, after an enormous number of extinctions of entire species, on the tip of one twig of the evolutionary tree, there may emerge a species with the special properties that make us able to worship the Creator.[56]

This level of suffering and cruelty is problematic for most kinds of natural theology. Kitcher therefore uses the presence of these kinds of natural evil and their extent to dismiss theological claims about a loving God. He adds:

> Our conception of a providential Creator must suppose that He has constructed a shaggy-dog story, a history of life that consists of a three-billion-year curtain-raiser to the main event, in which millions of sentient beings suffer, often acutely, and that the suffering is not a byproduct but constitutive of the script the Creator has chosen to write.
>
> To contend that species have been individually created with the vestiges of their predecessors, with the junk that accumulates in the history of life is to suppose that Intelligence—or the Creator—operates by whimsy. The trouble is that the charge doesn't go away when the action of the Creator is made more remote. For a history of life dominated by natural selection is extremely hard to understand in providential terms. . . . There is nothing kindly or providential about any of this, and it seems breathtakingly wasteful and inefficient. Indeed, if we imagine a human observer presiding

over a miniaturized version of the whole show, peering down on his "creation," it is extremely hard to equip the face with a kindly expression.[57]

If natural selection was a natural law necessary for the creation of a diverse and fully functioning universe, then Paulsen's analysis of how LDS theology escapes the problem of evil would seem to make sense. In fact, if less cruel methods were available and God did not use them, then theologians must adduce (presumably very tricky) arguments about how this method can be reconciled with attributes of love and kindness.

Mormon doctrines of the creation and the fall may (with some adventuresome speculation) also provide a rescue for the deep problem that Kitcher identifies. Mormon theology contains an inherent dualism positing that a spiritual aspect of existence mediates the consciousness of humans, plants, animals, and, indeed, the Earth itself. We have very limited details about how these spirit and material worlds interface with each other; however, taking evolution as a given natural law offers some possibilities for making the unimaginable cruelty of life, the creation, and the fall at least coherent.

Biology has long since abandoned vitalism, and modern biologists see no necessary reason to view organisms as anything more than biological machines. However, one of the acknowledged hard problems in philosophy of mind is the idea of subjective consciousness. Such consciousness seems to extend beyond the usual kinds of explanatory gaps that science fills. Philosopher of science Colin McGinn believes that a biological explanation of consciousness is forever beyond the purview of science because, no matter how completely we understand the correlations made by science between brain states and consciousness, consciousness, with its qualitative feel, can be experienced and recognized only from within subjective experience.[58] Granted, we must be careful in claiming that science will never figure out such and such a problem, a claim that sets up a "God of the Gaps" dilemma, which scientific advances repeatedly undermine. Still, providing scientific access to personal subjectivity does seem to be an inherently intractable problem. We can imagine a world unfolding strictly according to the forces of natural selection in which organisms are nothing more than biological machines—Cartesian wet robots, if you will. A Mormon-type creation, then, would be the union of these creatures (including a human body) with spirit material that allows these machines to become sentient and experiential beings. Such a union would link a consciousness-bestowing element to the material aspects of the world.

Speculating even further afield, we could conceive of the fall, less literally, as likewise a process of a spiritual and material coming together. This view smacks more of a kind of Gnosticism or Platonism, but even so may be worth exploring. Adam and Eve, in this view, would be the first of Heavenly Father's spirit children to be linked to one of these biological machines, with the traditional animating creation taking place as a union between spirit and evolved material. As a result of this union, all humans and all creatures participate in the fall—as a fall into materiality. In some sense, perhaps the participants even choose their participation. Continuing this line of thought, we see that Christ must then, as LDS thought commonly holds, redeem all creation.[59] Rather than causing a fall as a necessary imposition on all sentient creatures, Adam and Eve open the possibility of a participatory fall, during which conscious experience enters the world.

In this view, the natural evils of the living world did not begin until the fall and form part of the price of experience, not only for humans but for all creatures. Humans participate as God's children (as per LDS theology), but their role is more to act with Christ in bringing redemption to the world of experiencing beings. Christ's atonement becomes truly universal, opening the opportunity for both the resurrection and the permanent bringing together of the spiritual and the material. This step joins experience and material existence. I argue that Mormonism, in this way, provides an answer that escapes natural theology and the deeper problem of evil, while making Christ's atonement truly universal. This approach also allows a reconciliation with traditional views of Adam and Eve as real living persons—the first instance of sentience and the literal spirit children of God (agreed, we don't know what that means exactly). This approach also provides something vital to the world through the fall since, in a very technical sense, there was no death before the fall.

This kind of evolutionary-based view of the fall also releases God from naive views that he is culpable for it. There is something inherently troubling about God's setting up Adam to fail and fall. By analogy, it is as if I blame a mouse killed in my mousetrap for its desire for cheese rather than blaming myself for having baited and placed the trap.

However, this approach also has troubling aspects. If we remove God's consciousness-inducing spirit children from the biotic world, then, logically, we have to accept that beings like Neanderthals had no consciousness. Since it is well established that many early hominins had religious practices, created art, and made intricate tools, it is hard to argue that they had no vestiges of phenomenal consciousness. This idea is also highly dualistic, but in very Mormon rather than Cartesian ways.

2. Design in Mormon theology

How important to our theology is the idea that God is the designer in creation? Natural theology, starting with Augustine, has made the design and complexity of the universe one of the evidences of God through creation. These early theologies even held that God's attributes could be read from the features of the natural world. As underscored by Xenophon's claim that "signs of forethought" in Nature attest design (quoted earlier), this move to see design as evidence of Deity's involvement in creation obviously predates Christian theological speculation. Currently, we know that the natural law of evolution through natural selection[60] can fully explain the complexity of life on Earth (and presumably life elsewhere). Therefore, the question logically follows: Are the arguments for God from design necessary or important to a Mormon theology? Christian theologians and apologists have spilled significant quantities of ink over design, but why this question matters deserves some examination. For example, in relation to the embodiment of God, did he design his body?

It seems circular to make Paleyesque arguments for design that do not mesh well with some of Mormonism's foundational tenets, especially since arguments from design had become problematic long before Darwin. Scottish philosopher David Hume pointed out that design implies nothing about a designer and speculated that the designer of the universe could have been anything from an evil demon to a largely incompetent committee.[61] (The many blunders and inefficiencies found among Earth's organisms were apparent even in Hume's time, the eighteenth century.) If God's embodiment implies some sort of biology, then the design comes from elsewhere. LDS thinkers have speculated since the time of Joseph Smith and Orson Pratt that God works within natural law. If this principle includes evolution through natural selection, it seems that attempts to distance ourselves theologically from evolution could be a grave error. Thus, if we interpret the theory of evolution in a Mormon framework, it constitutes a potentially helpful and perhaps even necessary explanation for an embodied God, rather than merely posing problems for natural theology.

3. Embodiment in Mormon theology

We believe that, in some sense, we were created in the bodily image of God. We use scriptures like Ether 3:6, where the brother of Jared sees the Lord's finger, which was "as the finger of a man," to orient this belief. We also believe that "the Father has a body of flesh and bones as tangible as man's; the Son also" (D&C 130:22). These scriptures present problems for a non-teleological process such as evolution by natural selection—but perhaps not as many problems as we might first think. Evolutionary biologist Simon Conway Morris argues that, given the vastness of the universe and the limited number of solutions to the biological engineering problems of surviving in a planetary ecosystem, humans, or something like them, might be an inevitable evolutionary product.[62]

For example, reptile ichthyosaurs, mammal dolphins, and fish all have evolved very similar shapes to solve the problem of moving gracefully in oceans. These evolutionary convergences can take on very specific biological forms. Sabertooth cat-like predators who fed on large grassland mammals evolved as both marsupials (mammals with a pouch, like kangaroos and wallabies) and as mammals with placentas (e.g., bats, horses, and lions). Both marsupial and placental sabertooths were very similar in shape, ecological niche, and size. Both evolved from small rat or small opossum-like precursors. The universe is unimaginably large. Why? Allowing evolution to flower into something human-like could be one of the reasons. Philosopher James E. Faulconer asks an intriguing question about God's embodiment:

> The bodies of flesh and bone with which I am familiar do not shine, have blood, cannot hover, can be wounded and die, must move through contiguous points of time-space. In short, they are not at all like the bodies of the Father and the Son. So what does it mean to say that the Father and the Son have bodies? In fact, does it mean anything at all? When I use the word "body" in any other context, I never refer to something that shines, can hover, is immortal, and moves through space seemingly without being troubled by walls and doors. Given the vast difference between what we mean by the word "body" in every other case and that to which the word refers in this case, one can legitimately ask whether the word "body" has the same meaning in this case that it has in the others.[63]

One could also legitimately ask: Is God a *Homo sapiens*? Is God a mammal? Scientists have speculated on what a bipedal hominid evolved from avian precursors might look like. Would it have leftover structures like a pygostyle (a reduced fusion of vertebrae) instead of a tail? Slime molds can take very complex shapes in some of their life history stages. Can we imagine a human body that evolved from slime molds on another planet? It seems that many of our human features are part and parcel of our being mammals. Could being a mammal be a contingent feature of our evolution rather than an eternal part of our resurrected bodies? I don't have any answers to these questions, but they don't seem to be so problematic that they cannot be answered in ways that allow evolution as the mechanism of creation. These sorts of considerations significantly reduce problems of teleology, or God's presumed purpose for human beings.

4. Teleology in Mormon thought

If God, of necessity, used evolution to achieve his purposes, what does that say about his being able to act in the world? I need to add a cautionary note here. When I say God *uses* evolution, I recognize that, in talking about a Creator, it is possible that words like *allows* or *provides a space for* may be more appropriate. Nevertheless, if we embrace an evolutionary perspective, God's intervention, our petitionary prayer, and divine action to bring about his purposes become thorny issues. A nice thing about the magical view of creation is that it is no problem at all to imagine God intervening in the world. Why use evolution through natural selection in a nonteleological fashion if waving a magic wand was possible? In fact, if God can and sometimes does intervene, then why doesn't he do it all the time? Why *didn't* he do it during the Creation? This question opens an intriguing possibility: the necessary place of consciousness in divine interventions.

In Mormon thought, getting a physical body is important. Obviously, having a body means that we become part of the material world, as Faulconer speculates: "Our experience of the body, the only standard we have for understanding embodiment, suggests that to say that God has a body is to say that his omniscience and omnipotence must be understood in ways quite different from traditional Christianity because embodiment implies situated openness to a world. In other words, divine embodiment also implies that God is affected by the world and by persons in his world."[64]

So there seems to be something deeply important about physicality and spirit coming together. Could it be that the physical world can be manipulated only through consciousness-mediated direct action? Or through this kind of body that unites spirit and physical matter? When I read the scriptures, I see a God who makes arrangements for irreplaceable records to be kept, preserved, and maintained through conscious effort. He implies that, if they are not, this knowledge will be lost and not brought back through his intervention. I see the Lamanites languishing in unbelief until the sons of Mosiah are inspired to go among them. Angels bear messages to other consciousnesses but do not seem to manipulate the world in interventionist ways. Almost all of the scriptures can be reinterpreted as acts of consciousness acting in the world. Christ's miracles, especially his resurrection, seem to be an exception, but much of how God works in the world seems to be that he communicates to and through conscious beings who then use their agency to act. Stories of people inspired to stop and help a widow take on new meaning if God cannot help the widow without us.

Speculative Conclusions

Evolution may bear on theology in other areas, and entire discourses could be developed on each of these topics. For example, studies on motherhood from the animal kingdom are providing great insights into the nature of motherhood in human beings.[65] Or consider the work of Joan Roughgarden, a biologist at Stanford University, who recently argued for a new model of evolution based not on selfish genetic forces (Richard Dawkins's "selfish gene" model) but on models of cooperation among creatures in a gendered and sexual context.[66] Her ideas on cooperation are a nice model for the kinds of human and perhaps divine society that Mormon theology posits—free agent interaction as part of a society of gendered minds. This area is new biological research, but it seems more promising than the selfish-gene model because it seems more attuned to the kinds of societies that we see forming in the natural world and that Mormon conceptions of theosis also model and predict.

Evolutionary views of creation also steer us into a deeper engagement with the natural world, as we see ourselves quite literally connected to the creatures and ecologies around us (discussed further in chapters 6 and 7). The idea that our world emerged from deep time through natural selection implies that the wonderful diversity we see around us is contingent, unique, and precious. This evolutionary stance provides arguments for better stewardship of the natural environment because its current state took an enormous length of time. Not only are the creatures of the earth here for us, but we are here for them. A Darwinian-influenced theology argues that care for creation becomes an important aspect of God's grace to the natural world through us.

A melding of evolution and theology also introduces another area important in Mormon thought. Perhaps the LDS conception of theosis (and the path that leads to exaltation) suggests a Darwinian selection process in which elements of trial, testing, and proving are inherent parts of progression through the first and second estates of premortal and mortal existence. Could natural selection drive emergence forward in an eternal context as well? Are classically conceived intelligences the sorts of entities subject to natural selection? Abraham 3:21-25 describes intelligences as varying in traits relevant for theosis such as intelligence, righteousness, obedience, and so on. (Recall that variation is the first condition necessary for natural selection to function.) Thinking of Christ as God's son means that we know at least one case in which traits were in some senses inherited—and heritability is the second condition necessary for natural selection. But how broadly this principle applies is, obviously, speculative. Lastly, these traits get selected—the third condition necessary for natural selection. Not only might evolution be the principle behind the beauty, wonder, and diversity of life in the universe, but it may also drive the selection processes that help produce our eternal destiny.

For me evolution is an empowering idea. Linking it to our theology provides answers to several perplexing questions. It suggests that there is something wonderfully important about embodiment and why physical access to the universe is so important. Our doctrines, informed by evolution, answer questions about why such a cruel and wasteful process was chosen for creation and resituate the problem of evil. I find easy adaptations to our most important and profound doctrines. I see no reason why Mormons cannot, fully and without apology, embrace Darwinian evolution. As Darwin concluded in his magnificent *On the Origin of Species*: "There is grandeur in this view of life, with its several powers, having been originally breathed into a few forms or into one;

and that, whilst this planet has gone cycling on according to the fixed law of gravity, from so simple a beginning endless forms most beautiful and most wonderful have been, and are being, evolved."[67]

Notes

1. Wesley J. Wildman, "Narnia's Aslan, Earth's Darwin, and Heaven's God," *Dialogue: A Journal of Mormon Thought* 43 (2010): 210-17.

2. Elie Wiesel, *Night*, trans. Marion Wiesel (New York: Hill and Wang, 2006), 5.

3. See, for example, the following articles in *Dialogue: A Journal of Mormon Thought*: Duane E. Jeffery, "Seers, Savants, and Evolution: The Uncomfortable Interface," 8 (Autumn 1974): 41-75; Michael R. Ash, "The Mormon Myth of Evil Evolution," 35 (Winter 2002): 19-38; David H. Bailey, "Mormonism and the New Creationism," 35 (Winter 2002): 39-59; and David H. Bailey, "Scientific Foundations of Mormon Theology," 21 (Summer 1988): 61-79. See also Trent D. Stephens and D. Jeffrey Meldrum, *Evolution and Mormonism: A Quest for Understanding* (Salt Lake City: Signature Books, 2001); William E. Evenson, "Evolution," *Encyclopedia of Mormonism* (New York: Macmillan, 1992), 2:478; Eldon J. Gardner, "Organic Evolution and the Bible," in *The Search for Harmony: Essays on Science and Mormonism*, ed. Gene A. Sessions and Craig J. Oberg (Salt Lake City: Signature Books, 1993); William E. Evenson and Duane E. Jeffery, *Mormonism and Evolution: The Authoritative LDS Statements* (Salt Lake City: Greg Kofford Books, 2005); Howard C. Stutz, *"Let the Earth Bring Forth": Evolution and Scripture* (Draper, UT: Greg Kofford Books, 2011). More recently, a "Gospel Topics" essay on LDS.org approvingly cited highly technical evolutionary theory in defense of the Book of Mormon. See "Book of Mormon and DNA Studies," https://www.lds.org/topics/book-of-mormon-and-dna-studies.

4. Christian Illies, "Darwin's a Priori Insight," in *Darwin and Philosophy*, ed. Vittorio Hösle and Christian Illies (Notre Dame, IN: University of Notre Dame Press, 2005), 58-82.

5. Daniel C. Dennett, *Darwin's Dangerous Idea: Evolution and the Meanings of Life* (New York: Simon & Schuster, 1996). For an interesting rebuttal to Dennett's description of Darwin's idea as dangerous, see Conor Cunningham, *Darwin's Pious Idea: Why the Ultra-Darwinists and Creationists Both Get It Wrong* (Grand Rapids, MI: Wm. B. Eerdman's, 2010).

6. Kevin N. Laland et al., "Conceptual Barriers to Progress within Evolutionary Biology," *Foundations of Science* 14/3 (August 2009): 195-216.

7. Xenophon, *Memorabilia*, trans. E. C. Marchant, Loeb Classical Library (Cambridge, MA: Harvard University Press, 1923), 57.

8. Interestingly, President Spencer W. Kimball played off this idea in "Absolute Truth," *Ensign*, September 1978, 3.

9. Barbara Forrest, "The Wedge at Work: How Intelligent Design Creationism Is Wedging Its Way into the Cultural and Academic Mainstream," in *Intelligent Design Creationism and Its Critics: Philosophical, Theological, and Scientific Perspectives*, ed. Robert T. Pennock (Cambridge, MA: MIT Press, 2001), 5-53.

10. Niels Henrik Gregersen, "Emergence: What Is at Stake for Religious Reflection?," in *The Re-Emergence of Emergence: The Emergentist Hypothesis from Science to Religion*, ed. Philip Clayton and Paul Davies (Oxford: Oxford University Press, 2006), 279-322.

11. Kent C. Condie, "Premortal Spirits: Implications for Cloning, Abortion, Evolution, and Extinction," *Dialogue: A Journal of Mormon Thought* 39 (Spring 2006): 35-56.

12. James E. Faulconer, "Divine Embodiment and Transcendence: Propaedeutic Thoughts and Questions," *Element: A Journal of Mormon Philosophy and Theology* 1 (Spring 2005), http://www.smpt.org/docs/faulconer_element1-1.html.

13. *Theosis* is the term most often used within Eastern Orthodox Christianity to describe the process of attaining union with God including a certain likeness. This term and others like it (*deification, divination*) do not map perfectly onto LDS conceptions of "becoming like God" or "exaltation." For one discussion on this topic, see Jordan Vajda, "Partakers of the Divine Nature: A Comparative Analysis of Patristic and Mormon Doctrines of Divinization," *FARMS Occasional Papers* 3 (2002), http://publications .maxwellinstitute.byu.edu/periodical/occasional-papers-3.

14. When asked if Mormons believed that God was once a man, LDS Church President Gordon B. Hinckley responded: "I wouldn't say that. There was a couplet coined, 'As man is, God once was. As God is, man may become.' Now that's more of a couplet than anything else. That gets into some pretty deep theology that we don't know very much about" (quoted in Don Lattin, "Musings of the Main Mormon," *San Francisco Chronicle*, April 13, 1997, http://www.sfgate.com/cgi-bin/article.cgi?file=/chronicle/archive /1997/04/13/SC36289). President Hinckley seems to have been referring primarily to the question of God's past rather than humanity's future. See Blair Hodges, "Did President Hinckley downplay deification?," *By Common Consent* (blog), January 2, 2012, http:// bycommonconsent.com/2012/01/02/did-president-hinckley-downplay-deification/.

15. Ursula Goodenough, "The Sacred Depths of Nature: Excerpts," *Zygon: Journal of Religion and Science* 35 (September 2000): 567-86.

16. These ideas are found in Joseph Smith's King Follett discourse. See "Mormon Literature Sampler: The King Follett Discourse," http://mldb.byu.edu/follett.htm.

17. Blake T. Ostler, *Exploring Mormon Thought: The Attributes of God* (Salt Lake City: Greg Kofford Books, 2001), 359-60; and Neal A. Maxwell, "Patience," *Ensign*, October 1980, 28.

18. James McLachlan, "Fragments for a Process Theology of Mormonism," *Element: A Journal of Mormon Philosophy and Theology* 1 (Fall 2005), http://www.smpt.org/ element.html; Andrew Miles, "Toward a Mormon Metaphysics: Scripture, Process Theology, and the Mechanics of Faith," *Element: A Journal of Mormon Philosophy and Theology* 4 (Spring 2008); and Dan W. Wotherspoon, *Awakening Joseph Smith: Mormon Resources for a Postmodern Worldview* (Claremont, CA: Claremont Graduate University, 1996).

19. Gregersen, "Emergence," 299.

20. David N. Livingstone, "Evolution and Religion," in *Evolution: The First Four Billion Years*, ed. Michael Ruse and Joseph Travis (Cambridge, MA: Belknap, 2009), 348-69.

21. Many interesting responses to evolution from Jewish, Islamic, and Hindu sources posit a personal God who acts in the world. Buddhist responses are less troubled by evolution because of its inherent naturalism. I am not including them in my analysis because Christian responses make an interesting model for creating LDS-compatible theologies, both of which must include ideas of the fall and the atonement, which are not present in the same ways in non-Christian religions. Discussions of various other religious perspectives can be found in Philip Clayton, ed., *The Oxford Handbook of Religion and Science* (New York: Oxford University Press, 2008).

22. Creationists, including "intelligent design creationists," sometimes try to distinguish between micro- and macroevolutionary processes that biologists do not recognize. Macroevolution refers to the timescale at which evolutionary change is considered and is not a different kind of evolution, as is often implied by such groups. For example, it is not uncommon to find people who claim that they believe in micro-evolution (meaning something like the changes that might be found among different breeds of dogs) but not macroevolution. To a biologist that is the equivalent of claiming, "I believe in inches but not miles."

23. Gilles Deleuze, "Lecture Course on Chapter Three of Bergson's *Creative Evolution*," *SubStance: A Review of Theory and Literary Criticism* 36/3 (2007): 72–90.

24. Michael Vaughan, "Introduction: Henri Bergson's *Creative Evolution*," *SubStance: A Review of Theory and Literary Criticism* 36/3 (2007): 7–24.

25. Vitalism was an idea with ancient roots but became prominent during the Enlightenment (seventeenth–eighteenth centuries). It posited that life was made possible by a force not present in nonliving things.

26. Henri Bergson, *Creative Evolution*, trans. Arthur Mitchell (1907; repr., New York: Barnes and Noble, 2005), 68; emphasis mine.

27. Pierre Teilhard de Chardin, *The Phenomenon of Man*, trans. Bernard Wall (New York: Harper & Row, 1959), 268; emphasis in the original.

28. Teilhard de Chardin, *Phenomenon of Man*, 313.

29. See, for example, David R. Griffin, *Reenchantment without Supernaturalism: A Process Philosophy of Religion* (Cornell, NY: Cornell University Press, 2000); and Alfred North Whitehead, *Process and Reality*, corrected ed. (New York: Free Press, 1978).

30. John F. Haught, *Deeper than Darwin: The Prospect for Religion in the Age of Evolution* (Cambridge, MA: Westview Press, 2004).

31. John F. Haught, *God after Darwin: A Theology of Evolution* (Boulder, CO: Westview, 2000), 42.

32. Arthur Peacocke, "A Naturalistic Christian Faith for the Twenty-First Century: An Essay in Interpretation," in *All That Is: A Naturalistic Faith for the Twenty-First Century*, edited by Philip Clayton (Minneapolis, Mich.: Fortress Press, 2007), 9.

33. Karl E. Peters, "Empirical Theology and a 'Naturalistic Christian Faith,'" in *All That Is: A Naturalistic Faith for the Twenty-First Century*, ed. Philip Clayton (Minneapolis, MN: Fortress Press, 2007), 102.

34. Celia Deane-Drummond, *Christ and Evolution: Wonder and Wisdom* (Minneapolis, MN: Fortress Press, 2009).

35. Deane-Drummond, *Christ and Evolution*, 57.

36. Pope John Paul II, *Truth Cannot Contradict Truth*, address to the Pontifical Academy of Sciences, October 22, 1996, http://www.newadvent.org/library/docs_jp02tc.htm.

37. One of the best, though often overlooked, extended analyses of Mormonism's adaptive relationship to the sciences is Erich Robert Paul's *Science, Religion, and Mormon Cosmology* (Urbana: University of Illinois Press, 1992).

38. Gary James Bergera, "The 1911 Evolution Controversy at Brigham Young University," in Sessions and Oberg, *Search for Harmony*, 23B42; James M. McLachlan, "W. H. Chamberlin and the Quest for a Mormon Theology," *Dialogue: A Journal of Mormon Thought* 29 (Winter 1996): 151–67; and James M. McLachlan, "The Modernism Controversy," in *Discourses in Mormon Theology: Philosophical and Theological Possibilities*, ed.

James M. McLachlan and Loyd Ericson (Salt Lake City: Greg Kofford Books, 2007), 39-83.

39. William H. Chamberlin, "The Theory of Evolution as an Aid to Faith in God and in the Resurrection," *White and Blue*, February 14, 1911, 4.

40. Quoted in Ralph V. Chamberlin, *The Life and Philosophy of W. H. Chamberlin* (Salt Lake City: Deseret Book, 1925), 158.

41. McLachlan, "Modernism Controversy," 39-83.

42. Chamberlin, *Life and Philosophy of W. H. Chamberlin*, 320.

43. Chamberlin, *Life and Philosophy of W. H. Chamberlin*, 254. The embedded quotations are from an unpublished essay by W. H. Chamberlin, "Berkeley's Philosophy of Nature and Modern Theories of Evolution."

44. Chamberlin, *Life and Philosophy of W. H. Chamberlin*, quoting from W. H. Chamberlin, "Berkeley's Philosophy of Nature and Modern Theories of Evolution."

45. Chamberlin, *Life and Philosophy of W. H. Chamberlin*, 255.

46. Chamberlin, *Life and Philosophy of W. H. Chamberlin*, 322.

47. John A. Widtsoe, *Rational Theology* (Salt Lake City: Signature Books, 1997), 46-47.

48. B. H. Roberts, *The Truth, the Way, the Life* (Provo, UT: BYU Studies, 1996), 240.

49. Richard Sherlock, "'We Can See No Advantage to a Continuation of the Discussion': The Roberts/Smith/Talmage Affair," *Dialogue: A Journal of Mormon Thought* 13 (Fall 1980): 63B78; and Jeffery, "Seers, Savants, and Evolution," 41-75.

50. Richard Sherlock, "A Turbulent Spectrum: Mormon Reactions to the Darwinist Legacy," in Sessions and Oberg, *Search for Harmony*, 69.

51. For example, in books like *Man: His Origin and Destiny* (Salt Lake City: Deseret Book, 1954).

52. P. Kyle Stanford, *Exceeding Our Grasp: Science, History, and the Problem of Unconceived Alternatives* (Oxford: Oxford University Press, 2006).

53. The phrase "the three pillars of eternity" is borrowed from Bruce R. McConkie, "The Three Pillars of Eternity," BYU devotional address, February 17, 1981, http://speeches.byu.edu/?act=viewitem&id=598.

54. David L. Paulsen, "Joseph Smith and the Problem of Evil," *BYU Studies* 39/1 (2000): 53-65. He is quoting from Joseph Fielding Smith, comp., *Teachings of the Prophet Joseph Smith* (Salt Lake City: Deseret Book, 1974), 181.

55. Smith, *Teachings of the Prophet Joseph Smith*, 60.

56. Phillip Kitcher, *Living with Darwin: Evolution, Design, and the Future of Faith* (Oxford: Oxford University Press, 2007), 123.

57. Kitcher, *Living with Darwin*, 124.

58. Colin McGinn, *The Mysterious Flame: Conscious Minds in a Material World* (New York: Basic Books, 1999).

59. Sheila Taylor, "The Hope for Universal Salvation," *Element: A Journal of Mormon Philosophy and Theology* 2 (Fall 2006), http://www.smpt.org/element.html.

60. Illies, "Darwin's a Priori Insight," 59, holds that evolution is in fact one of nature's principles and is a priori true.

61. David Hume, *Dialogues Concerning Natural Religion* (Mineola, NY: Dover, 2006), 35-38.

62. Simon Conway Morris, *Life's Solution: Inevitable Humans in a Lonely Universe* (Cambridge: Cambridge University Press, 2003).

63. Faulconer, "Divine Embodiment and Transcendence," 1.

64. Faulconer, "Divine Embodiment and Transcendence," 18.

65. Sarah Blaffer Hardy, *Mother Nature: Maternal Instincts and How They Shape the Human Species* (New York: Ballantine Books, 1999).

66. Joan Roughgarden, *Evolution's Rainbow: Diversity, Gender, and Sexuality in Nature and Humans* (Berkeley: University of California Press, 2004); and *The Genial Gene: Deconstructing Darwinian Selfishness* (Berkeley: University of California Press, 2009).

67. Charles Darwin, *On the Origin of Species: The Illustrated Edition* (New York: Sterling Publishing, 2008), 513.

4

The Current Philosophy of Consciousness Landscape: Where Does LDS Thought Fit?

> *so much depends*
> *upon*
>
> *a red wheel*
> *barrow*
>
> *glazed with rain*
> *water*
>
> *beside the white*
> *chickens.*

—William Carlos Williams[1]

LOOKING OUT OF MY WINDOW ACROSS MY LAWN, I see a red toy wheelbarrow tipped over, abandoned beside the sidewalk. Its redness is something I experience distinctly. Undeniably. I might be deceived and there is no red wheelbarrow there. Maybe someone painted one on the window and I am confused, or maybe I am lying mad in a hospital bed and dreaming. Perhaps it is a hallucination. It could even be I am the victim of a maniacal government experiment where they are stimulating my brain in a way that makes me think I am seeing a red wheelbarrow. Nevertheless, whatever the cause, *for me* it is clear—I am seeing a red wheelbarrow. I am conscious that there is a red wheelbarrow. I am a being that, as Descartes first pointed out, experiences qualia.[2] As Descartes put it: *Cogito ergo sum* (I think, therefore I am).

79

What is consciousness? How does it arise? What are its correlates in the neuroarchitecture of our brain? What can science tell us about consciousness? *Can* science tell us anything about consciousness? Recently there has been a surfeit of books on consciousness from philosophical, biological, and psychological perspectives. These differing perspectives come to a variety of conclusions with little apparent agreement on how to even approach the problem of consciousness, let alone solve it. Nonetheless, there is value in examining how one's own worldview fits into the large picture of consciousness studies. LDS doctrine offers a unique and coherent view of consciousness and its place in the universe. This chapter introduces some of the current ideas being discussed in consciousness studies. The challenge of writing a short introduction to such a broad topic is that, of necessity, I must leave out much and risk pleasing no one. Despite this task's built-in inadequacies, I hope to stir thinking stimulated by a wide variety of researchers and philosophers. My purpose is not to answer many of the nuances of consciousness studies and their relation to LDS thought, but rather to point out an interesting area for further research.

The approach I take here is to examine several threads about consciousness that might be loosely captured under the heading "The Philosophy of Biology." Given this approach, I will not be exploring other specific philosophic movements that parallel this area of thinking. Since studies about the philosophical nature of biological consciousness are an amalgamation of brain science, evolutionary biology, psychology, and philosophy, my focus will be on current problems receiving attention in the philosophy of science. However, some grounding on the other areas of consciousness studies will be necessary for understanding certain areas of overlap among the disciplines. While this review is neither comprehensive nor focused in one area, I hope that it is sufficient to begin a dialogue with other scholars interested in consciousness studies and its relationship with LDS thought.

Introduction: The Hard Problem

Consciousness has been defined as "those subjective states of sentience or awareness that begin when one awakes in the morning from a dreamless sleep and continue throughout the day until one goes to sleep at night, or falls into a coma, or dies, or otherwise becomes, as one would say, 'unconscious.'"[3] This definition is not very precise. It does not capture the clarity that one would see in defining a plant or a mammal, in which case clear criteria can be set forth. Consciousness is elusive, and no single definition has satisfied everyone. Rather than a clearly articulated concept, consciousness can be thought of as a set of family resemblances. I hope to be explicit about what aspect I mean when I use the word *consciousness,* but to date the concept seems inherently vague.

Consciousness studies is usually divided into the "easy problems" and *the* "hard problem."[4] The easy problems, although actually quite difficult, are considered to be amenable to scientific exploration, for example, how the brain processes colors, which neural pathways are involved in specific behaviors, and how the brain communicates among its different components. While many of these problems remain unsolved and constitute the research agenda of neuroscience, they are scientifically tractable and researchers believe that they can one day identify the mechanisms they employ.

In contrast, phenomenal consciousness is *the* hard problem in consciousness studies.[5] Phenomenal consciousness is the aspect of consciousness identified by that "what it is to be like" feeling that we associate with personal subjectivity[6] and that subjective experience we have when seeing colors, hearing sounds, and so forth. It has several aspects: its sense of unity and irreducibility,[7] its continuity in space, its apparent lack of spatial dimension, and the ineffable quality of qualia—for example, the experience of seeing red, hearing music, thinking, and even thinking about our thinking.[8] In addition to the consciousness apparent in the present, we can also bring up past qualia in our mind. We are subjectively all aware of our nearly indescribable sense of being.

This "hard problem" is difficult because nothing in biology predicts the emergence of consciousness. If it were not for the fact that we experience this unique subjectivity, there would be no reason to postulate its existence. Furthermore, there are apparently no scientific methods to identify its presence or absence.[9] For example, if thinking machines from another galaxy without such consciousness were to examine our species biologically, they would have no reason at all to postulate consciousness.

Consciousness is also associated with a sense of what philosophers call intentionality, a technical term not to be confused with our ordinary use of *intend*, which means we are planning some course of action. Intentionality here means that our thoughts are about something or are directed toward a particular purpose. This "aboutness" is an active part of many of our conscious features: our thoughts, feelings, and sensations all are about something. Some argue that all mental states are intentional and are representative. Several philosophers have worked out a representational view of consciousness. They include Fred Dretske, who notes that the way an object is presented to the mind is conditioned on the way our senses represent that object in our mind. He argues that, in this view, all mental facts are representative facts.[10]

Consciousness Studies Overview

Descartes is often mentioned as the founder of consciousness studies, or the first person to carefully articulate the nature of the mind-body problem. He believed that the seat of consciousness lay in the pineal gland and argued that the mind and the brain were two separate things. He developed the idea of what was later termed the "Cartesian Theater," in which the mind observes the ongoing drama of our sensory input. The dualism that he espoused is still being argued about today.

Since that time, John Locke, David Hume, Immanuel Kant, Bishop George Berkeley, Ludwig Wittgenstein, Martin Heidegger, and Jean-Paul Sartre are among the many philosophers who have explored aspects of consciousness studies. While not explicitly exploring consciousness, Søren Kierkegaard devoted much of his writing to explications of subjectivity and its importance in understanding truth. Maurice Merleau-Ponty studied the relationship of consciousness and perception, arguing that the bodily nature of perception was intimately tied to consciousness.[11] Sigmund Freud developed the idea that the subconscious played an important part in our cognition and mental life. However, most of these philosophers did not engage directly with post-Darwinian biology—not that these philosophers are irrelevant to discussions of consciousness (for they certainly are relevant), but my purpose here is to explore where consciousness studies now stands in relation to mainstream philosophy of science, and space limitations preclude a more thorough exploration.[12]

Modern consciousness studies begin with two figures: Charles Darwin and William James. Darwin further anchored the world in scientific materialism as the de facto method of exploring the universe. While one need not assume strict materialism to use the scientific method, most recent explorations, including dualist positions, do. All modern positions on consciousness assume that the brain is the product of several million years of evolution.[13]

William James advanced modern studies of consciousness by tying studies of consciousness explicitly to psychology and brain science.[14] He was concerned with subjectivity and what its various states suggested about the nature of consciousness. Shortly after James, behaviorists like John Watson and B. F. Skinner discounted the value of subjectivity, thus influencing psychology away from the value of subjective information obtained through self-reports. In contrast, the last two decades have seen a resurgence of interest in subjectivity.[15] Since James's period at the turn of the twentieth century, three main schools of thought have gained prominence in explaining the nature of consciousness: functionalism, mysterianism, and dualism.

I will explore each perspective, how it relates to LDS ideas of consciousness, and how LDS views may contribute to current debates on the nature of consciousness. In particular, I examine the thoughts of Joseph Smith, B. H. Roberts, and other LDS thinkers, comparing them with current ideas in the philosophy and science of consciousness. The LDS doctrine idea that spirit and body constitute the substance of consciousness is, I will argue, a philosophically valid and coherent approach to consciousness.

Brain Science

Recent efforts in neuroscience have made great strides in understanding the brain and its correlates with consciousness.[16] New techniques, such as using radioactive emissions from labeled glucose to image metabolically active areas of the brain, have allowed researchers to explore which parts of the brain are active during certain behaviors. Single photon emission-computed tomography (SPECT) cameras can image these metabolically active areas on a computer, identifying which areas of the brain are active during given conscious and unconscious activity, including religious experiences. Using SPECT cameras, researchers investigated which areas of the brain are associated with religious experience.[17] They and others have speculated on the existence of a "God Module" in the brain that processes feelings of religious engagement. Some have argued from this hypothesis that God therefore consists of sensations generated by the brain. However, these two authors point out that much of the brain interprets and processes data gathered from outside ourselves. For example, the eye picks up light signals that the visual centers of the brain interpret, just as the ears pick up and process sound waves. It may be that the "God Module," if it exists, interprets real signals instead of manufacturing false impressions. Therefore, the existence of a "God Module" is uninformative on the question of God's existence.[18] Consciousness, such studies suggest, is not centered in one part of the brain. During consciousness, the entire brain is active; no single neural system seems responsible for inducing consciousness. The difference between conscious and unconscious states appears to be the specific type of neural activities occurring. During unconsciousness, signals among the neurons appear to be firing in lockstep at a given frequency. So while there is as much neural firing going on during periods of non-REM sleep, for example, the variance is very low. During consciousness, the variation in neural activity is strikingly high.[19]

Gerald Edelman and Giulio Tononi have found that the brain processes associated with consciousness are defined by a "dynamic core" of neural activity. They hypothesize that these neural pathways are being used in active consciousness through a Darwinian process of selection. For example, when you are driving home and suddenly remember to pick up milk, this remembrance would imply that the "remember to pick up milk" neural pathways and processes suddenly were selected for consciousness among the competing pathways and processes. Through computer simulation and brain imaging techniques, Edelman and Tononi's ideas are illuminating how the conscious brain coordinates and activates the neural processes associated with consciousness.[20]

Other methods of understanding the relationship between brain and consciousness include studies of patients with specific types of brain damage or other neural abnormalities.[21] Through these studies, researchers have associated various regions of the brain with behavioral correlates.

However, all of these studies give only the broadest generalizations about brain neurobiology. With 10^{10} neurons and as many as 10^{1000} possible connections in the brain, brain science is in its infancy in understanding how the brain works. For example, we lack a persuasive or widely accepted view of how memory works, how it is recovered, or what accounts for its indelibility. However, despite this lack of information about basic brain function, a group of neural scientists and philosophers of science are arguing that the final arbitration of what consciousness is and how it arises will ultimately be made by brain science. How well do these arguments succeed?

Functionalist materialists

Materialism—the idea that all causes are material and that the universe is closed to all but material objects and causes—is the most prevalent paradigm in the philosophy of consciousness today. While there are many materialist schools of thought, they share the underlying common assumption that the physical universe in toto is amenable to scientific discovery and manipulation. Functionalist materialists believe that brain science will eventually explain consciousness and that, if we understood all brain states, we would invariably understand consciousness. They see consciousness as an emergent property of the brain.[22]

Emergence theory has recently played an important role in how people view the universe. It is, in part, derived from chaos theory, which demonstrates that complex, unpredictable behavior of relatively simple systems can emerge in a way that understanding the system's simpler components cannot predict. An emergent property is a higher-level property that cannot be predicted from the lower-level processes that together make up the higher-level property. For example, water's liquidity would be hard to predict if all we had were single hydrogen and oxygen atoms; rather, liquidity emerges from the interaction of hydrogen and oxygen atoms and is completely explained by these interactions. However, given only the atoms and their properties, it would have been nearly impossible to predict all of the properties we see in water: for example, freezing at 0° degrees C, boiling at 100° C, its surface tension, and so on.[23] Consciousness, likewise, in this reading is an emergent property of brain function.

Materialist functionalists argue that brains are a kind of computer: the brain is the hardware and consciousness is the software, or the "wetware." This analogy, called strong AI (artificial intelligence), has been around since John von Neumann devised the first modern computers in the late 1940s. Von Neumann speculated that computers someday would be conscious and suggested that we would recognize consciousness in a machine when, in a conversation with a computer, we could not tell that it was not a human, regardless of what questions were asked. However, philosophers of science have rejected this view.

John Searle, for one, has pointed out the inadequacies of this materialist position and developed the now-famous Chinese Room argument.[24] In this argument, Searle takes the position that purely computational systems can never be conscious. He invites us to imagine a room in which a person submits questions written in Chinese to someone in the room. The answers that come back are written in fluent Chinese. One would naturally assume that the person in the room understood Chinese. However, in reality, the person in the room has a large book that is used to translate these questions. When the questions are submitted, she looks up the characters, then copies out the next line in the book, which always gives an appropriate answer to the question. She understands no Chinese whatsoever. In like manner, a computer can only take information, process it, and give whatever answer(s) are mandated by the specifics of its program. Consciousness, Searle argued, cannot arise in any computer program. The consciousness that arises from brains must be fundamentally different.

Roger Penrose likewise takes the position that strong AI is philosophically flawed and, further, that purely computational machines cannot produce conscious intelligence.[25] Ultimately, any computer or purely algorithmic machine is doing nothing more than executing a mathematical equation (granted, a potentially very complicated one) that can be written down on a piece of paper. It is hard to imagine how the execution of an equation could produce consciousness. Penrose argues strongly that quantum mechanics must play a role in consciousness—that "machines," biological or otherwise, must have more to them (possibly effects moderated by quantum mechanical influences) to produce consciousness.[26]

Some materialist versions suggest not only that the mind is an emergent feature of the brain but also that it arises epiphenomenally from the brain.[27] Consciousness is an after-effect that emerges solely because of the complex dynamics within the brain, and the mind plays no real role in directing conscious action or decision. It does not feed information back to the brain or "will" the brain to do anything at all. It is more like foam floating on water that plays no role in what is going on below the surface. Evidence for this view comes largely from the widely discussed experiments of Benjamin Libet, Nobel Prize-winning psychologist at the University of California, San Francisco.[28] Libet found that when he asked patients to flex their hands according to the position of a dot moving on a clock, the action of flexing, as initiated by a nerve impulse to do so, occurred *before* their conscious intention of doing so. However, others have interpreted Libet's experiments in ways that throw suspicion on the epiphenomenalist view.[29]

However, the emergence of the mind seems unique among other known examples of emergence behavior such as the liquidity of water. The liquidity of water is constitutive. Once we understand liquidity as a principle, we can go back to the basic components of H_2O and understand how liquidity arises. This is not true of the brain.[30] Currently there is no reductive materialist account of how the mind's emergence can be explained by the components and workings of the brain.

The biggest problem in understanding materialist versions of consciousness lies in explaining phenomenal consciousness—the subjective experience of, presumably, every person. There is no reason to speculate that consciousness is required to do the things that biological organisms have to do. Much of the consciousness literature proposes a thought experiment involving "zombies."[31] A zombie is a theoretical construct identical to a human in deed and action but completely without consciousness. For example, my zombie would be a doppelgänger constructed by replicating my body and brain, but it would lack consciousness of any kind. It would act like me and say the things I would say in the same circumstances. Even my wife and children would be unable to tell the difference between us. But there is a big difference. He (it?) has no conscious experience. The lights are on, but no one is home. There is no known biological reason that such a zombie could not exist, so why is someone (apparently) looking out the window? Why is there (apparently?) an observer of the Cartesian Theater?

The phenomenal nature of consciousness is so perplexing that some hardline materialists have chosen to deny the existence of consciousness and postulate that it is an illusion—although, in that case, I have to wonder whose illusion it is.[32] Daniel Dennett explains his thinking about the Cartesian Theater:

> Once we take a serious look backstage, we discover that we didn't actually see what we thought we saw onstage. The huge gap between phenomenology and physiology shrinks a bit: we see that some of the "obvious" features of phenomenology are not real at all: There is no filling in with figment; there are no intrinsic qualia; there is no central fount of meaning and action; there is no magic place where the understanding happens. In fact, there is no Cartesian Theater; the very distinction between onstage experiences and backstage processes loses its appeal. We still have plenty of amazing phenomena to explain, but a few of the most mind-boggling special effects just don't exist at all, and hence require no explanation.[33]

However, the commonsense experience of consciousness demands a more satisfying answer. Strong materialists have been accused of neglect in studying consciousness. Charles Siewert demonstrates this neglect by considering certain forms of blind-sight.[34] He argues that the most significant aspect of consciousness is the phenomenology of consciousness—which functionalist accounts ignore:

> The phenomenal features we have when we perceive, image, and think are not "mere sensations," but are themselves intentional features, abundant and subtly differentiated. And while it seems likely we would be able to engage in rather little intelligent behavior without consciousness, we value phenomenal features for more than what we think they enable us to do; and our valuing them in this way is enormously important for our attitude toward our own lives, and toward other people. Finally, an adequate philosophical or psychological theory of human thought and perception needs to account for, and not conflict with, how it seems to us to think and perceive—our having the phenomenal intentional features we have.[35]

The importance of the phenomenal nature of consciousness is illustrated by a thought experiment first articulated by philosopher Frank Jackson of Australian National University about a neurobiologist named Mary, who knows everything there is to know about the brain's processing of the color red.[36] She understands perfectly the neural pathways involved in processing red, the frequencies of light that contain red, and how they interact with the eye. She can objectively describe every activity in the brain involved in seeing red. However, Mary is color-blind and has never experienced the color red directly. Can Mary be said, then, to understand the color red? Suppose she then has some special surgery that allows her to finally see the color. At this point, it becomes clear that, despite a complete biological understanding of sensing the color red, there was something else that she never knew about red—the phenomenal character of experiencing red. This argument suggests that, even if we knew everything there was to know about the brain, the phenomenal experience of consciousness would not be explained fully. This explanatory gap is a failure in materialist explanations of consciousness.[37]

Materialists have also failed to provide testable hypotheses to determine when something is conscious and when it is not. Trying to decide if a slug or a fly is conscious has posed a difficult problem in materialist musings. Some, like Euan Macphail, have argued that only modern human children and adults are conscious, while human babies and animals are not,[38] while others argue that the higher vertebrates, at least, experience some sort of consciousness.[39]

Materialism, then, has failed to meet many of the benchmarks of what we recognize as a good theory of science. It makes no testable predictions. It has failed in many ways to provide testable hypotheses about any of its tenets. As an assumption, it provides no explanatory power to the extent that it demonstrates little merit in its application on the subject of consciousness.

Mysterian musings

"Mysterian" arguments are materialist in that they begin with the premise that our mind is the result of natural processes in the universe and is a natural part of the universe. There is no spirit animating the mind; biology completely describes the mind. However, the mind was adapted to solve specific sorts of problems encountered during the evolutionary history of our species on the planet. Because of these limitations, there may be questions that the mind is not capable of exploring. One of these, mysterians hold, is the problem of consciousness.

The mysterian view is that consciousness will always remain a mystery. Our mind is adapted to be good at specific tasks like solving the sorts of problems from which our mathematical knowledge is gleaned. The mind can tackle questions answered through the scientific method, for example by using rational thinking to solve the "if such and such, then such and such follows" type of problem. It can handle the type of questions best handled by the modern scientific method. However, our minds are not good at getting at problems like consciousness: "Our human intelligence is biased away from understanding consciousness. It is not that consciousness is objectively any more complex than the things we can understand; it's just that our faculties are not cut out to penetrate to its underlying nature."[40]

Mysterians point out that applying Gödel's theorem[41] to the scientific method itself suggests that reality has some problems that cannot be resolved using the scientific method. How much harder are questions that cannot even be addressed by the scientific method? Roger Penrose suggests that we must understand three worlds in order to understand consciousness: the mental world, the Platonic world of mathematic forms, and the physical world.[42] He argues that these worlds interact through quantum mechanics but that we do not yet know enough about the three worlds to make guesses about the nature of deep reality.

Does quantum mechanics in fact provide an answer? Many involved in consciousness studies have been intrigued with possible connections between the strange and counterintuitive world of quantum mechanics and the brain.[43] Quantum theory suggests that electrons orbiting the atom's nucleus are not like planets spinning around the sun, but rather are spread over a probability space. The famous uncertainty principle claims that how you observe or measure an electron affects its nature. Because of the indeterminacy of quantum effects, an escape from the rigidity of strict determinism seems possible if quantum effects can bubble up into the macro world where humans live. Penrose points out that microtubules in the brain are of such a size that quantum effects might play a role. The most advanced thinking in this area has come from a group studying quantum field theory, a recent advance in quantum mechanics. Physicist Giuseppe Vitiello from the University of Salerno has demonstrated that the entire brain is a large coherent quantum structure.[44] This structure allows for communication among the parts of the brain to be instantaneous and explains much about memory, such as its large storage capacity and duration.

So far, however, ideas associating consciousness and quantum theory have not yielded testable hypotheses and thus remain speculative. Searle has criticized them as just substituting one mystery for another.[45]

Dualist views of consciousness

Modern dualists, while embracing the evolutionary origin of the brain as a biological structure, argue that the mind and the brain are separate things. There are two types of dualists: substance dualists and property dualists.[46] Substance dualists hold that the brain is animated by a substance, soul, or spirit composed of something unavailable for physical observation or manipulation. Descartes thought that the universe contained two substances: *res extensa* (lit., "extended substance," or the materials that occupy space) and *res cogitans* (lit., "thinking substance," or another substance of consciousness).[47] Property dualists, in contrast, suggest that consciousness may be a property of possibly all matter and can be found anywhere that matter is complex enough to contain information.

Brain researcher John Eccles has best articulated the former position. He holds that the mind and the brain are separate entities analogous to

Karl Popper's three worlds.[48] The mind arises from Popper's World 2, with the mind and body interacting in the same way that World 1 and World 2 interact epistemologically. The substance in Eccles's theory is not a spirit or soul as defined in the typical religious sense of the word, but rather something that arises developmentally both in the ontogeny and evolutionary history of human brain development. But the substance of the mind consists of what he calls *psychons,* separate objects involved in the evolutionary development of the mind, which use quantum mechanics to influence the actual mind. These psychons form in association with specific dendrite bundles,[49] protoplasmic processes essential to the function of nerve cells. He sees the mind as existentially real and separate from the brain. It communicates with the brain, informs the brain with its will, and likewise is affected by the brain's perceptions of pain, pleasure, and other states derived from physical events:

> It is proposed that the self-conscious mind is actively engaged in searching for brain events that are of its present interest, the operation of attention, but it also is the integrating agent, building the unity of conscious experience from all the diversity of the brain events. Even more importantly it is given the role of actively modifying the brain events according to its interest or desire, and the scanning operation by which it searches can be envisaged as having an active role in selection.[50]

It is important to point out, in view of LDS theology to be discussed below, that these hypothesized psychons have no independent existence prior to the evolution of the brain and the appearance of life on earth.[51]

The challenges to substance dualism have been around since the time of Descartes. If another substance or property exists, how does it interact with the physical reality that materialists assume to be ultimate? And if it can interface with this reality, then should there not be ways to detect it? For example, because this substance interacts with brain states, it seems reasonable that some kind of detector, constructed using the same principles of physics that structure the brain, can be made to detect it. Early philosophers like Nicolas de Malebranche held that God was the source of the interaction. If my spirit wanted to move my arm, I willed it; and God sent the messages to the brain that it should be moved.[52] However, this proposal seems ontologically unsavory, and most philosophers and theologians have rejected it as too convoluted. Nonetheless, some of the ideas of a quantum interface between brain states as postulated by Penrose and Eccles allow an interface between this and another world quite easily, thus offering a possible defense of substance dualism.

The second form of dualism, property dualism, in contrast, avoids some of these problems. John Chalmers, director of the Center for Consciousness Studies at the University of Arizona, espousing a form of property dualism, suggests that consciousness is an independent attribute of the universe. Experience is an aspect of certain information states. He warns against construing this description as panpsychism, because it is not matter itself that is experiential. Rather, he suggests that certain configurations of matter that use or convey information as a system are experiential. The more complex the informational states, the greater the quality of experience. That is why highly complex physical objects like the human brain have a highly developed consciousness. Chalmers, after arguing that even a thermostat might have a rudimentary form of consciousness, suggests: "It may be that some are unwilling to accept the possibility of conscious thermostats simply because we *understand* thermostats too well. We know everything about their processing, and there seems no reason to invoke consciousness. But thermostats are really no different from brains here. Even once we understand brain processing perfectly, there will still seem to be no reason to invoke consciousness."[53]

Another form of property dualism, sometimes referred to as process dualism, suggests that consciousness is an irreducible fundamental feature of the universe. In considering an elementary particle's charge or the gravitational attraction of two bodies, there is ultimately no answer to the question of why these phenomena occur.[54] It's just the way the universe is constructed. The assumption that matter is composed of nothing but vacuous particles (i.e., they have no experience) has been challenged by process dualists like philosopher Alfred North Whitehead and theologian David Griffin of the School of Theology at Claremont Graduate University.[55] Griffin argues that the assumption that elementary forms of matter are without some form of awareness is unwarranted and instead contends that assuming otherwise makes for a more coherent theory of the underpinnings of the universe. Griffin, expanding on Whitehead's thought, argues that our own subjective experience with consciousness demonstrates that, at least in some form, consciousness is a natural part of the universe.[56] Why not assume that it is a phenomenon as basic as gravity? These process dualists suggest that, while less complete than our own consciousness, all things may have an awareness of sorts.

Panexperientialism posits that, like these physical properties of nature, consciousness is a fundamental property of the universe. There is no point in asking why—it just is. Whitehead speculated that all existing entities have some form of consciousness.[57] Particles of matter do not endure but are rather "throbs of experience."[58] These "Actual Entities," as he calls all particles in our universe, exist only for a short time, during which they form a relationship with all other actual entities. As actual entities go out of existence, they experience a "satisfaction," or a flash of experience. In the process of their annihilation, new actual entities form, integrating the past history of all the previous actual entities ("prehension," in Whitehead's terminology) that have led to its creation. This process continues for all time, creating all the experiences that occur in the universe.[59] According to this view, consciousness is therefore the result of a process, as the term *process dualist* implies. Panexperientialists claim their view runs counter to a kind of universal solipsism, one that denies consciousness to any of those without brains. However, just as there is no way to logically or scientifically argue for or against solipsism (because we have access only to our own subjectivity), panexperientialism can never be proved by standard methods.

This brief overview of consciousness theory and philosophy suggests that things are at best unsettled and at worst a mess. There seems to be no theory or idea tending toward a consensus. What these views have in common is the shared assumption that consciousness—at least, human consciousness—begins no earlier than birth and ends with death. Where do LDS doctrines fit in this melee?

LDS Views of Consciousness

Little has been written about LDS thought on consciousness as such. Implicitly, however, Latter-day Saints have both a unique and a profound view of consciousness as informed by modern scriptures, by prophets, and by theology. Three general concepts can be garnered from the scriptures: (1) the universe contains things that act and other things that are acted upon; (2) consciousness in its basic form is not created; and (3) consciousness can exist without the material world as we know it.

As to the first concept, assuming that the scripture below is making ontological claims (which may or may not be the case),[60] the universe contains two distinct types of entities: those that are to act and those that are to be acted upon: "And now, my sons, I speak unto you these things for your profit and learning; for there is a God, and he hath created all things, both the heavens and the earth, and all things that in them are, both things to act and things to be acted upon" (2 Nephi 2:14).

The scriptural underpinning for the second concept is a revelation received by Joseph Smith suggesting that there are two kinds of substances in the universe, spirit and element: "For man is spirit. The elements are eternal, and spirit and element inseparably connected, receive a fulness of joy" (D&C 93:33).

Third, another revelation clarifies the nature of matter: "There is no such thing as immaterial matter. All spirit is matter, but it is more fine or pure, and can only be discerned by purer eyes; we cannot see it; but when our bodies are purified we shall see that it is all matter" (D&C 131:7-8).

From the context of this scripture, it appears that *element* means the material world we experience through our physical senses, possibly enhanced with the instruments used in science. *Spirit* is a form of matter about which we know very little, except it is more "fine" than ordinary matter. What *pure* means is not clear, but we can assume that it is currently unavailable for observation from a scientific standpoint. Abraham 3:18-25 describes the organization of "intelligences" before the world. Of these the Lord says, "We will prove them herewith, to see if they will do all things whatsoever the Lord their God shall command them." This description implies that they were conscious beings capable of exercising free will. Doctrine and Covenants 93:29 points out that intelligence cannot be created or made. It is difficult to imagine intelligence without some sort of consciousness. Hence, these two scriptures seem to suggest: (1) consciousness, an attribute of a preexistent being, is an aspect of existence in the universe that is not created or made and is coeternal with God; and (2) consciousness can exist independently of the material world (as we know it) and is capable of growth and development. Therefore, ideas about consciousness are tied very closely to ideas about intelligence or intelligences.

Joseph Smith gave a further explication about the nature of intelligence in his King Follett discourse. There he taught that human beings have gone through a series of progressions from lesser to greater intelligence; their ultimate potential is to continue to grow until they reach a perfect state, like the level of existence God has reached. He explained, according to Wilford Woodruff's diary:

I am dwelling on the immutability of the spirit of man, is it logic to say the spirit of man had no beginning and or end[?] It does not have a beginning or end. . . . God never had power to create the spirit of man. . . . Intelligence is Eternal and it is self existing. . . . All mind . . . is susceptible of improvement[.] . . . The relationship we have with God places us in a situation to advance in knowledge. God has power to institute laws to instruct the weaker intelligences that they may be exalted with himself[.] This is good doctrine, it tastes good, I can taste the principles of eternal life, so can you, they are given to me by the revelations of Jesus Christ and I know you believe it.[61]

Joseph Smith points out that consciousness does not come into existence ex nihilo but has always existed in some form and is capable of growth and improvement. Although he did not clarify the nature of this consciousness much more before his untimely death, other LDS Church leaders and thinkers have speculated further on the nature of consciousness, incorporating the idea of intelligences.

One of the most prolific writers on this topic was B. H. Roberts (1857–1933). He served as president of the First Council of the Seventy and is considered one of Mormonism's preeminent thinkers and philosophers.[62] He was also one of the few LDS thinkers to discuss consciousness as such.

In *The Way, the Truth, and the Life*, a manuscript that was not published during his lifetime, Roberts explored the nature of consciousness. His definition differs somewhat from Searle's, which I quoted in the beginning of this chapter. First, Roberts differentiates between spirits and intelligences: "The difference between 'spirits' and 'intelligences' as herein used is this: Intelligences are uncreated entities, some inhabiting spiritual bodies—bodies composed of fine spirit elements, others are intelligences unembodied in either spirit bodies or other kinds of bodies."[63]

Roberts lists several attributes of intelligences such as consciousness, ability to perceive a priori principles (probably in a Kantian sense), imagination, memory, power to deliberate and to form judgments, freedom of will, and indestructibility. Although he does not explicitly mention phenomenal consciousness as an attribute of intelligences, he implicitly refers to it when talking about memory. As an example, he describes his memory of an orange tree and its blossoms, ascribing the same ability to intelligences.

Further elaboration of Roberts's definition of intelligence may be seen in his *Seventy's Course in Theology*, where he defines "Intelligence: Consciousness" by saying:

> [T]he term Intelligence is descriptive of the thing to which it is applied. Therefore Intelligence (mind) or Intelligences (minds), thus conceived are conscious. Conscious of *self* and of *notself;* of the *me* and the *not me.* Intelligence is that which sees itself, or is at once both subject and object. It knows itself as thinking, that is, as a subject; thinking of its self, it knows itself as an object of thought—of its own thought. And it knows itself as distinct from a vast universe of things which are not self; itself the while remaining constant as a distinct individuality amid the great universe of things *not self.* Fiske calls Consciousness the soul's fundamental fact; and the most fundamental of facts. It may be defined as the power by which Intelligence knows its own acts and states. It is an awareness of the mind. By reason of it an Intelligence, when dwelling in a body—as we best know it (man)—knows itself as seeing, hearing, smelling, tasting, touching; also as searching, and finding; as inquiring and answering; as active or at rest; as loving or hating; as contented or restless; as advancing or receding; as gaining or losing, and so following in all the activities in which Intelligences, as men, engage.[64]

Here Roberts seems to conclude that consciousness *is* self-consciousness. He attributes to consciousness qualities similar to those listed above, including several attributes of mind, the power of generalization, imagination, the power of forming new mental combinations, and the power of deliberation. He also notes that consciousness is a fundamental fact of the universe.[65]

In any event, it is clear that Roberts endows intelligences with many of the same properties of consciousness that human beings find in themselves. He would agree that not all have the same degree of intelligence— God has the greatest measure of that attribute—but he clearly argues that intelligence involves some sort of conscious experiences.

Other early LDS theologians have also speculated on the origin of consciousness. For example, apostle Orson Pratt (1811-81) anticipated the modern process theologies of Whitehead and Hartshorne by speculating that intelligence is a property of all elementary particles. After posing the question "What is intelligence?," he speculates that "it must either be a property of material atoms, or the result of the combination or contact of these atoms." He then argues that indeed material atoms must be possessed of some sort of rudimentary intelligence, which is eternal in nature and uncreated.[66] It must be kept in mind that his view of elementary particles preceded Niels Bohr's early twentieth-century articulation of our current understanding of the nature of the subatomic world and that he was looking at atoms as the fundamental building blocks of the universe. How his position would change with the new view of quantum electrodynamics we can only speculate.

Like Pratt, apostle John A. Widtsoe (1872–52) also viewed the world as largely panexperiential. In 1951, the year before he died, he wrote:

> We live then in a living universe which in all its component parts is intelligent. In addition to matter-energy, there are in the universe personal intelligences, having consciousness of varying degrees of advancement. These possess all the attributes of individuals. They have power of action. They can learn. They can act for themselves in their surroundings. Some of them are the men and women of earth.
>
> The highest of the universe intelligences is God. He possesses supreme knowledge and power. Indeed we have reason to believe that his knowledge is the sum of the knowledge possessed by all existing personal intelligences and that his power is the sum of the powers of such personal beings. His work with the intelligences inferior to his own constitutes the gospel story.
>
> In this universe of one eternal world are matter-energy and personal intelligences. Energy itself may be a form of intelligence, making all matter, to some degree, alive and intelligent. The whole universe is alive. The story of eternity is the interaction of matter-energy and personal intelligences. The things in the universe are under the control of law. To the extent that universal law is unchangeable, a limitation is placed upon all intelligences, who, as they rise, learn to control or use the law.[67]

Widtsoe seems well-informed about the modern Einsteinian view that energy and matter are two sides of the same coin. He even speculates that energy may be involved in consciousness.

Roberts, Pratt, and Widtsoe exemplify one interpretation of the nature of intelligences from scripture and the early teachings of Joseph Smith. Another is found in the writings of then-apostle Joseph Fielding Smith (1910-70; President of the Church, 1970-72) and his son-in-law Bruce R. McConkie, a member of the First Council of Seventy (1946-72) and later an apostle (1972-85). Both men are less explicit and more cautious in their speculation about intelligence or intelligences. They taught that intelligence prior to a spirit birth was unorganized and that individual consciousness did not exist before spirits were organized.

Smith wrote in 1956: "Some of our writers have endeavored to explain what an intelligence is, but to do so is futile, for we have never been given any insight into this matter beyond what the Lord has fragmentarily revealed. We know, however, that there is something called intelligence which always existed. It is the real eternal part of man, which was not created nor made. This intelligence combined with the spirit constitutes a spiritual identity or individual."[68]

McConkie wrote in *Mormon Doctrine*: "The intelligence or spirit element became intelligences after the spirits were born as individual entities. (Abr. 3:22-74.) Use of this name designates both the primal element from which the spirit offspring were created and also their inherited capacity to grow in grace, knowledge, power and intelligence itself, until such intelligences, gaining the fulness of all things, become like their Father, the Supreme Intelligence."[69]

Rex Sears, in his dissertation for Harvard University, contrasts the difference between McConkie's view of intelligences and Roberts's view, stressing that Roberts thought in terms of personal intelligences rather than merely a life force:

> No current church sponsored publications endorse any interpretation of the doctrine of uncreated intelligence but the highly influential, recently deceased Mormon apostle Bruce R. McConkie held that intelligence is the uncreated and uncreatable substance out of which individual spirits are formed. . . . Roberts does not explicitly address McConkie's view in the article in which he defends his own view, suggesting that McConkie's view was not in circulation at that time. Roberts's explicitly opposes the view, no longer (so far as I am aware) in circulation, that intelligence refers to something like the intelligent life force of a conscious individual, which the

parents of our spirits (God the Father and his spouse) transmit to their offspring. . . . It is this intelligent life force which has no beginning, being transmitted from parent to child through unending generations, but each discrete individual imbued with this force does have a beginning.[70]

However, the two views are not necessarily incompatible. Process theologians like David Ray Griffin suggest that, while all things have experience, for elementary particles this level of consciousness is very low.[71] He argues that only in organized structures such as the brain is consciousness fully realized. This result occurs by bringing unorganized conscious entities into a kind of unity that allows a higher level of consciousness.[72] Smith and McConkie argue only that God organized the intelligent stuff of the universe and make few claims about what that intelligence was like, leaving room for both the speculation of Roberts, Pratt, and Widtsoe and their own. The single point upon which all agree is that consciousness can exist without a mortal body and that it is eternal (at least in some sense)—that it cannot be created or made.[73]

The idea that our fundamental consciousness is eternal has not changed significantly between Joseph Smith's early statements about intelligences and the present day. While ideas about consciousness are not explicitly clear in Joseph Smith's original teachings on the subject, as Van Hale explains,[74] subsequent prophets have taught that we move, by a "birth" process, from being an intelligence to being a spirit created in the physical form of our Heavenly Parents to our current stage of development where spirit and matter have been temporarily joined.[75] After the resurrection, this temporary bond will be made permanent (Alma 11:43-44). Harold B. Lee, then an apostle, emphasized the fundamental unity of these three stages of existence:

As I thought about it I remarked that we do use words rather loosely when we speak of the "life before this, and this life, and the next life," as though we were a cat of nine lives, when as a matter of fact, we only have one life. This life we speak of did not begin with mortal birth. This life does not end with mortal death. There is something that is not created or made. The Scriptures called it "intelligence," which at a certain stage in the pre-existence was organized into a "spirit." After that spirit had grown to a certain stature it then was given the

opportunity by an all-wise Father to come into another stage
for its development. It was added upon, and after having lived
its span and having attained to its purpose in mortality, another change took place. We go, not into another life in fact,
but into another stage of the same life. There is something
which was not created or made, and something which does
not die, and that something shall live on forever.[76]

LDS teachings are unique among current arguments about consciousness. It is clear that we have a dual nature: body and spirit. But the nature
of consciousness as it relates to spirit matter is not understood and has not
been revealed. Because of our dual nature, one might be tempted to call us
substance dualists; but from the writings discussed above, it is clear that
we could be viewed as property dualists when it comes to the broader view
of the nature of the universe that includes spirit matter. Therefore, the
common distinction of property or substance dualism is not meaningful
from the perspective of an LDS theology and perhaps should be avoided.

However, it is clear that we embrace some form of dualism. There is
more to our consciousness than just the physical brain. Consciousness
existed prior to the brain and can exist for some time without it—for
example, prior to the resurrection. It is important to keep in mind that
an LDS view of consciousness is not incompatible with materialist assumptions about the origin of the brain through evolution.[77] Rather, it
is in assumptions about the nature of the mind where LDS views differ.

Dualism has fallen out of favor with consciousness philosophers
not because dualism stands on a shakier philosophical basis, but rather
because the nature of the dualism posited to exist is not detectable and
therefore not amenable to scientific exploration, a position untenable under current philosophical paradigms. For example, Daniel Dennett states:
"This fundamentally antiscientific stance of dualism is, to my mind, its
most disqualifying feature, and is the reason why in this book I adopt
the apparently dogmatic rule that dualism is to be avoided *at all costs.* It
is not that I think I can give a knock-down proof that dualism, in all its
forms, is false or incoherent, but that, given the way dualism wallows in
mystery, accepting dualism is giving up."[78]

Dennett thus acknowledges that dualism is a coherent, valid way to
view the universe. He is rejecting it "dogmatically," however, because
science cannot get its hands on dualism. But other than by assumption,
there is no more philosophical warrant for this hardline materialist

position than that articulated in LDS theology, which is informed by revelation.

Conclusions

Some theologians have argued that dualism must be eliminated from religious discourse if there is to be any dialogue between neuroscience and theology.[79] However, that position seems to be more a result of indispensable materialist assumptions than of any argument that nondetectable substances cannot exist. Ironically, strict materialism may undermine the advancement of science and miss or ignore a more accurate view of the universe's development. For example, string theory predicts up to eleven dimensions, only four of which we have access to.[80] Assuming that the universe consists only of what we can perceive may cause strict materialists to miss important insights. The dualist position is further defensible when enhanced by the belief that God can and does communicate with humans. There is no reason a priori to assume that only that which we can physically sense exists in the universe. This possibility seems especially likely when we consider subjective knowledge as a source of truth.[81] So far science, despite its importance and power in explaining the physical world, has been unable to shed much light on the nature of consciousness. But consciousness is a puzzling aspect of the universe that needs explaining.[82]

LDS theology is graced, in addition to the above arguments, by the idea that God is in communication with us, his children, and has revealed that there is considerable more to the physical universe than we can observe with the instruments of our invention. Thus, dualism, while a philosophically valid position, is complemented by continuing revelation, supporting the belief that our consciousness is a combination of brain and spirit and placing LDS theological views in an internally coherent philosophical framework as far as consciousness is concerned.

Notes

1. William Carlos Williams, "XXII," *Spring and All* (New York: Contact Editions / Dijon: Maurice Darantière, 1923).

2. Qualia are the individual elements of experience. A pain, the experience of seeing a color, and the sound of a note of music are all examples of qualia.

3. John R. Searle, *Consciousness and Language* (Cambridge: Cambridge University Press, 2002), 7.

4. David J. Chalmers, "Facing Up to the Problem of Consciousness," *Journal of Consciousness Studies* 2/3 (1995): 200-19; and Güven Güzeldere, "Problems of Consciousness: A Perspective on Contemporary Issues, Current Debates," *Journal of Consciousness Studies* 2/2 (1995): 112-43.

5. Benjamin Libet, "Solutions to the Hard Problem of Consciousness," *Journal of Consciousness Studies* 3/1 (1996): 33-35; and William S. Robinson, "The Hardness of the Hard Problems," *Journal of Consciousness Studies* 3/1 (1996): 14-25.

6. Thomas Nagel, "What Is It Like to Be a Bat?," *Philosophical Review* 83 (1974): 435-50.

7. John R. Searle, "Reductionism and the Irreducibility of Consciousness," in *The Nature of Consciousness: The Philosophical Debates*, ed. Ned Block, Owen Flanagan, and David J. Chalmers (Cambridge, MA: MIT Press, 1997), 451-59.

8. William Seager, *Theories of Consciousness: An Introduction and Assessment* (London: Routledge, 1999), 44-45; John R. Searle, *The Mystery of Consciousness* (New York: New York Review of Books, 1997), 28-29; and Charles P. Siewert, *The Significance of Consciousness* (Princeton, NJ: Princeton University Press, 1998), 85-99.

9. Alvin I. Goldman, "Can Science Know When You're Conscious? Epistemological Foundations of Consciousness Research," *Journal of Consciousness Studies* 7/5 (2000): 3-22.

10. Fred Dretske, *Naturalizing the Mind* (Cambridge, MA: MIT Press, 1995), 1-38; and Michael Tye, *Ten Problems of Consciousness: A Representational Theory of the Mind* (Cambridge, MA: MIT Press, 1995), 100-105.

11. Glenn Braddock, "Beyond Reflection in Naturalized Phenomenology," *Journal of Consciousness Studies* 8/11 (2001): 3-16.

12. Excellent reviews on the nature of consciousness are found in Karl Popper and John C. Eccles, *The Self and Its Brain* (New York: Routledge, 1977), 148-224; Güven Güzeldere, "The Many Faces of Consciousness: A Field Guide," in *The Nature of Consciousness: Philosophical Debates,* ed. Ned Block, Owen Flanagan, and Güven Güzeldere (Cambridge, MA: MIT Press, 1998), 1-67; and Seager, *Theories of Consciousness.*

13. Merlin Donald, *A Mind So Rare: The Evolution of Human Consciousness* (New York: W. W. Norton, 2001), 92-148; Steven Mithen, "Handaxes and Ice Age Carvings: Hard Evidence for the Evolution of Consciousness," in *Towards a Science of Consciousness III: The Third Tucson Discussions and Debates*, ed. Stuart R. Hameroff, Alfred W. Kaszniak, and David J. Chalmers (Cambridge, MA: MLT Press, 1999), 281-96.

14. William James, *Principles of Psychology* (1890; repr., New York: H. Holt, 1952), 8-52.

15. See my discussion in chapter 2, "Randomness, Contingency, and Faith: Is There a Science of Subjectivity?"; and B. Alan Wallace, *The Taboo of Subjectivity: Toward a New Science of Consciousness* (New York: Oxford University Press, 2000), 3-13.

16. Donald, *Mind So Rare;* J. Allan Hobson, *Consciousness* (New York: Scientific American Library, 1999), 96-99; James Newman, "Putting the Puzzle Together, Part 1: Towards a General Theory of the Neural Correlates of Consciousness," *Journal of Consciousness Studies* 4/1 (1997): 47-66; James Newman, "Putting the Puzzle Together, Part II: Towards a General Theory of the Neural Correlates of Consciousness," *Journal of Consciousness Studies* 4/2 (1997): 100-121.

17. Carol Rausch Albright, "The 'God Module' and the Complexifying Brain," *Zygon: Journal of Religion and Science* 35/4 (December 2000): 735-44; Andrew B. Newberg and Eugene G. d'Aquili, "The Creative Brain/The Creative Mind," *Zygon* 35/1 (2000),

53-68; and Andrew Newberg, Eugene d'Aquili, and Vince Rause, *Why God Won't Go Away: Brain Science and the Biology of Belief* (New York: Ballantine Books, 2001), 113-27.

18. See Michael Shermer, *How We Believe: The Search for God in an Age of Science* (New York: W. H. Freeman, 2000), 65-69; and Michael Spezio, "Understanding Biology in Religious Experience: The Biogenetic Structuralist Approach of Eugene G. d'Aquili and Andrew Newberg," *Zygon: Journal of Religion and Science* 36/3 (September 2001): 477-84.

19. Gerald M. Edelman and Giulio Tononi, *A Universe of Consciousness* (New York: Basic Books, 2000), 70-75.

20. Edelman and Tononi, *Universe of Consciousness*, 70-75.

21. Martha J. Farah, "Visual Perception and Visual Awareness after Brain Damage: A Tutorial Overview," in Block, Flanagan, and Güzeldere, *Nature of Consciousness*, 203-36; F. X. Vollenveider, A. Gamma, and M. F. I. Vollenweider-Scherpenhuyzen, "Neural Correlates of Hallucinogen-Induced Altered States of Consciousness," in Hameroff, Kaszniak, and Chalmers, *Towards a Science of Consciousness III*, 99-110.

22. Narika Newton, "Emergence and the Uniqueness of Consciousness," *Journal of Consciousness Studies* 8/9-10 (2001): 47-60; and Michael Silberstein, "Converging on Emergence: Consciousness, Causation and Explanation," *Journal of Consciousness Studies* 8/9-10 (2001): 61-98.

23. Searle, *Mystery of Consciousness*, 80-86.

24. Searle, *Mystery of Consciousness*, 11-12, 80-86.

25. Roger Penrose, *Shadows of the Mind: A Search for the Missing Science of Consciousness* (Oxford: Oxford University Press, 1994), 12-16.

26. Harry T. Hunt, "Some Perils of Quantum Consciousness: Epistemological Pan-Experientialism and the Emergence-Submergence of Consciousness," *Journal of Consciousness Studies* 8/9-10 (2001): 35-45.

27. Robert Van Gulick, "Reduction, Emergence and Other Recent Options on the Mind/Body Problem: A Philosophic Overview," *Journal of Consciousness Studies* 8/9-10 (2001): 1-34; and Francis Crick and Christof Koch, "Towards a Neurobiological Theory of Consciousness," *Seminars in the Neurosciences* 2 (1990): 263-75.

28. Susan Blackmore, *The Meme Machine* (Oxford: Oxford University Press, 1999), 225-28; and Benjamin Libet, "Unconscious Cerebral Initiative and the Role of Conscious Will in Voluntary Action," *Behavioral and Brain Sciences* 8/4 (December 1985): 529-66.

29. Owen Flanagan, "Conscious Inessentialism and the Epiphenomenalist Suspicion," in Block, Flanagan, and Güzeldere, *Nature of Consciousness*, 357-73.

30. Todd E. Feinberg, "Why the Mind Is Not a Radically Emergent Feature of the Brain," *Journal of Consciousness Studies* 8/9-10 (2001): 123-45.

31. Allin Cottrell, "Sniffing the Camembert: On the Conceivability of Zombies," *Journal of Consciousness Studies* 6/1 (1999): 4-12; and Owen Flanagan and Thomas Polger, "Zombies and the Function of Consciousness," *Journal of Consciousness Studies* 2/4 (1995): 313-21.

32. Blackmore, *Meme Machine*, 225; and Daniel C. Dennett, *Consciousness Explained* (New York: Little Brown, 1991), 219-34.

33. Dennett, *Consciousness Explained*, 434.

34. In blind-sight, certain parts of the brain experience damage, resulting in blindness, even though nothing is wrong with the visual processing parts of the brain; however, the direct link between the images seen by the eye and interpreted by the brain cannot be passed to consciousness. Persons with this type of blind-sight can "guess"

with almost 100 percent accuracy what object is being held before them but claim no ability to see it.

35. Siewert, *Significance of Consciousness*, 338.

36. Frank Jackson, "Epiphenomenal Qualia," *Philosophical Quarterly* 32 (1982): 127-36; and Frank Jackson, "What Mary Didn't Know," *Journal of Philosophy* 32 (1986): 291-95.

37. Joseph Levine, "On Leaving Out What It's Like," in Block, Flanagan, and Güzeldere, *Nature of Consciousness*, 543-55; and Colin McGinn, "Can We Solve the Mind-Body Problem?," in Block, Flanagan, and Güzeldere, *Nature of Consciousness*, 529-42.

38. Euan M. Macphail, *The Evolution of Consciousness* (Oxford: Oxford University Press, 1998), 204-37.

39. Donald R. Griffin, *Animal Minds: Beyond Cognition to Consciousness* (Chicago: University of Chicago Press, 1992), 17-18.

40. Colin McGinn, *The Mysterious Flame: Conscious Minds in a Material World* (New York: Basic Books, 1999), 65.

41. Gödel's theorem showed that within an axiomatic system are true theorems that cannot be proved within the system itself.

42. Penrose, *Shadows of the Mind*, 348-92.

43. Henry P. Stapp, "The Hard Problem: A Quantum Approach," *Journal of Consciousness Studies* 3/3 (1996): 194-210; and Evan Harris Walker, *The Physics of Consciousness* (Cambridge, MA: Perseus, 2000), 216-37.

44. Giuseppe Vitiello, *My Double Unveiled: The Dissipative Quantum Model of Brain* (Philadelphia: John Benjamins, 2001), 67-86.

45. Searle, *Mystery of Consciousness*, 84.

46. Robert Van Gulick, "Reduction, Emergence and Other Recent Options on the Mind/Body Problem: A Philosophical Overview," *Journal of Consciousness Studies* 8/9 (2002): 1-34.

47. Max Velmans, "The Relation of Consciousness to the Material World," *Journal of Consciousness Studies* 2/3 (1995): 255-65.

48. Popper defines three ontological worlds. World 1 is composed of physical elements and includes everything from inorganic and biological objects and artifacts of human design such as art, machines, and books. World 2 is the subjective world of knowledge, perception, memories, and other informational states of subjective experience. World 3 is knowledge in an objective sense, such as the knowledge contained in libraries, human culture, and the paradigms of science. Karl Popper, *The Logic of Scientific Discovery* (New York: Harper and Row/Basic Books, 1959); and Popper and Eccles, *Self and Its Brain*, 36-50.

49. John C. Eccles, *How the Self Controls Its Brain* (New York: SpringerVerlag, 1994), 88.

50. Popper and Eccles, *Self and Its Brain*, 373.

51. Eccles, *How the Self Controls Its Brain*, 178, acknowledges that animals have some consciousness.

52. Popper and Eccles, *The Self and Its Brain*, 184.

53. David J. Chalmers, *The Conscious Mind*, ed. Owen Flanagen (Oxford: Oxford University Press, 1996), 296.

54. Teilhard de Chardin, *The Phenomenon of Man*, trans. Bernard Wall (New York: Harper & Row, 1955), 54-60.

55. David Ray Griffin, *Reenchantment without Supernaturalism: A Process Philosophy of Religion*, ed. William P. Alston (Ithaca, NY: Cornell University Press, 2000), 94-128;

and Alfred North Whitehead, *Process and Reality*, corrected ed. (New York: Free Press, 1978), 46-51.

56. David Ray Griffin, *Unsnarling the World-Knot: Consciousness, Freedom, and the Mind-Body Problem* (Berkeley: University of California Press, 1998), 90.

57. Whitehead, *Process and Reality*, 18-20, viewed consciousness as arising only in complex individuals. He identified "prehensions" as the basic type of experience.

58. Shimon Malin, "What Does Quantum Mechanics Imply about the Nature of the Universe?," in Hameroff, Kaszniak, and Chalmers, *Towards a Science of Consciousness III*, 313-16.

59. Whitehead, *Process and Reality*, 20-26.

60. This caveat is important to keep in mind along with my discussion of scriptural literalism in chapter 1.

61. Andrew F. Ehat and Lyndon W. Cook, eds., *The Words of Joseph Smith: The Contemporary Accounts of the Nauvoo Discourses of the Prophet Joseph* (Provo, UT: Religious Studies Center, Brigham Young University, 1980), 346; spelling and capitalization standardized and terminal punctuation added.

62. Truman G. Madsen, "Philosophy," in *The Truth, The Way, The Life: An Elementary Treatise on Theology*, ed. John W. Welch (Provo, UT: BYU Studies, 1996), 595-617. This volume contains Roberts's treatise of the same title as well as several essays by later scholars. Subsequent references to Roberts's treatise are to this work.

63. Roberts, *The Truth, The Way, The Life*, 255.

64. B. H. Roberts, *Seventy's Course in Theology*, 5 vols. (Salt Lake City: Deseret News, 1907-12), 4:2.

65. Roberts could be read as falling into the trap of denying consciousness to anything but humans, since most of these attributes would deny consciousness to animals. However, I do not believe that this was Roberts's intent. At the time of his writing, little was understood about an animal's reasoning power or mental abilities. Therefore, Roberts may not have considered animal consciousness at all. But I think he would be inclined to argue that, for example, a cat might fit these parameters. A cat is clearly aware of its spatial bounds (e.g., it does not move out of the way of a tree falling in the far distance), makes decisions (it chooses between lying by the fire or on the couch), and so on.

66. *The Essential Orson Pratt* (Salt Lake City: Signature Books, 1991), 33.

67. John A. Widtsoe, *Joseph Smith: Seeker after Truth, Prophet of God* (Salt Lake City: Bookcraft, 1951), 150.

68. Joseph Fielding Smith, *Answers to Gospel Questions*, 5 vols. (Salt Lake City: Deseret News, 1957-67), 4:127.

69. Bruce R. McConkie, *Mormon Doctrine*, 2nd ed. (Salt Lake City: Bookcraft, 1966), 84.

70. Lannie Rex Sears, "An Essay in Philosophical Mormon Theology" (PhD diss., Harvard University, 1996), 34.

71. Consciousness philosophers, including materialists, dualists, and process thinkers, all speak of "degrees" or "orders" of consciousness, implying that an ape, say, has a higher order of consciousness than a slug. LDS theology also describes a similar ordering of intelligences (Abraham 3:19). These ideas are similar enough that the ideas of "degree" in the secular view of consciousness and LDS views on "orders" of intelligences seem to be talking about the same thing.

72. Griffin, *Unsnarling the World-Knot*, 77-116.

73. For a more speculative view of the nature of intelligences, which places LDS theology in a postmodernist framework, see Daniel Wright Wotherspoon, "Awakening Joseph Smith: Mormon Resources for a Postmodern Worldview" (PhD diss., Claremont Graduate University, 1996), 210-32.

74. Van Hale, "The Origin of the Human Spirit in Early Mormon Thought," in *Line upon Line: Essays on Mormon Doctrine*, ed. Gary James Bergera (Salt Lake City: Signature Books, l989), 115-44.

75. Charles R. Harrell, "The Development of the Doctrine of Preexistence," *BYU Studies* 28/2 (Spring 1988): 75-96.

76. Harold B. Lee, "Address at the Funeral of Edwin Marcellus Clark," April 5, 1955, Harold Bingham Lee Addresses (1939-73), quoted in *Teachings of Presidents of the Church: Harold B. Lee* (Salt Lake City: Church of Jesus Christ of Latter-day Saints, 2000), 9.

77. Trent D. Stephens and D. Jeffrey Meldrum, *Evolution and Mormonism: A Quest for Understanding* (Salt Lake City: Signature Books, 2001), xvii-xix.

78. Dennett, *Consciousness Explained*, 37; emphasis in original.

79. Philip Clayton, "Neuroscience, the Person and God: An Emergentist Account," *Zygon* 35/3 (September 2000): 613-52; and Nancy R. Howell, "Ecofeminism: What One Needs to Know," *Zygon* 32/2 (June 1997): 231-41.

80. Brian Green, *The Elegant Universe* (New York, Norton, 1999).

81. Steven L. Peck, "Randomness, Contingency, and Faith: Is There a Science of Subjectivity?," *Zygon: Journal of Religion and Science* 38 (March 2003): 5-24.

82. See chapter 10, "My Madness," where I relate a personal experience that made consciousness an even greater puzzle to me.

5

Life as Emergent Agential Systems: Tendencies without Teleology in an Open Universe

Biology has something relevant to say to theology and vice versa,[1] and as a biologist I would like to hone in on some aspects of life that may gesture to perspectives that cross disciplinary lines. In particular, I would like to draw on the work of Henri Bergson, long ignored in biology. However, he is growing in relevance as problems in understanding what life is and how it enfolds in an emergent universe become more pressing and perplexing.

Life is a relationship among various kinds of agents interacting at different scales in ways that are multifarious, complex, and emergent. Life is always part of an ecological embedding in communities of interaction, which in turn structure and influence how life evolves. Evolution is essential for understanding life and biodiversity.

Evolution is underwritten by random genetic mutations and other sources of variance that arise in the chemically based genetic structures that underpin life on Earth. Natural selection sifts through mutations, which occur at random and without regard to the environment in which they arise, and finds those organisms better suited to the local environment in which those particular life forms find themselves. In addition, the stochastic nature of survival, the accidents and contingency of living in a dangerous world, ensures that genetic drift will also play an important role. These two processes structure the kinds of organisms that inhabit our planet by forging them in ways that are conditioned on the randomness and contingency of local environments. The history of evolution is one of false starts, dead ends, accidents, and mistakes. This, as seen through the lens of science, suggests a lack of teleological aim for the forms of life on this planet. Does this imply that the universe is therefore without certain tendencies? I would like to explore this question in detail by first looking at aspects of biology that appear over and over again in the history of life on Earth as broadscale patterns and regularities. Second, I would like to examine what is known about the "arrow of complexity," the tendency of life to increase in complexity over time and how this creates opportunities for emergence and creativity to arise. Finally, I would like to explore these repeated aspects in light of the work of Henri Bergson, particularly that found in his *Creative Evolution*.[2] This may point to certain kinds of teleology that might be permissible from an evolutionary perspective. Teleology of a certain kind is being rethought in biology[3] and may be explored profitably in religion vis-à-vis biology.[4] I will focus here, however, on tendencies, as a new way to view the kind of teleology that seems to play a role in theological constructions that imbue the universe with certain ends.

Life on Earth as Structured by Evolution

Evolution by natural selection is an a priori principle according to Christian Illies.[5] As given, it requires no empirical content to frame, nor is it a particular law in a given universe. Philosopher Daniel Dennett calls it a sorting algorithm,[6] but it always holds under the following conditions:[7]

    a. Variation in traits.
    b. Selection on trait differences (different variants leave different numbers of offspring).
    c. Trait attributes are to some extent inherited by "offspring" from "parents."

These things are sufficient for evolution to occur. This process works whether the subjects are chemicals, digital computer programs, or beans in a jar—anything. This description of evolution by natural selection is not really in dispute. It is obviously just a procedure, in a functional sense, that sorts things based on some selection criteria, usually determined by some environment in which the traits vary on how well they fare in that environment.

A claim of evolution by natural selection is a claim that the system you are working with is one in which these conditions hold. Life on Earth seems just the sort of thing where these conditions are met. The claim that some group is a Darwinian population is the claim that it meets these criteria. In application however, it can be complex and messy, as philosopher of biology Peter Godfrey-Smith writes in his book *Darwinian Populations*:

> Darwinian populations are collections of things that vary, reproduce at different rates, and inherit some of this variation. The basic features of these collections are startlingly routine—births, lives, and deaths, with variation and inheritance. But Darwin saw that this set-up, this arrangement of ordinary features, is an extraordinarily important element of the world. Darwin's description was empirical and concrete. The last century's work has included a series of moves towards abstraction, attempting to say what is essential about the Darwinian machine—which features are not dependent on the contingent particularities of life on Earth.[8]

Variation on Earth, the first requirement for evolution by natural selection, arises through the random process of mutations. These random mutations are expressed in a particular environment and survive differentially based on how well they do in that particular environment. So over time, at the level of local environment, there is a kind of "matching" between the environment and the organisms that inhabit it. However, it is only in that local environment that any sort of direction can be observed. In such a system there can be no goal or aim toward which evolutionary change is moving—only local adaptation given the context of mutational changes.

However, even though this process draws on the randomness inherent in the genetic structure of life, there yet appear to be tendencies, repeated patterns, regularities, and strategies in which life engages at multiple levels. This seems to belie the idea that evolution is just randomness being co-opted for local environments, because there seem to be aspects of life that bubble up over and over again, suggesting that there are things about life that appear to be tendencies of life itself, not just specific forms that reappear to solve specific engineering problems,[9] but regularities that are used by many forms of life in many ways.

To begin, some effort in dissecting what life is may be useful. Eugene Thacker carefully unpacks some of the differences between "life" as such and "life forms."[10] Starting with Aristotle, he draws a useful distinction between the two concepts. Life is more than a nominalistic category and more than a summation of the instances of life forms. Life is something with properties, the exploration of which gives us a sense of what is possible in the world of actually realized life forms. What features of life seem to be repeatedly instantiated in the instances of life on Earth? Are there tendencies to which life seems drawn? There have been nice explorations of this from the theological side. John Milbank in particular pays attention to the distinction between the instances of life and what constitutes and frames it,[11] but here I want to draw on distinctions from the biological sciences and tease out how these might be relevant to more philosophical and theological considerations, especially as informed by Bergson's thought. First, let us examine a few of these tendencies as seen in empirical studies of the biological sciences.

Examples of Tendencies Seen Repeatedly in Life

It is useful to consider the history of life on Earth and point out key aspects of its evolution that highlight features that argue against disenchanted reductive views of nature, and perhaps even suggest a very Bergsonian view of the creative nature of evolution. I suggest that an ecological emergent view helps us see life as a nonessentialist unfolding that is established by dynamic networks of cooperating entities, which in turn allow for further creativity, innovation, and freedom in the universe.

Let me be clear how I am using *creativity* here. It is clear that life on our planet has responded to unique environments through evolutionary-innovated solutions to the challenges it faces through the three processes described above. These are creative in that they did not exist before their appearance in life forms. They are novel (granting that they might have appeared "new"' in several independent events) and creative in just this sense.

The universe is structured, as Latour suggests, such that "entities (as broadly construed) have struck a hard bargain with reality to allow stable configurations of chemicals that allow life to get started."[12] How life got started on Earth from its chemical precursors remains an open scientific question, upon which progress is being made. As we learn more about early planetary environments, and as we discover how frequent life is in the universe through surveys of distant solar systems, the question of how life begins will likely become clearer. Once life is off the ground, there seem to be repeated patterns. While there is nothing specifically teleological about life on Earth in the sense that there are specific Platonic-like forms to which life is heading, there are repeated strategies that evolve independently, that seem constitutive of how life proceeds biologically on Earth.

1. Life solves engineering problems

The first tendency I want to examine is that evolution solves engineering problems. While organisms on Earth have evolved in a number of distinct directions, life forms in similar circumstances have sometimes arrived at similar solutions for surviving well. For example, life on Earth has had multiple species evolve to solve the problem of swimming in the sea. Fish from chordate ancestors evolved into something with a torpedo shape, terminal tail movements to produce forward thrust, and fins to stabilize their motion. In addition to the initial evolutionary radiation of the fishes, this strategy for living in water has also evolved at least twice from vertebrate terrestrial organisms. In looking at the body "designs" of dolphins and ichthyosaurs, their similarity to fish and to each other is immediately apparent. Thus, solving engineering problems can create some startlingly specific designs.

Another example is found in sabertooth cats that evolved independently from separate rat-like precursors in both marsupial and placental mammalian lines.[13] Biologist Simon Conway Morris speculates that given this propensity, it may mean that the human shape and form may be inevitable in the universe on similarly constituted planets with similar ecological underpinnings.[14]

This allows us to ask how the evolutionary trajectories of specific life forms have evolved. Moreover, there are more general tendencies that seem to be repeatedly repeated in vastly different organisms and seem to underpin what makes life a successful enterprise in increasing complexity and innovation in the universe. And while specifics are non-essentialist and lack formal (in the Platonic sense) underpinnings, there are repeated patterns that allow for increased complexity. These other tendencies are usefully examined by looking at attributes of organisms closer to the chemical basis of lifelike bacteria. (There would have been a temptation in previous eras, when a Great Chain of Being was seen to structure life, to call these simpler, or more recently "less evolved," but given the complexity we are discovering in the microbial world, abandoning such notions seems important.) These are representatives of an early instance of cellular life, and these organisms have continued to evolve since their emergence on Earth to be successful contenders in the struggle for existence on this planet.

2. A trend toward individuality, then to societies of individuals

There is a trend toward individuality. Let me be specific about what I mean by that. Individuals are always collections of other individuals. In this I follow the work of Thomas Pradeu and Leo Buss, who have rigorously explored how societies of entities form from individuals to individuals.[15] So while humans might be rightly called an ecology—for example, we are a conglomerate network of ancient bacteria (mitochondria), cells, and commensal species of bacteria and fungi, all necessary for our survival—we are tightly bound as an entity and functionally interact and survive as individuals. This appearance of such tightly bound "systems" allows individuals to be identified and delineated in ways that go beyond a nominal approach. For example, Pradeu uses the immune system's host recognition system to delimit what belongs to the individual and what does not.[16]

The first instances of life were likely the simple packaging of chemical systems creating an inside and an outside—to put it crudely, a "me" and a "not me." If we look at a prokaryotic cell, we see definitive structures that carve it from the common chemical milieu.

This move to individuality occurs at multiple scales in a back-and-forth movement between societies of individuals framing the creation of new kinds of individuals that have as their makeup other individuals. This means that while individual objects are the foundation of life, these individuals can be composed of other confederations of objects and individuals. Life seems to move from individuals to an ecology and society of individuals that create new individuals, which in turn frame new ecological and societal relationships. This is one of life's strongest tendencies. An example may be helpful here.

Bacteria are an especially good example of this in light of their supposed simplicity. The societal and ecological relationships of bacteria constitute an area of growing interest, in part because of the surprises they hold.

For example, bacteria have social-communicative networks that enhance their ability to survive. Quorum sensing—the ability of a bacterial population to communicate with other conspecifics to perform coordinated activities like the building of a protective film that offers them protection, allows the use of shared resources, and provides opportunities for greater dispersal—has been seen as one of the more important discoveries of microbiology in recent years.[17] Communication through detecting and sending chemical signals allows others within the film to assess the condition and structure of the population. In addition, through quorum sensing, biofilms can provide a shared resource to other species. For example, oxygen-using bacteria can use the boundaries of the film where the gas is more abundant, while abiotic species, which thrive in the absence of oxygen, can exploit more anterior positions, providing food and chemical resources that are beneficial to the bacteria on the edges secreting the biofilm, thus supporting commensal relationships among differing species. These cooperative relationships establish ecological networks that take place on multiple scales and among very different species.

A spectacular example comes from the relationship between the bioluminescent bacteria *Vibrio fischeri* and the squid *Euprymna scolopes*.[18] The squid contains a light organ that allows the colonization of the bacteria. The organ provides specific nutrients to the bacteria that allow for its own thriving. The bacteria can live individually among the oceanic plankton. However, using quorum sensing, when the population reaches a certain size, the bacteria turn on genes that produce the bioluminescence. This is a benefit to the squid because by glowing it reduces its shadow as seen by predators looking toward the surface lit by a bright moon. So both species benefit. It is a complex dance between two different species, on vastly different size scales, which have to coordinate their behavior with other members of the population. This attribute of life to move to social cooperation to solve complex problems is ubiquitous in Earth's biota.

Another move made by life along this continuum of individuality and societal relationships is the differentiation and specialization of individual function for the benefit of the whole. The most extreme example of this is where individuals give up their potential for reproduction. But differentiation of individual roles is quite common in the microbial world and includes things like domicile creation, cooperative hunting, specialized food provisioning, specialized defenders, specialized dispersal forms, altruistic suicide, and communication.[19]

Two examples can be mentioned. The first is the jellyfish-like Portuguese man-o'-war (*Physalia physalis*), which is not a single organism but rather a colony of individuals.[20] Although each individual has taken on a different role—for example, some are stinging cells, while some are part of the air bladder—the "organism" itself is a colony. Only the individuals that have differentiated into gametophores reproduce, so, much like a beehive, only a few of the individuals retain the ability to reproduce. Another example is the slime mold, which similarly creates fruiting bodies and other types of cells, which will reproduce.[21] Some form a stalk to facilitate dispersal.

So we see that within life the repeated strategy of cooperation, differentiation, and individuation is ubiquitous from the smallest to the highest scales. Also important to explaining life on Earth is understanding its vast, growing complexity since its inception 3.5 billion years ago, when abiogenesis got off the ground. What allows this clear increase in complexity? In part it seems to be the bootstrapping that occurs as complexity generates more complexity.

It is in such social communities that we first find individuals leaping forward in creative networks that allow for greater complexity and creativity in the life forms that structure life on Earth. In so doing, they exemplify the three separate but entangled trends that allow novelty in life on Earth to emerge: complexity, cooperation, and sociality.

3. Niche construction

Another tendency of life can be illuminated in the creative power described by niche construction theory. Niche construction theory was developed in the early 1980s and, while growing in influence, is still a nascent field.[22] While a complete accounting of the main features of this theory is beyond the scope of this paper, the basic idea is easy to grasp. Life evolves in contexts; that is, the struggle for life is always embedded in an environment. It is clear that this environment is not static and is in constant flux, but while we often take note of that, we fail to acknowledge that what is causing and substantiating that flux is life itself, creating a constant back-and-forth between organisms and the environment they inhabit. This not only changes the habitat for the biotic creatures that initially found themselves in the environment in question, but creates new opportunities for survival and evolutionary change among all the organisms living within that context.

The American beaver is an oft-cited example of niche construction. These North American animals build large dams that block streams and change the environment significantly. They cut down and move trees to make their dams and lodges, creating ponds, which can in turn create wetlands, provide habitat for fish and birds, and restructure completely the ecological community. Their presence provides new energy flows that can allow new levels of complexity and opportunities for evolutionary directions to expand. Dawkins uses the beaver as an example of the extended phenotype for his gene-centered view of evolutionary change.[23] However, he misses the changes that feed back and forth between the beaver and its environment. Dawkins assumes a static landscape that misses much of how life structures and restructures itself. Niche construction theory suggests that the landscape is in constant flux and that life unfolds generously, from more to more. In the evolution of ecology it can be truly said, "For to every one who has, will more be given, and he will have abundance; but from him who has not, even what he has will be taken away" (Matthew 25:29 RSV).

Niche construction is key in understanding how life unfolds. That it is missing in current reductive thought becomes very apparent in the models that are used to construct evolutionary explanations and predictions. A good example is the failure of the "climbing Mount Improbable" models that have been used to explain evolutionary change.[24] As philosophers of science have noted, all such models have in some sense failed to capture the fact that life forms have increased in complexity as life progressed over evolutionary time scales.[25] (Stephen Gould is an exception, strangely arguing that complexity has not increased.)[26] Kevin Korb and Alan Dorin argue that models have failed to reproduce the increase in complexity that is obvious in the directional arrow of complexity—things move from lesser to greater complexity.[27] Most models of evolutionary processes have missed the obvious trend of increasing complexity that is apparent in the fossil record. Korb and Dorin argue further that this is because niche construction theory has been ignored and that using static landscape models misses this feature of nature. They argue that to capture this feature, only simulation models are adequate for the task because they are able to target what life actually does—change the selective landscape in which it evolves, thus providing increases in complexity. The metaphor that Dawkins uses of climbing Mount Improbable fails because the complexity of life is a moving target. Life changes the nature of the landscape. I will come back to this momentarily.

This suggests that life is constantly reinventing itself, changing, be-coming more than it was, unfolding in new and creative directions. In short, life on Earth is emergent. This is clear from the empirical evidence we have about the way life has unfolded on this planet; moreover, this may be a distinguishing feature of life itself, as it is hard to imagine a kind of life that could evolve without this kind of creative necessity that allows it to adapt to the new circumstances it must confront.[28]

Life created an oxygen atmosphere, which allowed for more complex autotroph-like fungi and plants to create more niches. Following this, motile animals evolved, more niches opened, and plants invaded bare and lifeless landmasses, which in turn provided more niches. The transformation of life on Earth has been the story of increasing complexity, opening and creating new niches, and advances in sociality, cooperation, and coevo-lution. A wildly emergent world full of genuine surprises has been the result. It seems possible that this is a general feature of life in the universe.

4. Emergence and complexity

Niche theory introduces the possibility of emergence. Let me be careful with that word because it has come to mean many things to many people and tends to be a fraught concept. I am defining it in the sense of Mark Bedau, who argues for three types of emergence.[29] In all three types, the foundational concept is the idea that a property is emergent if it is a prop-erty that can be possessed by the macro scale but cannot be possessed by the micro scale. The classic example of this is an avalanche comprised of overloaded snowbanks. An accumulation of snowflakes composes an avalanche, but individual snowflakes possess no property of avalanches.

As noted above, Bedau divides emergence into three kinds: nominal, weak, and strong. The first, nominal emergence, is emergent in the sense that wholes are dependent on their parts and are autonomous in the sense that parts do not have the properties of the whole. For example, a herd of zebras is a herd just as a result of individual zebras aggregating in a certain way. The herd emerges because of individual behavior.

At the other end of the spectrum of emergence, strong emergent properties are characterized by supervenient powers that create irre-ducible causal influences. In this sense, emergent properties, although dependent on microlevel properties, create causal powers that cannot be reduced. These are thought to be extrascientific in that they can-not in principle be explored through reductive methods. The subjective experience of the mind is the only example that is usually given, and there is skepticism that strong emergence is a coherent concept.

Falling between these kinds of emergence, weak emergence is defined in this way: the system's global behavior derives just from the operation of microlevel processes, but the micro-level interactions are interwoven in such a complicated network that the global behavior has no simple explanation. Getting more specific, Bedau argues that weak emergence is underivable except through simulation, and he suggests that microlevel changes are dependent on the situation in which they find themselves and which allows for the updating of their reaction. A clear example of weak emergence would be a beehive, in which individual bees are making "decisions" based on the needs of the hive and its situation within the hive. A bee can assess the conditions and needs of its hive and change its behavior accordingly. Within a beehive, individual bees are not only making decisions but also exchanging information with each other and assessing the situation within the hive and with the outside world in complex ways that make the hive much more than an aggregate of bees, in the sense that a herd of wildebeest is just an aggregate. Although one can see that a herd is a continuum and there is some assessment going on within it (e.g., what is my neighbor looking at, and why is it so nervous?), it is not as complex as the hive, nor is its behavior as complex. The information exchange used to create such a complex network as a hive is also more abundant.

The beehive is especially intriguing because the colony that emerges appears to be a new kind of individual, one where the entire hive becomes the unit of selection. Some individuals have given up their reproductive capability to allow for something new.

This outline has given a sense of the main themes of life: individuation, sociality among individuals, ecological relationships among the biotic and abiotic worlds, niche construction, and emergent complexity. It is difficult to assess whether these are necessary features of life in our universe, as we have access to only one actual instantiation of life, this Earth. However, we have hints from studies of artificial digital life that these may be necessary, as simulations have seemed to have had limited success in replicating aspects of life's complexity without them.[10]

Life, then, may be a combination of contingency in that specific forms that emerge are novel (given resemblances created by solving certain engineering problems as noted) but conditioned on the three themes discussed above.

Henri Bergson: Life as Tendency

From the above it is clear that there are tendencies in the way that life has evolved on Earth: individuality, societies of interacting individuals, creation of habitat through niche construction, increasing complexity, and the emergence of novelty.

These tendencies suggest possible universal aspects of the deep structure of the universe. Note that this hunch is not mysterious, nor does it argue for some sort of intelligent design to force these tendencies into existence. However, these aspects do seem to appear over and over in the life histories of Earth's organisms, as well as in simulations of artificial life, making it a wager worth considering.

Henri Bergson, in his book *Creative Evolution*, argued that for life to evolve creatively there must be an initial push, a striving that allowed for life to press forward into new creative ventures. This élan vital was structured into the beginning of life's forward motion and continues from duration to duration. In the gap between these durations, Bergson poses the existence of opportunities for creativity to blossom and provide fodder for adaptive evolutionary processes. His creative evolution is not merely evolution in a Darwinian sense, as life is seen as endowed with certain tendencies. Paul-Antoine Miquel makes this explicit in his study of Bergson:

> What is life, according to Bergson, then? First of all, life is not adaptation by divergence of characters. This is the difference with Darwin: there is for Bergson an internal impetus, which can be described by neither the principle of divergence, nor the law of natural selection. *It is a tendency acting through its counter tendency.*[31]

Paula Marrati points out that for Bergson life has an essence and that essence of life is a tendency to a "motion" that creates divergence.[32] This is the élan vital in which life finds its creativity and complexity.

There is a temptation in biology to dismiss Bergson's idea of a first impulse as a kind of vitalism, in which the élan vital functions as an influencing force that moves life in certain directions or provides the necessary spark that animates life and in some sense defines what it means to be alive. However, this reading is not quite correct, as life for Bergson is the movement or tendency to push through negative influences by dividing itself in new, creative, and emergent ways.[33] This is largely congruent with the findings of biology. Since the modern synthesis of Darwinian biology and genetics, the idea of a first impulse can be translated into our current conceptions of evolutionary change in ways that accord with how they currently stand. Bergson's view of life is borne out by our current understanding of evolutionary biology.

In *Creative Evolution*, Bergson argues that this forward impetus is structured by "durations" that specifically provide a temporal "place" in which creativity could arise. However, there may be other, differently structured "places" that provide this kind of creativity in the moments between durations. Let me unpack this.

For example, randomness itself can be viewed analogously with Bergson's élan vital, with random mutation marking the end of a duration and the mutation becoming the source of creativity, like Bergson's initial push. This is much more complex than I can describe in this article, but in broad brush it is possible to see how randomness plays out in life on Earth. Empirical observations of randomness seem to capture everything that Bergson required for this initial impulse. Embedded in the structure of the universe is a push forward from the constant stream of randomness that unfolds and the sorting of the randomness according to local environmental conditions.

Life's processes are often mischaracterized as a simple reductive scheme, but that misses some of life's most astonishing features. Bergson criticized this as *finalism*, in which the whole history of space-time was given in its totality—as a god outside of time might view it, in which everything is determined and fixed from the moment of creation. This "whole" can be seen in philosopher Daniel Dennett's idea of a design space, which he uses to argue for a deterministic universe, because there are only so many possible combinations of DNA that produce viable "creatures." From a given starting point, the unfolding of different life forms must wander around in this design space, driven by local selection regimes, but the set is finite, and the steps must be small ones. Richard Dawkins uses the same notion in his view of "climbing Mount Improbable," in which he demonstrates how evolution can entirely explain the designed complexity of life on Earth. Dennett and Dawkins are right that evolution completely explains complexity, but the question that deserves some consideration is, where does the design space itself come from? Of course, that question is in principle unanswerable from a scientific perspective.

One of the interesting things about the flat naturalism that is rarely commented on is the "given all at once" (as Bergson called it) nature of the static landscape. In a deterministic universe with all the possibilities being fixed from a God's-eye perspective, the entire landscape of physical reality is fully given: from the perspective of space-time, the entire complex structure of the universe is just a static "now" and is fully present. The question of the source of the landscape seems especially odd from the point of view of a strict deterministic naturalism. Such a point of view assumes, and it seems to me it must assume, a metaphysics in which the marvelous landscape of bacteria, beavers, eyeballs, and ecological niches is given completely from the initial starting event (such as the Big Bang) because the unfolding of the universe, in this view, is entirely deterministic and noncreative. The entire extant landscape must be all there from the first moment. What unfolds must be necessary and conditioned on this given landscape and must be given a priori to the universe's unfolding. Strict flat deterministic naturalism, then, shares a stance with naive creationist views that assume that the entire landscape is present in its entirety. If it is determined, it must be "all there" or "given," as Bergson suggests. In this sense ontological materialism actually embeds an easy creationism.

This idea of an ontological design-space approach also misses the precise point that Bergson made: where do the creativity and complexity come from in the design spaces conjured to explain the evolution of life? This brings up a related question—what aspects of life (as opposed to life forms) seem to be those that give us broadscale principles of what life is?

The richness of the universe appears to argue for even higher levels of creativity, opportunity, and grace (where *grace* is defined as what is given at a given time).[34] Unlike the apprehension of biological reality described earlier in this chapter, the flat landscape seems to be missing something essential, namely, the creative nature that seems inherent in evolutionary processes, which create new landscapes on which to work using the tendencies inherent in life itself.

Bergson saw this as a key aspect of what we mean by "life," as Keith Ansell-Pearson explains:

> Bergson then turns his attention to life. It is necessary, he argues, to deal with tendencies that are to be explained by the necessity of living. By "living" Bergson means the formation of distinct material zones, in short, bodies. It is my own body

and that of others that I have the most right to distinguish in the continuity of the universe. A body is led by its various needs—the need for food, or the need for self-preservation, for example—to distinguish and constitute other bodies. It is the life of living bodies, therefore, that establishes a primary discontinuity within matter: "To establish these special relations among portions thus carved out from sensible reality is just what we call living."[35]

This seems to coincide nicely with the habit of life to seek individuality, but does so not by positing a fixed design space like Dennett's, but through the tendency of life to create now openings for life through processes like niche creation.

Bergson's view captures aspects of life that the kind of landscape Dennett posits misses in its static givenness; it is ironic that Bergson is principally remembered, at least in biology, for the élan vital, when in fact he wrote extensively against teleology (or "finalism," as he called it). It seems to me that this flat naturalism is an insidious teleology in which the entire landscape is given and organisms move through it with the only possibilities being those that appear in this static landscape. Bergson notes:

> To speak of an end is to think of a pre-existing model which has only to be realized. It is to suppose, therefore, that all is given, and that the future can be read in the present. It is to believe that life, in its movement and in its entirety, goes to work like our intellect, which is only a motionless and fragmentary view of life, and which naturally takes its stand outside of time. Life on the contrary progresses and endures in time.[36]

He notes that life is what we now might call emergent and contextualized only on what has gone before, but not as if following a landscape. He continues:

> But, in the adaptation of an organism to the circumstance it has to live in, where is the pre-existing form awaiting the matter? The circumstances are not a model into which life is inserted and whose form life adopts [think of Dennett's

design space here]. This is indeed to be fooled by a metaphor. There is no form yet, and the life must create a form for itself, suited to the circumstances that are made for it. It will have to make the best of these circumstances, neutralize their inconveniences and utilize their advantages—in short, respond to our actions by building up a machine which has no resemblance to them. Such adapting is not repeating, but replying—an entirely different thing.[37]

He is not imagining life here as an intelligent agent, and he fully supports the idea that evolution is what does the replying, but he suggests that life is creative in just the sense that there are novel responses and opportunities embedded within the evolutionary process, just as niche theory would imply.

This suggests that there may be the possibility of a new Bergsonianism that recognizes that his views are compatible with our current understanding of biology. It appears that creative evolution has relevance today as we look at life as having just the kind of tendencies that Bergson described in his important work.

Theological Implications of the New Bergsonianism

Are there theological implications in Bergson's creative evolution? I would like to focus on some aspects of his theory that might be of value in interpreting theologies of creation. First, what we see unfolding in life on Earth seems to imply the nonclosed nature of the cosmos—that life is ongoing, creative, and emergent. The flat naturalism that posits an intact design space would imply that there is some sort of creation more like that of the intelligent designer of creationism in which God's role is to nudge things along that would otherwise be improbable, but the flat landscape is still given up front. However, an open universe in which niches create new opportunity and infinite possibilities suggests, as John Haught terms it, endless promise.[38] This does not forestall certain ends; as I've shown above in certain kinds of universes, certain engineering problems seem to recommend certain ends. This kind of openness does not limit theologies of divine purpose, but it does necessarily do away with teleological specifics that creation is less than a continuing process.

Again, turning to Bergson:

The truth is that adaptation explains the sinuosities of the movement of evolution, but not its general directions, still less the movement itself. The road that leads to the town is obliged to follow the ups and downs of the hills; it adapts itself to the accidents of the ground; but the accidents of the ground are not the cause of the road, nor have they given it its direction. At every moment they furnish it with what is indispensable, namely, the soil on which it lies; but if we consider the whole of the road, instead of each of its parts, the accidents of the ground appear only as impediments or causes of delay, for the road aims simply at the town and would fain be a straight line. Just so as regards the evolution of life and the circumstances through which it passes—with this difference, that evolution does not mark out a solitary route, that it takes directions without aiming at ends, and that it remains inventive even in its adaptations.

But, if the evolution of life is something other than a series of adaptations to accidental circumstances, so also it is not the realization of a plan. A plan is given in advance. It is represented, or at least representable, before its realization. The complete execution of it may be put off to a distant future, or even indefinitely; but the idea is nonetheless formidable at the present time, in terms actually given. If, on the contrary, evolution is a creation unceasingly renewed, it creates, as it goes on, not only the forms of life, but also the ideas that will enable the intellect to understand it, the terms which will serve to express it. That is to say that its future overflows its present, and cannot be sketched out therein in an idea. There is the first error of finalism.[39]

This opens the possibility of tendencies without teleology, in which the universe really does bring out certain features. These appear again and again. Could these features allow for the consideration of a universe, unfolding into new and perhaps nonteleological ways, and speak to divine purpose—one without the need for a God to intervene in specific ways as in the flat design space and those envisioned by intelligent design and Dawkins's Mount Improbable?

It also speaks to the uniqueness of life because it is novel and open-ended and gives reasons for preserving, perhaps as a theological mandate, the treasures of this ongoing creation. It gives reasons for supposing that there is something precious and sacred about life on Earth because it has not been manufactured like a boat crafted for a purpose; rather, creation is exemplified by life itself as manifest in the history and unfolding of the universe. This kind of open, unfolding view of creation highlights the importance of ecological considerations in the world.

The word *process* is appropriate here because there seem to be affinities with this ecological view of creation and process theologies, as distinct from Paleyesque kinds of natural theology or theo-drama views of theologians like Celia Deane-Drummond.[40] However, this new Bergsonianism may point to a new kind of natural theology based not on the specifics of life forms but on general tendencies of life like sociality, individuation, complexity, and creativity.

Finally, emergence seems to imply that the universe is becoming freer and more open-ended in certain senses, and that freedom further implies that the universe itself generously creates new levels, based on features of life that seem ubiquitous and move back and forth in ways that are agential and individualized, that grow in complexity, and that emerge in beauty as a magnificent universe.

Notes

1. See Conor Cunningham, *Darwin's Pious Idea: Why the Ultra-Darwinists and Creationists Both Get It Wrong* (Grand Rapids, MI: William B. Eerdmans, 2010).

2. Henri Bergson, *Creative Evolution*, trans. Arthur Mitchell (1907; repr., New York: Barnes and Noble, 2005).

3. Daniel W. McShea, "Upper-Directed Systems: A New Approach to Teleology in Biology," *Biology and Philosophy* 27 (2012): 663–84; and Jeffrey Wattles, "Teleology Past and Present," *Zygon: Journal of Religion and Science* 41 (2006): 445–64.

4. Jeremy Sherman and Terrence W. Deacon, "Teleology for the Perplexed: How Matter Began to Matter," *Zygon: Journal of Religion and Science* 42 (2007): 873–901; and Lyman A. Page, "Teleology in Biology: Who Could Ask for Anything More?," *Zygon* 41 (2006): 427–34.

5. Christian Illies, "Darwin's a Priori Insight: The Structure and Status of the Principle of Natural Selection," in *Darwinism and Philosophy*, ed. Vittorio Hosle and Christian Illies (Notre Dame, IN: Notre Dame University Press, 2005).

6. Daniel C. Dennett, *Darwin's Dangerous Idea: Evolution and the Meanings of Life* (New York: Simon & Schuster, 1996).

7. Richard Charles Lewontin, "The Units of Selection," *Annual Review of Ecology and Systematics* 1 (1970): 1–18.

8. Peter Godfrey-Smith, *Darwinian Populations and Natural Selection* (Oxford: Oxford University Press, 2009), 107.

9. For example, those explored in Simon Conway Morris, *Life's Solution: Inevitable Humans in a Lonely Universe* (Cambridge: Cambridge University Press, 2013).

10. Eugene Thacker, *After Life* (Chicago: University of Chicago Press, 2010).

11. John Milbank, "Immanence and Life," 2001, available at http://theologyphilosophycentre.co.uk/papers/Milbank_StantonLecture2.pdf.

12. Graham Harman, *Prince of Networks: Bruno Latour and Metaphysics* (Melbourne, Australia: re.press, 2009), 23.

13. See Stephen Wroe, Michael B. Lowry, and Mauricio Anton, "How to Build a Mammalian Super-Predator," *Zoology* 111/3 (2008): 196-203.

14. Morris, *Life's Solution.*

15. Thomas Pradeu, *The Limits of the Self: Immunology and Biological Identity* (Oxford: Oxford University Press, 2012); and Leo W. Buss, *The Evolution of Individuality* (Princeton, NJ: Princeton University Press, 1987).

16. Pradeu, *Limits of the Self.*

17. Andrew B. Goryachev, "Design Principles of the Bacterial Quorum Sensing Gene Networks," *Wiley Interdisciplinary Reviews: Systems Biology and Medicine* 1/1 (2009): 45-60.

18. Spencer V. Nyholm et al., "Recognition between Symbiotic Vibrio Fischeri and the Haemocytes of Euprymna Scolopes," *Environmental Microbiology* 11 (2009): 483-93.

19. Bernard J. Crespi, "The Evolution of Social Behavior in Microorganisms," *Trends in Ecology and Evolution* 16/4 (2001): 178-83.

20. Ellen Clarke, "The Problem of Biological Individuality," *Biological Theory* 5 (2010): 312-25.

21. John Tyler Bonner, *The Social Amoebae: The Biology of Cellular Slime Molds* (Princeton, NJ: Princeton University Press, 2008).

22. A good overview is John Odling-Smee, Kevin N. Laland, and Marcus W. Feldman, *Niche Construction: The Neglected Process in Evolution* (Princeton, NJ: Princeton University Press, 2003).

23. Richard Dawkins, *The Extended Phenotype: The Long Reach of the Gene* (Oxford: Oxford University Press, 1982).

24. Richard Dawkins, *Climbing Mount Improbable* (New York: W. W. Norton, 1996).

25. Mark A. Bedau, "The Evolution of Complexity," in *Mapping the Future of Biology*, ed. Anouk Barberousse, Michael Morange, and Thomas Pradeu (New York: Springer, 2009), 111-30.

26. Stephen Jay Gould, *Wonderful Life: The Burgess Shale and the Nature of History* (New York: W. W. Norton, 1989).

27. Kevin B. Korb and Alan Dorin, "Evolution Unbound: Releasing the Arrow of Complexity," *Biology and Philosophy* 26 (2011): 317-38.

28. This is explored further in Stuart A. Kauffman, *Reinventing the Sacred: A New View of Science, Reason, and Religion* (New York: Basic Books, 2008).

29. Mark A. Bedau, "Downward Causation and Autonomy in Weak Emergence," in *Emergence: Contemporary Readings in Philosophy and Science*, ed. M. A. Bedau and P. Humphreys (Cambridge, MA: MIT Press, 2008).

30. See Korb and Dorin, "Releasing the Arrow of Complexity."

31. Paul-Antoine Miquel, "Bergson and Darwin: From an Immanentist to an Emergentist Approach to Evolution," *SubStance* 36/3 (2007): 42-56; emphasis in original.

32. Paula Marrati, "Time, Life, Concepts: The Newness of Bergson," *Modern Language Notes* 120 (2005): 1099-111.

33. See Hisashi Fujita and Roxanne Lapidus, "Bergson's Hand: Toward a History of (Non)-Organic Vitalism," *SubStance* 36/3 (2007): 115-30.

34. This reading of grace is put forth in Adam S. Miller, *Badiou, Marion and St Paul: Immanent Grace* (London: Continuum, 2008).

35. Keith Ansell-Pearson, "The Reality of the Virtual: Bergson and Deleuze," *Modern Language Notes* 120 (2005): 1112-27, citing Bergson, *Oeuvres* (Paris: PUF, 1959), 334; and Bergson, *Matter and Memory*, trans. Nancy M. Paul and W. Scott Palmer (New York: Zone Books, 1991), 198.

36. Bergson, *Creative Evolution*, 34.

37. Bergson, *Creative Evolution*, 39.

38. John F. Haught, *Deeper than Darwin: The Prospect for Religion in the Age of Evolution* (Boulder, CO: Westview Press, 2003).

39. Bergson, *Creative Evolution*, 68.

40. Celia Deane-Drummond, *Christ and Evolution: Wonder and Wisdom* (Minneapolis, MN: Fortress Press, 2009).

6

Death and the Ecological Crisis

AFTER TEACHING CLASS YESTERDAY, I hastily grabbed one of those over-packaged lunches so indispensable to those in a hurry to gulp down something quickly. This one was canned tuna salad and crackers. I felt guilty at the amount of unnecessary material piling up as I squirreled through the packaging to find my meal. I was taken aback and shocked at what I found myself entangled in: a plastic outer covering with cardboard back, a can holding the tuna salad and its pop-top lid, a separate wrapper for the crackers, and a little plastic spoon in yet another little plastic wrapper. I knew better than this—I am an ecologist for heaven's sake. I felt tricked and shamed, betrayed by my own hurry and hunger into buying something that produced a small heap of rubbish and clutter. I looked at the remnants of a small lunch multiplying around me and looked around guiltily, hoping none of my students walked by during this moment of indiscretion. I moved to extract the food from these layers of cardboard, plastic, and aluminum. Visions of overflowing landfills danced through my head, and feeling a sneaky avarice I loaded the salad onto the cracker and took a bite. It *was* tasty. It was quite good, but there was something hidden in that bite so disguised and camouflaged that I almost missed it. I had been focused on the failures of Western civilization in generating unprecedented waste. But I had forgotten something even more fundamental. Buried forgotten in all that packaging was a life, hidden, unattended, unacknowledged, and even unrecognizable—a being processed from all its rich biological complexity to the simple categories of taste, color, and texture. During my hurried lunch, nothing of the lived life smashed into that processed can bubbled into my consciousness;

127

nothing reminded me that an animated creature had died to make my meal. That life, a miracle that exists as far as we know only on this planet, was masked and hidden. The unlucky tuna that (who?) had once cut through the ocean as a powerful living being—a breathing, free creature, a vital agent—had ended up packaged and unrecognizable in a convenient quickie lunch product. Even the word *tuna* for me had not been associated with a life; it had become the particular flavor of a product, one among many that I might choose. The juicy mass in the can, which bore the stamp of patterns pressed from the lid, was merely a lump of whitish, firm-textured food that went well mixed with pickles and mayonnaise. Just a choice of tastes I might enjoy to ease my hunger, but the significant detail that there was a life taken to provide that meal only made it into my mind by the most unlikely of routes, and on another occasion might not have even entered into my head at all. So it is with most of us. Our food is pleasantly presented and death forgotten.

This is where I take a different turn. I might be expected at this point to construct an argument against eating meat and for the virtues of vegetarianism. But I am not going there. I am going to posit that we've forgotten the place that death plays in the cycles of the earth, that there is something missing in our culinary habits that is important to reacknowledge. As Mr. Spock reminds us in the episode "Wolf in the Fold" as the *Star Trek* adventurers contemplate an alien force that feeds on the "life force" of others: "In the strict scientific sense, Doctor, we all feed on death, even vegetarians." That vegetarians are likely to have forgotten that a death was involved in their verdure seems to stem from our mammalian prejudice that somehow plants are such an "other" form of life that that their death doesn't really count in our tally sheet of what matters. Carnivore or vegan, death is a part of every aspect of our survival, but this fact we've somehow pushed to the margins of our consciousness. This has implications.

What is our relationship with death? Our own death can hardly fail to capture our attention, as Heidegger and Freud argued and tried to push to the center of our conscious concern. Death has been part of the human horizon of awareness for a long time. We've had to kill for a long time. Observations of chimpanzees hunting and killing monkeys give us our first hint that our common ancestor knew how to take a life.

Moving forward in time, we note that the very first member of our genus *Homo* knew how to jog toward death. If you inspect the fossilized skeleton of a *Homo erectus* from the neck down, even physical anthropologists who spend their life among such bones are hard-pressed to tell it from an anatomically modern human. This striding bipedal form came into being a long time before we developed the rational soul that Aristotle so cherished with its capacity for language and formal reason. Why this physical form? To run. Our body is apparently engineered by nature to run. Dennis Bramble at the University of Utah has pointed out that we are one of the best runners in the animal kingdom.[1] Not that we are particularly speedy. Indeed, almost anything can outrun us in a sprint. (Have you ever tried to catch a chicken? I will be asking you to do so later.) But at running a goodly distance, we are champions. Only the dog and horse are even in our league. Everything about us from the way our foot and knees are constructed to the way our torso swings free from our hips and our stable, forward-staring head is designed to jog for leagues. Not walking, mind you. Running.

The story seems to be that our roots lay in scavenging and piracy. Picture a band of *H. erectus* sitting around, the low foreheads encasing a slightly smaller brain, not quite allowing speech, but enough brains in place to make the same-shaped hand axes for over a million years (these were magnificent for crushing bones). These beasts (perhaps grouped in the shade of an Acacia tree), so much like us and yet so different, are highly social—like the common ancestor that sprouted both us and the chimps. Maybe this band is grooming one another; maybe gestures are becoming more advanced, suggesting the first motion toward symbolic representation. But then suddenly, ten kilometers away, black dots appear hovering above the horizon—vultures. The reposing apes immediately leap to their feet and they run. Men, women, and children all run together toward the circling vultures (except maybe the mothers with new infants—maybe them too). There is strong selection to get there quickly. The pride of lions that made the kill will devour most of it posthaste, and what they leave will be snatched hurriedly by hyenas, jackals, and other scavengers. The band arrives at the kill and manifests the other trait that in all the animal kingdom only we and, presumably, our ancestors can do well. They pick up rocks and throw them. They have both speed and stunning accuracy at flinging rocks at their scavenger competitors and predatory providers. Although we cannot know for certain that they were as highly developed pitchers as we are (since throwing ability is a brain function and does not fossilize well), the anatomy for throwing is there, and we may see the roots of baseball in this volley of well-aimed projectiles that drive the lions from their kill. Then with their well-made stone axes they chop off their booty and sit down to a sumptuous meal. Anthropologist Richard Wrangham suggests they may have even cooked it.[2]

These, however, are likely kills without reflective awareness. Like a wolf shredding the carcass of a caribou, death is just food. However, at some point later in the evolution wandering toward humanity, we became aware of death as a possibility for our own existence—necessarily as part of a burgeoning self-awareness. The thought must have appeared for the very first time in one of our ancestors, perhaps as he or she slices open the hide of a freshly killed antelope—"Hey, this will happen to me someday!," the Paleolithic equivalent of a kind of Cartesian cogito, "Things die, ergo I will too."

As evidence of this awareness of mortality much later than *Homo erectus* in our family tree, we see that Neanderthals buried their dead with ceremony. Neanderthals did not mate with our species as evidenced by DNA analysis, but they shared a common ancestor with us about 600,000 years ago. The famous Regourdou burials show that death was something to acknowledge and mark in special ways. Here Neanderthals buried a person with ceremony: the body carefully positioned with the skull and arm bones of a bear carefully arranged in ritually symbolic ways. Of course, no one knows what these things actually meant to this species of near-human—whether they are sending their dead lavishly into the next life or honoring their memory, we cannot say. Their intentions are long gone, but we do recognize what they were doing. The hermeneutics of this other species' burial preparations brokers an easy familiarity, and the meaning of their actions seems consistent with our ways of being human today. The evidence for funeral rites in modern humans is recognized from about 28,000 years ago, when two children were buried ceremoniously at Sungir, Russia, covered carefully with red ochre. But for the origin of these rituals, we must go further back in time because they likely came from some ancestor common to both us and Neanderthals. Since DNA evidence suggests that our last common ancestor was around 600,000 years ago, death has been marked for at least that long. Interestingly, these death rituals seem part and parcel to the development of art, symbolic language, and the creative advancement of our tool culture. All these features of ritual awareness are what put the "modern" in anatomically modern humans.

This preoccupation with death seems not only focused on our own demise. Much of the art seems to be a call to participate in the death of our prey. The caves in Altamira, Spain, may be spiritual strivings to control aspects of the living world. Again, we see this recognition of death and its role in life. Our ancestors seemed highly attuned to recognizing and participating in these cycles of death and life.

Paying attention to death is something almost uniquely human. Certainly, mother apes and monkeys mourn over the loss of their offspring. Both chimpanzees and baboons will carry a dead baby around for days like a limp doll, mourning over its loss and trying to care for it as if it were alive. But neither animal pays much attention to the body of a dead compatriot. Primatologists Dorothy Cheney and Robert Seyfarth describe in their book *Baboon Metaphysics* a baboon sitting down for lunch next to a dead acquaintance whose mangled body had been stuffed into the fork of tree by a satiated leopard.[3] Most higher animals divide the world into "agent things" and "non-agent things." We do. As agent things, we expect to make choices, to act in explainable ways. In considering why the coyote moved from that place to this, we might reason that it was to find food, to look for a mate, or to find a place to sleep. All agent behavior is steeped in teleology. There is purpose to an agent's action, a kind of embedded rationality that transcends the taxonomic descent from human to slime mold. Even an amoeba is acting as an agent as it turns toward the light. So agents act with purpose. Non-agents are the things in the world that are acted upon.

But for most creatures, once something is dead, it is no longer an agent. It enters into the world of non-agency and, if not eatable, treated as an artifact of the landscape like a stone or anthill. This is true of even our nearest simian relatives. This is not true for humans, however. (Nor, oddly enough, for elephants, which upon meeting the bones of a relative or acquaintance will reverently handle the bones and pass them among the herd as if remembering the animal whose bones they were. Even more striking, the more intimate two elephants were in life, the longer one will handle and caress the bones of the other.)

This distinction in our mind between agent and non-agent is very deeply embedded in our nature. And it may be the roots of our religious propensity itself. Richard Boyd argues that when we fill the world with angels and spirits, fairies and helping ancestors, these are category mistakes. They are agent explanations for what seems teleological in nature. Why did I happen on this roebuck while hunting? There is a purpose even in that; therefore agents must be involved. Good luck and bad luck and their manipulation find their root in teleological explications that need agents, so we provide them. This distinction runs deep, and it is in the transitions from life to nonlife that we find our greatest mysteries. Our deepest magic has always been in this transition from agent to non-agent; whether in ourselves or our prey, there is mystery here worth marking, meditating on, and trying to manipulate. Birth and death—it is here that mystery begins and ends.

These mysteries may be what make us most human. Our capacity for compassion, our empathetic response, may be rooted in our recognition of our mortality and the mortality of other creatures—and the absolute dependence of our lives on theirs. We are embedded in life. Connections weave around us in the ecosystem services that provide for our maintenance and continuance. In cold scientific terms, all life is sustained through the transfer of energy, from the sun to the primary producers like plants and algae, to the secondary producers that eat the plants, on up through a food web of energy exchange, recycling through the earthy decomposers that support again the growth of plants in soils. Energy and material are exchanged, co-opted, stolen, given, and recycled. While describing it thus in modern ecological terms is accurate, these are things we recognized and celebrated very early in our human history. These cycles were recognized in rituals, noted in preparations for the hunt, and honored and maintained through spiritual practices that recognized the relationship between life and death.

But what is happening?

Death has become other and foreign. Something unpleasant, banished to the nether regions of our culture. We engage with it usually as distant tragedy as the headlines report the loss of a soldier's life, or a massacre, or another natural disaster that takes a number of lives. We are rightly horrified at such events, but we are rarely touched by them intimately. We don't see the torn bodies of our solders (and recently my government remains determined that we don't even see the caskets of our fallen heroes); we don't see the swollen corpses of tsunami victims except as passing frames in panoramic shots of devastation from which we shudder and turn away. Our funerals are quick, quiet affairs where death is dressed up in its finest suit of clothes and quickly gotten out of the way. This is not to say that death does not impact us; of course it does. But death seems to be considered among the most unnatural of occurrences for which we spend a great deal of time and energy avoiding and trying to stop. We deny death until it happens. But I don't want to focus on human death per se. While I think our lack of seeing death in the natural cycles of our life has implications for the way we handle the death of those we love, I think also there is a deep lack of understanding of the role death plays in supporting life itself. Our life.

Our disacquaintance with death has implications that I think hurt us. Some of our most horrible cruelties occur because we have distanced ourselves from one of the main ebbs and flows of life. Death is a part of life: the death of both animals and plants. Just because plants are such a foreign form of life, sometimes we devalue and excuse their death and do not recognize that life and death rely on one another.

Rituals of death may be necessary to reacquaint us with the fact that life feeds on life. It may be that the rituals of our ancestors kept the relationship between life and death present so that taking a life never became mundane or taken for granted such that they became desensitized to their connectedness with these processes. Today our sanitation of and separation from death draw us way from the cycles of life. When we mask death's meaning behind sanitized packaging, we lose—we have to lose—the reverence and fragility bound up in knowing that our lives depend on the lives of other living things. Is it any wonder that we are in the midst of a worldwide ecological crisis when we have no awareness that our lives rely on ecosystem services? How can we value life when we don't understand the role that life itself plays in our continuance? Death and life are inexorably intertwined. We feed upon the life of others. We have to. We have no direct accesses to the sun's energy itself, so we must take it from those who do. But in masking these cycles and necessities, we are losing this reverence that we see going back to the very first creatures that we identify as human. It is in that reverence that we will find the attitudes and perspectives that will make taking care of our planet something of ultimate concern. When we understand that life takes life, we then can put ourselves in a context of meaning. We can develop a sense of gratitude to those of both vegetable and animal origin that contribute to our place in these cycles. Many of my friends in the environmental movement see vegetarianism as a higher form of environmental awareness, and I agree there are good reasons for eating lower on the food chain. But to me this often becomes a blatant form of anthropocentrism. It devalues our history as scavengers and hunters and pretends we've outgrown our roots. It can become a form of elitism and arrogance that purports to put us on some sort of higher plane than the predators of the earth. We pretend we have reached a higher level of enlightened thinking. It buys into the conception that predation is bad and that we are above that sort of thing. It separates us from the very cycles I'm describing. I rarely meet vegetarians who are any more aware that a life has gone into their falafel than their neighbors are aware that a life has gone into their hamburger. Both groups have had their participation in life's cycles masked and attenuated. Both have forgotten our connection to the ecological cycles that gift and sustain life.

Many of the abuses that we see in our food production (which have not changed much since Sinclair's *The Jungle* and which provide one of the good reasons for being a vegetarian) could be cured if we developed a deeper reverence for life and a more profound recognition of life's processes. Let's try a little experiment. I want you to go and get a live chicken. Kill it yourself. Put its head on a chopping block and remove it in a violent downward swing of an ax. You may have to borrow someone's place in the country. If you do it in the mall parking lot, you will likely be arrested. Watch the blood stream from the still-beating heart. You will get some blood on you quite likely. You'll see it transition from a living agent, which a few minutes ago was blinking and tilting its head trying to get a better look at you, to something motionless and still (well, after a few minutes it will be still). Now pluck its feathers, pull its viscera from its abdominal cavity, and cut its parts into its familiar useable pieces: drumstick, breast, thigh, and so forth. Cook as desired. Finish this essay when you're done eating.

Of course, you didn't do it. Some of you were horrified at the suggestion. Can it be that this horror may be the root of our ecological crisis? Let me unpack this a little. Some of you were horrified because of the violence of this act. It is an unpleasant and nasty business. Yet you would have no problem popping into a Kentucky Fried Chicken eatery and noisily eating the finger-licking-good pieces snuggled cozily in the greasy bucket—not realizing that someone, somewhere had to do that very thing—perhaps in an even more violent and cruel way, necessitated by the millions of chickens that must be so processed.

Others of you were horrified at death itself. Killing another being is something untoward, unethical, and unwarranted—a gaggle of *un*'s that humans should move beyond in our enlightened status at the pinnacle of evolution. We have ethical responsibilities because we have moved beyond the limits of other, nonconscious animals. Rationality has brought us responsibility that necessitates our moving beyond what our primitive cousins the wolf, the bear, and the lion must still engage. We are not like them, even though we understand that they are just animals and playing the role that nature demands of them. We are something better and other. Thoreau says it in *Walden*:

> Is it not a reproach that man is a carnivorous animal? True, he can and does live, in a great measure, by preying on other animals; but this is a miserable way,—as any one who will go to snaring rabbits, or slaughtering lambs, may learn,—and he will be regarded as a benefactor of his race who shall teach man to confine himself to a more innocent and wholesome diet. Whatever my own practice may be, I have no doubt that it is a part of the destiny of the human race, in its gradual improvement, to leave off eating animals, as surely as the savage tribes have left off eating each other when they came in contact with the more civilized.[4]

Predators. We are not like them. We are better. We stand above Nature—not in relationship among its entities and processes.

The first horror of killing is based in the unpleasantness of causing death, and it is unpleasant; the second, in a kind of arrogance, twin vices that separate us from nature and root our current culture in an active separation of what it means to be a human living nestled in connections and complexities that are necessary for life itself in all its diversity. By recognizing death's role in life, we gain a reverence for life that is deeply embedded in our real nature as one of Earth's creatures. Our responsibility derives not from just our rationality, which allows us to act on our impulses, but from our power to do harm. And that harm is exponentially enhanced when we are disconnected from, and other than, Nature. Our care for this world ultimately must come from a connection with Nature, including a connection with death. This connection engenders reverence. When the death behind our food is masked in packaging that hides the life behind that food, our connection to and reverence for life are damaged. The abuses of the modern slaughterhouse can be countenanced only by separating us from the lives of the creatures processed there (even the word *processed* seems to remove us from the fact that we are killing). Were we to wield the knife, or even watch the knife wielded, our use of animal flesh would be as reverenced as the gift it is.

So am I proposing we go back to slaying our own food so that we can maintain the connection between life and death? Perhaps. But actually, my proposal is much more modest. Next time you open a can of tuna, eat a piece of chicken, or put a fork into a salad, pause a moment and remember the life given for this meal. Reverence that life and for just a moment situate yourself deeply within the cycle of life and death. Life matters. Death matters. Both rely on each other.

Notes

1. Dennis M. Bramble and Daniel E. Lieberman, "Endurance Running and the Evolution of *Homo*," *Nature* 432 (2004): 345-52.

2. Richard Wrangham, Edge: World Question Center, 2008, http://www.edge.org/q2008/q08_9.html#wrangham.

3. Dorothy L. Cheney and Robert M. Seyfarth, *Baboon Metaphysics: The Evolution of a Social Mind* (Chicago: University of Chicago Press, 2007).

4. Henry D. Thoreau, *Walden: A Fully Annotated Edition* (New Haven, CT: Yale University Press, 2004), 207-8.

PART
TWO

7

An Ecologist's View of Latter-day Saint Culture and the Environment

DEAD HORSE CAMP WAS HIDDEN DEEP in the southern Wyoming Rockies. Owned by the Wyoming State Mental Hospital, it was a retreat for those suffering the wounds of mental illness. Each year my father, a social worker, would take our family there for a few weeks while he assisted the staff with patients who were spending the summer in the Rockies. For some this was a place of healing. For me it was a magical time. Next to the camp was a large beaver pond over which we would pole an old wooden raft. As we floated over the calm surface, we could see through the clear water a buildup of matted vegetation. If I looked over the edge of the raft, I could see the denizens of another world. Over the top of the vegetation glided an amazing assortment of strange and bizarre creatures. Dragon-like insect larvae (although I did not know what they were then) walked slowly over the vegetation. I would hover over them, spying on their every movement, like Homer's god spying on the Athenians. For hours my friends and I would lie with our faces over the edge of the raft, floating lazily over the pond, watching the comings and goings of these strange creatures. I believe this is where the ecologist in me was born.

However, it was shooting the leopard frogs that now forces itself out of the depths of childhood as my most vivid memory. I had two guns up there, a pump-action BB gun and a .22 rifle. I was raised by a father who loved to hunt. From September to June we lived on game: deer, elk, moose, antelope, and rabbit. By the time we went back to beef, it seemed a wonderful treat.

Every morning that summer, my brother and another boy staying at the camp and I would walk around the pond, "plugging" frogs with our BB guns. Fanning out along the shore, we would sneak up on one, take aim, and shoot it in the back. We would pile the massacred victims in an old gallon can and take our trophies back to camp to show everyone our hunting prowess. I remember an old lady we called "The Witch," a wizened patient with yellow skin, who was horrified at what we were doing. She scolded us, wagging a bony finger, "You boys ought not to do that!" We laughed at her; they were just frogs.

I vividly remember the sequence of feelings associated with shooting the frogs. It started with the intensity and excitement of the hunt—slowly, we would make our way through the tall reeds bordering the pond. There was a sense of expectation and anticipation as we walked, guns forward, slightly hunched as we had seen John Wayne do in *The Green Berets.* We would stalk quietly, looking carefully near the water's edge for the telltale bump in the water that signaled the presence of our quarry. There was a moment of strong exhilaration bubbling up into my stomach as I quickly aimed at the frog. The puff from the air gun gave a sweet sound, and the thud of hitting the helpless beast remains clear and distinct in my mind. Right after the kill, however, there was a momentary feeling of wrongness. A heavy stillness. A feeling of sin. For a few minutes I knew I had betrayed something inside me, that it was a wrong as clear as the buzz of the flies I heard all around me. But the feeling was easily swept away. Triumph returned with the verbal applause of my hunting companions, and a sense of pleasant satisfaction quickly drove out the negative feelings as we placed our lifeless quarry into the gallon can.

But something else happened that summer for which that sense of wrongness could not be removed. I was hunting for squirrels along the edges of the camp, my .22 caliber rifle at the ready. Suddenly in front of me up popped a woodchuck. It was an enormous beast—a magnificent rodent, nearly as large as our cocker spaniel, standing upright before me. It was turned to the side, looking down the hill I had been creeping along. I slowly got to my knees and took careful aim. It was the shot of a lifetime. The bullet entered one shoulder and came out the other. The animal dropped to the ground limp and lifeless. With a whoop of joy, I ran up to it and turned it over. Along its breast ran a line of nipples, full and ripe, dripping milk. A feeling of sickness swept over me. I knew in that instant I had killed not only this woodchuck but its babies as well. I looked around for a hole, thinking maybe I could raise the babies myself, but could not find one. I went back to the body and looked at the wounds gaping from both shoulders. Its teeth were exposed—set in a deathly grimace. I don't remember what I did with it. I don't remember if I skinned it as my brother did the badger he shot. It seems like I would have, but I don't remember. My memory is vivid, however, on the rows of nipples dripping milk. That is as clear as if it had happened yesterday. Something in that killing sucked the joy of hunting out of me.

A change came in me after slaying the mother woodchuck. It occurred slowly. I would like to say that I had a sudden change that forever caused me to never take the life of an animal, but it was not that kind of change. It was slow and uneven. In the years that followed, I still hunted rabbits with my father, but I remember more often than not as I raised my gun to kill a rabbit, I would watch it in my sights for a while but then would remove my finger from the trigger and lower my gun. Sometimes I would shoot, but the excitement of the hunt was waning. In the death of that woodchuck, a new sensibility began to find its way into my life. In many ways this new awareness acted as a midwife in my birth as an ecologist. I looked at nature differently after that. Its wonders became more apparent, its beauties something to ponder more deeply. Things were not placed in the world for my unfettered use. I felt for the first time that things were not placed on the earth for my pleasure in their destruction. It strikes me as odd that my appreciation for nature came in the form of a needless death, but so it was.

In telling this story, I have never felt the need to condemn those that do hunt. I still hunt, although I try to hunt with a sense of gratitude for the life I take, and I hunt only with the intent to provide meat for my family. I also know that for many families with whom I grew up in Moab, it was a way of life; it was their connection with wild lands and places. It fed their families, and they took the provision and thanked the Lord for meat to eat. Hunting rooted them to earth—to the great chain of being.

Western Culture

This was not true of all hunters. Some had attitudes and perceptions of nature that harken back to my days of plugging frogs without thought or conscience. Such people seem twisted and strangely broken, as I was.

I was raised a member of the Church of Jesus Christ of Latter-day Saints. That didn't seem to mean anything about how we should relate to the earth. While growing up, the closest I came to understanding that there might be a relationship between our religion and nature came during conference at our stake center, listening to President Spencer W. Kimball give his address "Don't Shoot the Little Birds." But at least among those I knew in Moab, the talk did not change anyone's behavior. I remember a discussion with several men in the ward who interpreted the entire talk as simply "Eat what you kill." That aphorism alone summed up the entirety of President Kimball's message. If there was a relationship between nature, the church, or some sort of environmental ethic, it was never discussed by the members I knew, either at our church meetings or outside. In Boy Scouts we learned (and I don't think this is true anymore, as I have sensed a growing conservationist attitude within Scouting) that nature was to be tamed—bent for our enjoyment. In all my years as a youth growing up in the church, I never heard expressed the idea that nature was something that mattered for its own sake. Certainly, it was the context of many of our activities—the matrix that framed much of our lives. But its protection, its value, and its fragility were never mentioned. It was there, much as the air that we breathed, unnoticed and not reflected on, and used as needed.

Each year as Scouts we would earn money for our boating trip to Flaming Gorge by cutting down pole pines. We would go to the nearby La Sal Mountains and cut down as many as we needed (there appeared no limit to the supply) and sell them to local people who were building or repairing fences. If the word *environmentalist* was used, it was to degrade or belittle someone. "Your mother is an environmentalist" was a cutting remark that could be settled only with a fistfight. While on a recent fishing trip with some good Latter-day Saint men who otherwise would never swear, I observed that they could not say the word *environmentalist* without putting the word *damn* in front of it.

What do we make of this? Are Latter-day Saints anti-environmental, as some claim?

Sadly, my impressions of the relationship between many of those in my religion and the environment seem consistent with the way many people negatively view us. As an ecological insider, it is clear to me that most ecologists view Mormonism as an enemy of nature. They often assume that to be a Mormon ecologist is an oxymoron. Many of our recent legislators have declared open season on the environment and have the worst environmental record of any state's representatives. This is true both of Utah-specific legislation and national environmental programs.[1]

However, I strongly believe that this attitude within the church is a holdover from our western United States culture and its history of anti-government feelings and "Leave us alone!" sentiments. Because so many members of the church in Utah and its surrounding areas have been raised with these western attitudes, western culture is often conflated with church culture. What is needed is to educate the Saints in their true culture as it is found in the gospel. How can this education proceed?

From my experience with church members, I see that they have a profound love for nature. They love camping, hunting, and spending time in the wilderness. What are we to make of this dichotomy between how we are perceived and how we feel? Many of those who express outrage at the mention of environmentalism are Scouters who profess a strong conservation ethic. They have profound memories of being in wilderness areas, which they speak about with love and passion. But talk to these same people about environmental protection and they vehemently denounce it and claim such legislation is supported only by extremists and malcontents. When I suggest anything to my good Latter-day Saint family and friends about global warming, the worldwide loss of species, or the protection of our wild areas, they scoff not only at the idea that we should be concerned about these things but that there is even such a problem that needs attention. This attitude has disillusioned many of our finest Latter-day Saint environmental thinkers. It has polarized and separated people into camps that isolate us on issues that need unanimity and reconciliation if they are to be addressed. Sadly, some people who have a strong desire to protect and preserve the planet have left the church over what they perceive as anti-environmental feelings among church members. And some Latter-day Saints question whether one can be a good member of the church and still be an environmentalist. It is too often the case that those on both sides of the issue promote uninformed stereotypes that help maintain differences. These differences then become exaggerated, polarized, and entrenched.

Perceptions and Realities

To get past these differences, we need to understand the roots of current LDS attitudes and from where these perceptions arose. I would like to explore reasons why I think Latter-day Saints have been perceived as anti-environmental and whether such perceptions are justified. I will also offer suggestions on how to move beyond stereotypes and divisive line drawing and how Latter-day Saints can bring a unique perspective of caring for creation that is environmentally friendly, scientifically informed, and faith centered. These views and observations are informed by my own experiences of both growing up in Mormon culture and becoming an ecologist. These views are meant only as personal observations and are not comprehensive; they are given to open more discussion on this topic.

To do this I would like to explore these issues in the context of Don Browning's practical theological ethics. He writes from a perspective of hermeneutic realism and practical theology. "Hermeneutic realism" is the view that understanding rests in dialogue—that pure objectivity is impossible not only in ordinary discourse but in science as well. He has used this framework as a way to look at difficult ethical questions found in practical theology. He has identified five dimensions of moral thinking and practical reason:

> In a series of essays and books stretching from the early 1980s to the present, I have identified five dimensions of moral thinking or practical reason: (1) a visional level generally conveyed by narratives and metaphors about the character of the ultimate context of experience, (2) an obligational level guided by some implicit or explicit moral principle of a rather general kind, (3) assumptions about basic regularities of human tendencies and needs, (4) assumptions about pervasive social and ecological patterns that channel and constrain these tendencies and needs, and (5) a level of concrete practices and rules that are informed by all the foregoing dimensions. . . .
>
> A hermeneutically conceived practical theological ethics should proceed as a dialogue involving all five of these dimensions. According to this view, practical-theological ethics begins with a problem, crisis, or question that exposes the practical thinker's preunderstanding at each of the five levels.[2]

Using this framework, I want to explore various aspects of LDS belief or practice and the modern environmental movement. By making these dimensions explicit, I hope to open a dialogue between these currently widely separated groups. I believe it will be useful to see how these dimensions structure the context for an LDS environmental viewpoint.

I express my own observations in what follows. This is not meant to be an analysis of objectively obtained data, but if my observations are biased, it is because there are little data on LDS attitudes about the environment. My observations are based on my interactions with church members in family, church, and educational settings (I teach environmental science at Brigham Young University). These are observations about American Latter-day Saints only. I hope these thoughts may be useful both for the Saints trying to understand more about environmentalism and for environmental thinkers curious about how LDS beliefs structure attitudes about the environment. I doubt there is a consensus on anything I'm about to say, but I hope to capture broad trends that can be explored by sociologists more rigorously and that can be either confirmed or refuted.

Dimension 1: The Ultimate Context of Experience

Latter-day Saint view

Latter-day Saints view this life as a continuation of one that began in the premortal life, where people lived as literal sons and daughters of God. Earth and the known universe were created for our sake. All that exists from the level of stars to bacteria are present to propel human salvation and advancement forward toward greater knowledge and glory. In an eternal biological sense, we are of the same species as God. Latter-day Saints also believe that the earth has a fixed, finite temporal life and that at some point it will die and be recreated in a celestial state. They also believe that the most important truths are revealed to humans through prophets. Truth can be garnered through the scientific method and rational discourse, but these truths must cohere with revealed truth, which always has priority. This viewpoint structures both LDS theology and praxis. Therefore, Latter-day Saints look upon this earth life as a stepping-stone to greater things. Of ultimate concern during this earthly sojourn are those things that will be taken into the next life, such as family relationships (structured by married couples and children) and priesthood-defined power and its associated ordinances. Interestingly, LDS doctrine includes the notion that the earth has a spirit and is alive in some sense, and that it can "feel" the wickedness of the earth's inhabitants, including the degradations of sin and pollution produced by the human family (see Moses 7:48).

Modern environmental view

Conversely, most biologically based environmental ethics are based on the overwhelming physical evidence presented by geology, genetics, physiology, anatomy, and sophisticated mathematical modeling that the earth came into being 4.5 billion years ago and that life has evolved through the Darwinian process of natural selection and genetics. Humans are one of many species that have occupied the earth since life's appearance over 3.5 billion years ago. The value of life comes from the recognition that it demonstratively exists in only one place in the universe and that its rarity and diversity are unique objects that have value in and of themselves, or may be practically useful and necessary for human survival. Truth is gathered only through the scientific method and rational discourse.

Comparison

At first glance these two viewpoints might seem irreconcilable because the reason for the existence of humans moves from being central to accidental. However, LDS biologists have argued that, while not central to ultimate concerns, the mode of creation remains an open theological question and that one viewpoint does not preclude the other.[3] There is widespread belief among Latter-day Saints that these fundamental contexts *are* incompatible. The reason for this animosity is due more to historical accidents than to any revelatory instruction on the Latter-day Saint side or even a reasoned response from either side. Shortly after Darwin published the *Origin of Species*, several prominent scientists such as Huxley and Hooker used Darwin's theory to support an atheistic agenda. While some religious people immediately set about reconciling their beliefs with new scientific claims, the reaction of many in the religious community was to entrench and counterattack against Darwinism. Because these two camps became antagonistic, Darwin's theories became associated with atheism and biblical creationists became vocal opponents of the theory.[4] These entrenched attitudes and misunderstandings continue to this day despite notable attempts at reconciliation.

Unfortunately, this ideological war unnecessarily spilled over into many Latter-day Saints' viewpoints on evolution. This created an attitude of suspicion toward science in much of Mormon culture.[5] This anti-science stance is still prevalent in my conversations with members of the church throughout much of the United States, but I personally find it most prevalent in rural Utah. An anti-environmental stance may in part be explained by these feelings, as most of the evidence for environmental degradation is coming from the same scientists who promote evolution. The attitude seems to be "If scientists can be so wrong about the origin of life, can we trust them when it comes to claims of an environmental crisis?"

Dimension 2: An Obligational Level and Moral Code

Latter-day Saint view

The LDS worldview outlined briefly above has a profound effect on the way Latter-day Saints view ethical and moral responsibilities and priorities. There are several ways that this perspective can be understood. One reading is that since the earth was created for our benefit, we have unrestricted use of its resources and that in all things humans have priority over the natural world. This priority may include employment, recreation, or other needs. This rationale is largely unsupported by scripture or by prophetic discourse, yet it is widespread among members of the LDS community.

Hugh Nibley has often chided the Saints for this environmental attitude. For example, he writes: "Man's dominion is a call to service, not a license to exterminate. It is precisely because men now prey upon each other and shed the blood and waste the flesh of other creatures without need that 'the world lieth in sin' (D&C 49:19–21). Such, at least, is the teaching of the ancient Jews and of modern revelation."[6]

Another reading for a strong LDS environmental ethic is promoted by scholars such as George Handley who argue that humans, as God's children, have responsibility as stewards of earthly blessings.[7] Their thoughts have been articulated elsewhere, so I will not elaborate here except to say that this stance offers a strikingly powerful environmental ethic.[8]

Modern environmental view

The justification for mainstream environmental ethics is surprisingly weak since it is derived from a scientifically based viewpoint, which typically does not engage in moral judgments. This weakness has been acknowledged by several prominent environmental thinkers.[9] While there is no teleological reason for doing so, still it is argued from a Rawlsian sense of justice that we do not have any intrinsic superiority as a biological entity and therefore must respect the right of our fellow beings to exist.[10] It is also argued from a utilitarian perspective that nature needs protection because its processes and services are necessary to human needs and prosperity. Yet if we live in a contingent and purposeless universe, it is hard to muster reasons why we should preserve anything, for by definition everything is doomed in the end anyway. But any ethical system must be based on a sense of fairness and openness within a context that either things matter in and of themselves or they have utility for humans and therefore should be protected and preserved.

Comparison

LDS theology provides a strong environmental ethic. Reasons for caring for creation are clear and justified from scripture, prophetic utterances, and the teachings of LDS leaders and scholars. Ironically, Latter-day Saints as a people have not lived up to their highest teachings. There appears to be little awareness of these teachings among the general populace of the church, and many members in Utah seemed to have embraced a sociopolitical environmental viewpoint structured by historical antigovernment sentiments formulated in the early history of Utah.

Conversely, some of the most vocal LDS environmentalists have failed to capitalize on the environmental teachings promoted in the scriptures and in the teachings of the prophets. Instead they have faulted the church for its members' lack of attention to embracing the environmental movement's perspective of a scientifically based ethic. For example, Terry Tempest Williams, arguably Mormonism's most articulate environmental advocate, largely couches her arguments for an environmental ethic from the perspective of mainstream environmental discourse. This has had the effect of making her ineffective in communicating her valid concerns about the environment to her own people.

Dimension 3: Assumptions about Basic Regularities in Human Needs and Tendencies

Here both Latter-day Saints and mainstream environmentalists share many of the same needs. Both share a need for love, adequate housing, fresh water, healthy and readily available food, and enough income to provide the basic essentials of life. How these necessities are structured and provided, however, may differ.

Latter-day Saint view

Latter-day Saints are taught from an early age to be frugal. Church leaders have repeated that we are to "Use it up, wear it out, make it do, or do without."[11] The church has an extensive welfare system to ensure that the basic necessities of life are available to those in need.

Home storage and production are encouraged, and instruction on how to process, maintain, and keep food is conducted on a regular basis at ward and stake levels. Members have been encouraged by their prophets to keep their yards, fences, and holdings in good repair. The church sets an example of this, and the beauty and care of its temples are exemplary. People are taught to live within their means and to stay out of debt. Again, regular instruction on family finances at ward and stake levels is conducted regularly. Preparing for the future is seen as an important part of church culture. Planning for an education and fruitful employment is emphasized at every level. For example, with the Perpetual Education Fund, the church is helping third world members gain an education to improve their possibilities for future employment. In short, the church encourages development in social, educational, physical, and spiritual areas of life.

Of paramount importance in LDS culture is the family. The importance and eternal nature of families are stressed. Mothers are encouraged to stay at home with their children. As a result, LDS families tend to be larger than their counterparts in other faiths.[12] Latter-day Saint women tend to have children at a rate about 60 percent higher than the national average.[13] Issues of overpopulation rarely concern the general church membership, who believe that bringing children into the world is one of life's greatest privileges and responsibilities.

Modern environmental view

The environmental movement is concerned with the long-term health of the world's ecosystems. The fundamental object is to live sustainably so that the things that we enjoy can be enjoyed by future generations. The environmental movement, then, encourages prudent resource use, recycling, and the protection of ecological systems. It assumes that the world is in a state of crisis caused by the assault of a growing population and indiscriminate resource use. The environmental movement seeks to protect what remains and encourage people to live within the carrying capacity of the earth. It recognizes that many ecosystems worldwide are under threat from global warming, habitat loss, species extinction, invasive species, and other anthropogenic changes. Mainstream environmentalists are aware that the earth has a given carrying capacity and that currently the human ecological footprint is high, owing to both large populations using limited resources and the increased use of resources through the spread of Western culture. Population control is often closely associated with the environmental movement. Nearly all of the texts used in environmental science classes have a chapter on overpopulation and its effects. Most of these texts do not consider the nuance of population numbers vis-à-vis the impact of individual members of the population (e.g., Western cultures have a much higher ecological footprint than do typical indigenous cultures).

Comparison

Ironically, the teachings of Latter-day Saints and the modern environmental movement have many outlooks in common such as frugality, the importance of reuse, the care of resources—in other words, exercising wise stewardship over our earthly blessings. Why is it that these two groups continue to be at loggerheads?

Latter-day Saint scriptures teach that the abundance of the earth is here for our use. Many assume that the Lord's statement "For the earth is full, and there is enough and to spare" (D&C 104:17) is made without qualification and that concerns about population are not an issue.[14] Population issues are one area where dialogue between Latter-day Saints and environmentalists is desperately needed because it remains an area where the two sides do not see eye-to-eye. However, as the scripture enjoins us, we have not lived up to our responsibility of caring for the poor; therefore both views are flawed and a dialogue is desperately needed.

This claim of unlimited abundance is often interpreted by some members to mean that there are no limits set on using and procuring natural resources. In addition, wealth is often mistakenly interpreted as a consequence of righteous living. Beyond the population issue, however, it is ironic that many environmentalists see Latter-day Saints as part of the problem rather than as part of the solution, when the LDS view does support (and even mandates) a strong environmental ethic. But part of the problem is, again, that Latter-day Saints have not lived up to their teachings. Hugh Nibley has been very vocal but largely ignored in his attempts to show the Saints the disparity between their beliefs and their actions. As a result, there is a perception within the LDS community and the mainstream environmental movement that the two groups have opposing goals and interests.

Dimension 4: Assumptions about Pervasive Social and Ecological Patterns That Channel and Constrain Tendencies and Needs

Both groups in America are heavily influenced by the values of Western culture. Most people in the United States own two or more cars, which are used to commute to work, shop, and provide access to recreation and entertainment. Large homes are situated with poor access to work and shopping areas and have led to what has been called urban sprawl. Economic realities constrain much of the interactions between people and their environment. Western culture is extremely "packaging heavy," meaning there are few food items, household goods, tools, automobile parts, or toys that do not come heavily packaged. This significantly increases the amount of waste produced and increases the stress on ecosystems that provide the raw materials for this packaging. Solid and liquid waste are handled by standardized methods over which individuals in this culture have little control. Recycling is unevenly practiced across the country, and Utah and other western states excluding California, Oregon, and Washington lag considerably behind in recycling efforts compared with other parts of the United States.

Latter-day Saint view

In addition to the constraints of Western culture, Latter-day Saints are busy. The symbol of the beehive for the state of Utah is an appropriate choice. A typical active member may have church responsibilities that can take from five to thirty hours a week, depending on the type of calling (with some leadership callings sometimes requiring the higher time commitment). In addition to this, they are expected to pursue their genealogy, attend a two-hour session at the temple as often as possible (typically about once or twice a month), visit from two to five members of the church as home or visiting teachers to ensure the families' needs are being met, assist in neighborhood service projects, hold a family home evening on Monday nights, be involved in community activities and projects, and attend stake and regional conferences. In large families where the husband is the sole breadwinner, the need to work longer hours creates an additional burden on many members. Finally, the number of LDS women needing to work outside their homes has increased, as the demands of large families are more difficult to meet by a single wage earner in today's economy. These demands constrain the amount of time Latter-day Saints can spend in other pursuits, including environmental concerns.

Modern environmental view

Most environmentalists are constrained by current Western culture and society. These constraints are often frustrating to environmentalists who are seeking ways to reduce the ecological footprint of Western culture. They must face the dilemma posed by the reality that people are unlikely to give up the comfort and convenience gained during the last one hundred years. Often environmentalists are perceived as being unrealistic and uncompromising in their demands for changes to our current cultural system. Because a growing body of information suggests that current rates of consumption are not sustainable if we are to maintain many of the earth's ecosystems, environmentalists tend to be alarmed, pessimistic, and negative about the future. This reduces their effectiveness in spreading their message, which seems to be filled with undue doubt and despair. This concern has led some environmental thinkers to make inflated and unfounded claims of doom, such as Paul Erlich's assertion that the 1980s and 1990s would be filled with massive starvation, war, and social destabilization. Some environmentalists' failure to be clear and accurate has created skepticism in the general populace about all claims made by the environmental movement, compromising its effectiveness in communicating genuine concerns.

Comparison

While there are many specific examples of Latter-day Saints who are active environmentalists, many tend to focus on other aspects of life, such as the demands that church membership places on people. As a result, many things, such as gaining an environmental awareness, can be a lower priority, and a reasoned and thoughtful response to environmental claims remains unexamined by many. From my experience, students in my environmental science class raised in typical Mormon households are not often knowledgeable about the scientific claims of environmentalism. Political conservatism formulated by popular talk radio personalities, ultraconservative political figures, and polemical Internet sites with inaccurate science reporting and presentations of anti-environmental thought and data (which are rarely screened to ensure data quality) seem to be the primary source of their information.[15] An undercurrent of an unreflective environmental negativism informed by these political philosophies seems pervasive with my students, family members, and ward members among whom I have lived. For example, on the topic of global warming, I am often greeted with surprise when I point out that there are few scientists now studying the issue who do not believe it is occurring. (Although there are a number of scientists not working in the areas of climatology, biodiversity, or ecology who will sign their names to long lists claiming that global warming is not a problem, researchers actively studying the problems are unified about the reality of global warming.) Understanding good science is important for helping Latter-day Saints understand the extent of the current environmental crisis.[16]

Dimension 5: A Level of Concrete Practices and Rules Informed by All the Foregoing Dimensions

Latter-day Saint view

Active Latter-day Saints often structure their existence around living good and righteous lives. Where they perceive ethical norms, they are usually committed and diligent about trying to bring those things into their daily religious practice. I am convinced that if caring for creation were couched in terms that made ethical sense, the Latter-day Saints could become leaders in the environmental movement. As it is, recycling is not seen as a priority, global warming is ignored, and wilderness protection and species preservation are seen as unnecessary and unwanted government interventions.

It will take good information by committed members of the church to lead the way to this change in behavior and perception. Such leadership is starting to bubble up, and I am optimistic that when the Latter-day Saints became better informed about the environment, they will rise to the occasion and make a difference in averting much of the growing degradation of earth's resources. This must be couched in gospel terms and not in those terms prevalent in mainstream environmental discourse, with its foundation in a naturalistic-materialistic view of humans' place in the universe.

Even though an LDS environmental ethic will not be based on materialist foundations, it is important that members be acquainted with the science behind the environmental movement. Latter-day Saints should understand that science is our best assessment of the current condition of the earth. It will be scientists working in ecology and environmental studies that will help us understand the threat to earth's continued maintenance. To act as good stewards, we need good information. The climate of mistrust of science by many members of the church needs to be addressed and examined. Caring for creation is an attitude that should become more prevalent in LDS culture and belief systems. The following might be seen as first steps toward becoming more environmentally aware:

1. Understanding the importance of caring for creation from a gospel perspective.
2. Having an attitude of stewardship in considering actions.
3. Learning the facts of environmental degradation from reliable sources.
4. Acting within our sphere of influence to take care of natural resources.
5. Seeking for understanding with others involved in the environmental movement and recognizing that drawing us-and-them lines is counterproductive for fostering healthy views of current needs regarding the environment.

Modern environmental view

The mainstream environmental movement must understand that the Latter-day Saint viewpoint is built on a different foundation than theirs. The mainstream movement has aspects that Latter-day Saints may not accept, such as population control, which goes against fundamental teachings. However, much can be agreed on, such as the protection and care of the earth and its creatures. The steps needed for the environmental movement to engage with LDS members in a more productive dialogue include:

1. Recognizing that Latter-day Saints have much to offer in the way of a perspective for caring for creation.
2. Seeking to understand LDS doctrines and practices and seeing how they might be used to offer an alternative to standard environmental discourse.

Comparison

While Latter-day Saints are not likely to embrace all of the current environmental movement's goals and desires, there is much overlap. It is in this area of overlap where dialogue and understanding can begin and where much good can be accomplished. I suggest the following as a way to open more dialogue and understanding between the two groups. Often in the history of the world, when two groups of people met, the differences in language, custom, and background caused misunderstanding that led to conflict. However, when the language is learned, the customs respected and appreciated, and the background assumptions made explicit, understanding can be achieved, differences worked out, and open intercourse established between the groups. I think this sort of understanding is possible for both Latter-day Saints and those in the environmental movement. To this end, I suggest that we recognize, respect, and appreciate each other's differences; work together on common goals and ideals; and read each other's literature, understand each other's method of discourse, and appreciate and respect our differences.

It is my hope that the view that Latter-day Saints are against the environment and its care and that nature is for their unrestricted use will be changed in the environmental community. I hope that the view among Latter-day Saints that environmentalists are litigious fanatics who deny people their freedom to use natural resources as they please will be replaced with an understanding and appreciation for their concerns about the global environmental crisis. I hope that by appreciating one another's differences and by engaging in open dialogue, we can work together on common goals that will protect the environment for future generations and make this world a clean and precious place to live.

Notes

1. I had a student compile and score the voting records of our state representatives over the last thirty years. I excluded any legislation that dealt with population control. With a few notable exceptions, Utah's representatives had among the poorest records of environmental protection in the nation.

2. Don Browning, "Feminism, Family, and Women's Rights: A Hermeneutic Realist Perspective," *Zygon: Journal of Religion and Science* 38/2 (2003): 317–32.

3. See chapters 3 and 5 herein and Trent D. Stephens and D. Jeffrey Meldrum, *Evolution and Mormonism: A Quest for Understanding* (Salt Lake City: Signature Books, 2001), 175.

4. Michael Ruse, *Can a Darwinian Be a Christian?* (Cambridge: Cambridge University Press, 2001).

5. I felt this directly in growing up in Moab. I remember my seminary teacher expressing his belief that there were no such things as dinosaurs. On my mission I actively taught that evolution was wrong, and I remember my surprise when I arrived at BYU and found that the book used in the zoology evolution class actually seemed to favor the idea. I also remember, after being "converted" to evolution while studying biology at BYU, being told by a religion teacher, "You will go to hell if you believe in this damnable doctrine." For a more detailed reading of the history of the relationship between science and Mormonism, see Erich Robert Paul, *Science, Religion, and Mormon Cosmology* (Urbana: University of Illinois Press, 1992).

6. Hugh Nibley, "Man's Dominion, or Subduing the Earth," in *Brother Brigham Challenges the Saints* (Salt Lake City: Deseret Book, 1994), 18-19.

7. George Handley, "The Environmental Ethics of Mormon Belief," *BYU Studies* 40/2 (2001): 187-211; and *Home Waters: A Year of Recompenses on the Provo River* (Salt Lake City: University of Utah Press, 2010).

8. See George B. Handley, Terry B. Ball, and Steven L. Peck, *Stewardship and Creation: LDS Perspectives on the Environment* (Provo, UT: Religious Studies Center, Brigham Young University, 2006).

9. See, for example, Max Oelschlaeger, *Caring for Creation: An Ecumenical Approach to the Environmental Crisis* (New Haven, CT: Yale University Press, 1994).

10. John Rawls, *A Theory of Justice* (Oxford: Oxford University Press, 1971).

11. W. Eugene Hansen, "Children and the Family," *Ensign,* May 1998, 58.

12. I have found much confusion on the use of birth control among the general populace of the church. While officially there is no doctrine on birth control, statements from some church leaders leave some ambiguity on the matter, and in conversations with other members of the church around the country, I find members practicing every possible interpretation: from the perspective that birth control is forbidden to the idea that there are no limits on how birth control is used. LDS .org states, "Decisions about birth control and the consequences of those decisions rest solely with each married couple." See https://www.lds.org/topics/birth-control. Abortion is forbidden with a few exceptions. See https://www.lds.org/handbook/handbook-2-administering-the-church/selected-church-policies/21.4#214.

13. Personal calculation based on 65 percent of Utah being LDS as reported in "Utah fertility rate tops the U.S. charts," *Deseret News*, Sunday, November 7, 2010, http://www.deseretnews.com/article/700079435/Utah-fertility-rate-tops-the-US-charts.html (accessed July 22, 2014).

14. It is clear from the context of the scripture that the earth is "full" only in the context of a Zion society where there are no poor. The scriptures following this verse discuss our responsibility to care for the poor.

15. A fascinating study of the spread of misinformation regarding climate change is Naomi Oreskes and Erik M. Conway, *Merchants of Doubt: How a Handful of Scientists Obscured the Truth on Issues from Tobacco Smoke to Global Warming* (New York: Bloomsbury Press, 2011).

16. See chapter 1 herein for a discussion of the benefits of the scientific community's peer-review system.

8

Reverencing Creation

As a BYU student in the early eighties, I earmarked part of my meager paycheck to help protect endangered whales. Since then "Save the Whales" has become so hackneyed that even unswerving environmentalists smile at its kitschiness. But at the time, I really was concerned with saving the whales (and still am). The great blue whale—along with many other cetacean species—was on the verge of extinction, and urgent action was needed.

However, a movement called "Food for Poland" had just been launched by one of my heroes, Eugene England.[1] It had been started to alleviate President Ronald Reagan's suspension of aid to the bedraggled satellite of the Soviet Empire, and the movement became the *causa sine qua non* for student activists. I was torn. I wanted to help, but what about the whales? On my stretched-too-far-already student budget, I could not afford both causes. The logic "Aren't starving people always more important than animals?" tore me in two. How could I in good conscience step away from my responsibility to succor my hungry brothers and sisters in what was an obvious and immediate need? I wrestled and twisted but could not decide which good to choose.

Finally, I decided to pray about it. I suppose I went into the prayer thinking that the Lord would tell me to support the people of Poland since it seemed somehow improper to put mere creatures above the spirit children of God. As I prayed, however, I became immersed in a profoundly affective spiritual experience. It was as if my mind's eye was being opened to how God viewed the whales—as if I suddenly inhabited a corner of his mind. I sensed that he loved them. More than that,

I became aware that he knew each of them as individuals, as if he knew their names and cherished each of them deeply—not as possessions or pets or useful creatures or lesser beings of any kind. He seemed to convey to me that the whales were fellow travelers through existence. Fraternal creatures of dignity and worth. Weeping, I stood up and wrote a check to the Save the Whales Foundation.

The vision (and that is how I represent it to myself, recognizing its personal and incommunicable aspects and meaning) has dimmed in its impact and in my memory, but I have never forgotten the experience. While I recognize that it was not your revelation, I share it because of how profoundly it altered the way I look at nature and its creatures, even informing my decision to become an ecologist. I wish I could say that I have lived up to that vision, but I have fallen short in many ways. But recently I have felt that I need to embrace that experience more fully. It deserves my attention and reverence.

We are in the midst of an ecological crisis. Throughout the world, ecosystems are facing monumental threats, maybe the most menacing since the Cretaceous extinctions that snuffed out the dinosaurs. The climate is changing under the influence of human outputs, ocean fisheries are disappearing, forests are being cleared for development at an alarming rate, coral reefs are dying in every ocean, and entire ecosystems are in chaos. These harms are well documented and scientifically established. I know of no ecologist or environmental biologist who would disagree with the foregoing assessment.[2] The church is beginning to emphasize our role in being good stewards of the earth.[3] But it still seems as though the dangers we face have not yet made much of an impact on many members of the church, some of whom even seem to bear some animosity toward environmentalism.

I became an ecologist because I love complexity and I love nature. When I look out at nature, I understand that much that is going on is not only invisible to us, but also deeply complex—manifold relationships playing themselves out among the living and nonliving things of our planet. These relationships form the structure and fabric within which we live. They touch us constantly, from the oxygen we breathe to the ecological cycles that sustain our lives in what seems like an almost alchemical process of combining sunlight, soil, air, and water. These cycles, and cycles within cycles, are constantly spinning around and within you. (Though you may not want to know this, you are quite an amazing ecosystem yourself, being a home for three to six pounds of very active bacteria.) Even so, much of this amazing complexity is taken for granted, ignored, and even despised.

That is why I want to write about reverence for nature. As members of the LDS Church, we have not lived up to our best selves or our best doctrines. But instead of preaching hellfire and brimstone, I'm going to take a page from the positive psychology playbook and say that our current state of mental misalignment with nature is irrelevant. What's important is that we work on getting better from wherever we stand. So let's get started.

When I was a graduate student in ecology, people were often surprised to find that I was a "Mormon ecologist." The Mormons had a reputation for being not only uninterested in environmental concerns but hostile to them. In fact, when the Ecological Society of America was planning to hold its national meeting in Salt Lake City, an active protest emerged against the idea because of the Utah legislature's abysmal environmental record. Among other hints that Utahns were not environmentally literate, the protestors focused on the apathy that some of Utah's residents have shown toward preserving our lands from thoughtless development.

In the mid-1990s, Max Oelschaeger complained in his book *Caring for Creation*, "The only denomination that has formally stated its opposition to ecology as part of the church's mission is the Church of Jesus Christ of Latter-day Saints."[4] At about the same time, Marshall Massey claimed that the church was formally committed to environmental inaction. A number of LDS scholars have responded to these kinds of statements, and explicit claims of Mormon environmental inaction or ecological antagonism are no longer common in print.[5] In my experience, however, the perception that Mormons are anti-environmentalist remains current in many environmental circles.

Sadly, I understand their perception. While I was growing up in Moab, one of the worst curses you could fling at someone was "Your mother is an environmentalist!" However, I had many friends in graduate school who were both Mormons and concerned environmentalists. I use the word *environmentalist* purposely because I find that many of my students who are emerging environmentalists try to distance themselves from the word because they feel it carries negative connotations. I want to unabashedly embrace the word and redeem it through new associations. I'm looking for an environmental awakening among my people, especially given the richness of our doctrines about the importance of the world we live on. And I think such an awakening is just waiting to happen.

One of my favorite scenes in *The Lord of the Rings* is when the hobbits Merry and Pippin stumble into Fanghorn Forest and meet an Ent called Treebeard, one of the shepherds of the trees. The forest is being destroyed by Saruman, an evil wizard. Treebeard explains that the Ents have been slow to act.

> Only lately did I guess that Saruman was to blame, and that long ago he had been spying out all the ways, and discovering my secrets. He and his foul folk are making havoc now. Down on the borders they are felling trees—good trees. Some of the trees they just cut down and leave to rot—orc-mischief that; but most are hewn up and carried off to feed the fires of Orthanc. There is always a smoke rising from Isengard these days.
>
> Curse him, root and branch! Many of those trees were my friends, creatures I had known from nut and acorn; many had voices of their own that are lost forever now. And there are wastes of stump and bramble where once there were singing groves. I have been idle. I have let things slip. It must stop![6]

He then adds, speaking of the Ents' sluggishness: "If I could make them understand the need; if I could rouse them: we are not a hasty folk. What a pity there are so few of us."

Treebeard calls an Entmoot—a grand council of the Ents—and the Ents *do* get roused. Suddenly the Ents are fully awake and ready to take action:

> The old Ent now took the hobbits back and set them on his shoulders again, and so they rode proudly at the head of the singing company with beating hearts and heads held high. Though they had expected something to happen eventually, they were amazed at the change that had come over the Ents. It seemed now as sudden as the bursting of a flood that had long been held back by a dike.[7]

In the end, the Ents completely demolish Saruman's terrible fortress—something no army in Middle Earth could have accomplished.

I hope that we Mormons need only the right sort of Entmoot of ground-root efforts to awaken to the threats we face. I think we can become a truly great force for the care and nurture of our planet.

But what must happen to awaken us? I've been pondering of late some of the ways people from other faiths and traditions have expressed their care for creation. For example, ecofeminist Starhawk, in her book *Earth Path*, offers the following blessing on—of all things—a compost pile.

> We offer gratitude to the great cycles of birth, growth, death, decay, and regeneration. We are grateful to all the beings who have made the great transformation, leaving the remains of their bodies here. We are grateful to all the hungry mouths that consume the dead. Blessings on the termite, the beetle, the ant, the spider, the worm. Blessings on the fungi and the bacteria, those that need the air and those that avoid it. Blessings on all the life in this pile that will transform decay to fertility, death to life. May I always remember that the cycle of life is a miracle. May I continue to feel a sense of wonder and joy in the presence of death and life. May I remember that waste is food, and may my eyes be open to opportunities to close the circle and create abundance and life.[8]

What assumptions go into such a blessing? First, that God cares about such things as compost piles. It shows an awareness of our dependency on the little things on earth—an acknowledgment that these diverse things matter to our health and well-being. The blessing requires some education about the workings of nature. It shows a deep reverence for the ecological cycles that make life possible. It takes seriously the idea that our spiritual lives can merge with nature and its care.

Such attitudes as we find in this blessing on a compost pile would go far in helping us sense how important and fragile our life support systems are and how essential their care actually is. Could we thoughtlessly use and abuse our wonderful lands and natural resources if we sensed a deep and important sacredness within them? If we truly asked blessings or gave thanks for the cycles and processes of nature, could we easily exploit or abuse nature as we have so quickly and carelessly done up until now? Could we glibly argue that certain of our companion species are less valuable than a new mall or housing development?

At first it may seem absurd to ask a blessing on a compost pile—maybe as absurd as making a sacred covenant with the creatures of the earth. However, in Genesis, after Noah disembarks from the ark, God says to him:

> And I, behold, I establish my covenant with you, and with
> your seed after you; *and with every living creature that is with*
> *you, of the fowl, of the cattle, and of every beast of the earth with*
> *you; from all that go out of the ark, to every beast of the earth.*
> (Genesis 9:9-10; emphasis added)

The Lord then establishes a covenant that he will never destroy the
earth with water again and sets a rainbow to mark this covenant. Then
the Lord adds:

> And I will remember my covenant, which is between me and
> you and every living creature of all flesh; and the waters will
> no more become a flood to destroy all flesh. (Genesis 9:15;
> emphasis added)

I don't take literally the idea that at one point in history there was a
worldwide flood and that an ark loaded with a sampling of at least one
pair from each species sailed upon it,[9] so why take literally the idea that
God made a covenant with the beasts of the earth? For me, the story isn't
about physical geology and biodiversity, but a metaphor for the deep concern the Lord has for what are often called the "lesser things of Earth."

Though there does seem to be a claim for humans as God's favorites
embedded in Mormon theology, I think it is crucial to note that the Lord
makes his covenant with Noah, his children "for perpetual generations"
(Genesis 9:12), *and* every living creature. Us *and* them. This suggests to
me that while we may be our Heavenly Father's ultimate concern, we
are not his *only* concern. Other creatures do matter to him—after all, he
commanded Noah to make sure they made it onto the ark. The ark and
the great deluge may be metaphorical, but the Lord's care is genuine,
deep, and important. His creation and its creatures matter. We have an
obligation to reverence and recognize his care for them.

To reverence something requires not just an acquaintance but an
intimacy. Notice in the compost blessing that there are specific references
to ecological processes. This knowledge comes from the past hundred
years of ecological study of the processes and activities of nature and the
discovery of the deep time that went into their unfolding. The Jewish
writer Abraham Joshua Heschel writes in his book *The Sabbath*:

Creation, we are taught, is not an act that happened once upon a time, once and for ever. The act of bringing the world into existence is a continuous process. God called the world into being, and that call goes on. There is this present moment because God is present. Every instant is an act of creation. A moment is not a terminal but a flash, a signal of Beginning. Time is perpetual innovation, a synonym for continuous creation. Time is God's gift to the world of space.[10]

I love the idea that creation is part of a long, patient becoming, the evidence for which we see in the fossils of this earth, in the DNA of every cell of our bodies, and in other creatures' bodies. Evolution ennobles the creation and Creator because it suggests that God is a gardener, not a magician.[11]

To picture the creation as the wave of a wand devalues it. Perhaps this is a reason we Latter-day Saints have sometimes not appreciated the immense work that went into creating the marvelous diversity amid which we live. The thought that millions of years have been required for the creation goes far in helping us appreciate the uniqueness and preciousness of our earth. As we look at nature, we are looking into deep creation through an eye fashioned out of elements gleaned from the remains of burned-out stars. Not a nature fashioned by the quick wave of a hand, but one that has required about 13.7 billion years to cultivate.

As Latter-day Saints, we have stunning reasons for preserving our planet. It is, after all, our permanent home. If we take seriously the idea that the celestial kingdom will be on this earth, we will understand that it is not a lifeless sphere to be used and abused. That we believe the earth was made to facilitate our eternal progression in no way allows us to operate from a position of power and disrespect. Rather, it deepens our responsibility and heightens the necessity of reverencing the processes that sustain the life we have been given.

Environmentalism seems not just a good idea, but a requirement.

Notes

1. For more about Eugene England's "Food For Poland" program, see Mitch Davis, Michael G. Sullivan, and Ronald J. Ockey, "A Bullet and a Vision: Food For Poland, 1982–1985," *Sunstone* 121 (January 2002): 46–47.

2. For a nice review of the evidence and an LDS perspective on climate change ethics, see George Handley, "Faith and the Ethics of Climate Change," *Dialogue: A Journal of Mormon Thought* 44/2 (Summer 2011): 6-35.

3. For example, Elder Marcus B. Nash of the First Quorum of the Seventy delivered an address at the Stegner Symposium on Religion and the Environment at the University of Utah called "Righteous Dominion and Compassion for the Earth," April 12, 2013, http://www.mormonnewsroom.org/article/elder-nash-stegner-symposium. The LDS Newsroom just added a Gospel Topics page entitled "Environmental Stewardship and Conservation"; see http://www.mormonnewsroom.org/article/environmental -stewardship-conservation. The Mormon Channel recently produced a beautiful short film called *Our Home*, available at https://www.youtube.com/watch?v=cGxYvos1DMw.

4. Max Oelschlaeger, *Caring for Creation: An Ecumenical Approach to the Environmental Crisis* (New Haven, CT: Yale University Press, 1996), 204.

5. Among the best of LDS responses is George Handley's moving book *Home Waters: A Year of Recompenses on the Provo River* (Salt Lake City: University of Utah Press, 2010).

6. J. R. R. Tolkien, *The Two Towers* (New York: Mariner Books, 2005), 76.

7. Tolkien, *Two Towers*, 91.

8. Starhawk, *The Earth Path: Grounding Your Spirit in the Rhythms of Nature* (New York: HarperOne, 2005), 168.

9. See chapter 11 herein; and for more on this topic, see Duane E. Jeffery, "Noah's Flood: Modern Scholarship and Mormon Traditions," *Sunstone* 134 (October 2004): 31-32.

10. Abraham Joshua Heschel, *The Sabbath* (New York: Farrar Straus Giroux, 2005), 100.

11. For more on evolution and Latter-day Saint theology, see chapter 3 herein.

9

Grace vis-à-vis Violence

The earth . . . was filled with violence.

—Moses 8:28

The grace of Lord Jehovah fills the Earth.

—Psalm 33:5[1]

VIOLENCE PERMEATES EXISTENCE. It is structured into the very fabric of the evolved life on Earth through the process of natural selection—a process that seems to have implications for theology, especially our relationship with divine grace. Violence also seems to enter into my life at multiple points. Unlooked for. Mixed with this grace. Yes, "mixed with grace," that is what I want to focus on: this inexplicable enfolding of contraries. Blessings and cursings. Grace and violence.

I am putting pen to paper on this subject because I was recently exposed to a lot of discussion about grace and mercy and other positive attributes of the Divine. Three particular things helped crystallize my need to say something about the place of violence in religious discourse. The first was from a discussion on NPR about domestic violence and its devastating aftermath.[2] The second was an Internet discussion on grace and where it might be situated in the structure of the universe. The third was a statement made by a woman at church who said that when she meets Jesus in the next life she hopes he will take her into his arms and all her sorrows will melt away forever. These three things—violence, grace, and the hoped-for undoing of violence through grace—seemed to tangle me up a bit. I need to explore it. Reflect on it. Sort it out. I offer six "studies" from my life that I hope can disclose something of this contradiction. Then I will try to unpack this vexing admixture of what I want very badly to be cleaner, clearer, more easily grasped. I want my relationship with God to be better ordered than it seems to be when I reflect on the presence of both violence and grace in my life.

Study 1

My brother and I are walking back from a small store in Winton, California. Suddenly, someone yells and approaches us from a pool hall across the street. Motorcycles line the front entrance. We've been warned not to go near it. An older boy approaches and says, "Do you want to fight?" I'm in seventh grade. He looks like a ninth grader. "No," I say. He calls out to a biker going into the pool hall. "There is going to be a fight!" Then without warning he balls his fist and with great speed and force strikes me brutally on the nose. It breaks in three places and blood sprays everywhere. I run. I run and run and run through the peach and almond orchards that craft the patchwork landscape of our agricultural community. I arrive home panting and terrified. I am cleaned up. My eyes wide, like a cornered fox, I don't stop panting for a long time after I've recovered from my run. For the next year I see my tormenter everywhere—no, I think I see him. He is not really there, but my brain is wired for fear so completely that it creates him in every dark corner, looking out of every classroom window I walk past, sitting in every car that drives by. I kneel and pray every morning under the almond trees that God will protect me from the enemy who is everywhere and is always, always looking for me.

Study 2

High School in Moab, Utah. Someone is shouting angrily in the hall. A teacher comes into our classroom and locks the door. "It's Silas," he says. The teacher is afraid. Silas is large. Violent. Goliath-like. And dangerous. He is drunk and shouting for a teacher whom he intends to harm. Were the same thing to happen in 2014, SWAT teams would be called, neighborhoods locked down, but at this moment in small-town time no one seems to think of getting the police involved. We all know Silas. Silas and I are not friends as such. He is a redneck and I am a hippie with hair that falls between my shoulder blades, but we are in the same Mormon ward and I used to date his little sister, and he likes me because I treated her well—so he's told me several times, anyway. He would not hurt me, I think. "I'll talk to him," I say, and the teacher unlocks the door and I go out. Silas is standing alone in the locker-lined hallway. The students have all gone for cover. He is silhouetted against light shining through the main entrance doors out of sight to the left, behind him, making of him a large shadow such that I can't make out the details of his face. He is staggering drunk and shouting the teacher's name and making threats. He has a bottle of something in his hands and he takes a drink and falls back awkwardly a few steps, almost tripping but not quite. As I walk down the hall toward him, it never occurs to me to be afraid. He stops shouting as I approach. He stares at me. He is a foot taller than me and strong as an ox. He *is* an ox. He has a three-county reputation for uncontrollable violence and, when provoked, for giving a disproportional response of consciousless brutality. There is no one that could take him on in a fight. No one. I reach him and take him by the arm and say, "C'mon, Silas, let's go home." He lowers his head and I lead him out and take him home. When we get to his house, he says "Thanks," pats me on the shoulder, and melts out of the car.

Study 3

Cob and I have wrapped towels around our fists and are fighting. He is an Apache from Idaho who was given the choice to go to prison or join the army. He joined the army. We are inseparable friends and troublemakers. Our sergeant hates us, as does our lieutenant. We get all the crap duty. But now we are in the barracks fighting—no rules. He is slower than me, and I hit him in the face hard three or four times for every one he lands one on me; but he outweighs me by thirty pounds, all muscle, and when he connects I feel it. We are both high, and after our match we stand shoulder to shoulder in front of the bathroom mirror, blood running down our faces, laughing our heads off at what a mess we've made. A fellow soldier walks in and sees us and says, "You guys are freaks." We laugh even harder. That night Cob gets in an argument with some man in a bar. It escalates and Cob goes outside to fight him. The man's friend and I go out with them. There is a lot of verbal posturing, but finally Cob and the man go at it. His friend and I stand watching. We look at each other and size each other up to see if their conflict has become ours. It has not. We both go back to watching the fight. No one wins. In the end, they are both standing with their hands on their thighs, breathing hard and blaming each other for the fight. Cob says something sort of funny. The other guy snorts and follows with a quip. They laugh and decide to go back in for a drink together. I'm tired. I go back to the barracks.

Study 4

I am standing at the top of the steps near the Spencer W. Kimball Tower at Brigham Young University. I am using crutches to move forward. A few months before, my wife and I were in a head-on collision with a drunk driver while on our honeymoon. Among other wounds, my front teeth and part of my maxillary were smashed out by the steering wheel—I feel hideous and self-conscious. Both of our injuries were extensive, and we spent several days in intensive care. Our families were warned to prepare for our deaths.

We both survived and were healing physically, but now, there in front of the Kimball Tower, a crush of peculiar fear and anguish overwhelm me. I stop walking and gasp for air. I can't see, and I feel as if my mind is being crushed out of existence. This is happening more and more frequently. I'm sure I am losing my sanity. The diagnostic possibility of post-traumatic stress syndrome has yet to arrive. I think it is just me dying slowly. Darkly. Crazily. I try to move forward, but the sorrow and anguish overwhelm me again; the mental suffering is fiercer than anything suffered physically in the wreck. I think, *This is what Jesus suffered in the Garden.* This is *that* kind of mental anguish. Then I think something unthinkable. I think, *He could not have suffered this much.* Years later I will discover that I want to put an adverb in front of *think*. I will want to put *inappropriately* or *stupidly* or maybe *arrogantly*. But right now I simply think what I think. And that is what I think. And the reason it enters my mind is because I honestly believe that if it were any worse, I would be crushed out of existence. And how could Jesus suffer more? If he were a God, he could *endure* more. Big deal. If one suffers to the limit of one's being, isn't that as bad as it gets?

And.

I am mad at God. Disappointed in God. Maybe I want to belittle his suffering because he did not protect me. He is not coming through for me the way I had been taught he would. He left me alone. Haven't I served a mission? Married in the temple? Am I not doing all that a good Mormon should? Why then is this happening? How could that accident happen on my honeymoon? We'd prayed for protection that morning. Why this?

Why was my bride torn in pieces, now scarred and wounded? Why was I broken and battered? And why, after it all, why cannot God stop the waves upon waves of panic, horror, and fear that are crushing the life out of me, cycling through my day like a monster? Priesthood blessings do not work. Prayers do not work. Why am I being made to drink the bitter cup? That was the *Lord's* job. *Not mine!*

Study 5

Timothy has been horrible. We are vacationing in the Great Smoky Mountains, and we are driving on empty roads to a trail we want to hike. This six-year-old has been picking on his brothers, backtalking, and being disobedient. We are at our wits' end. He is mocking our two-year-old and has gotten all three of his brothers crying. He says something smart to his mother and I snap. We are on a vacant road, and I tell him to get out of the car. Get out. He starts to beg. I say, "I've had it. Get out of the car." He does. I tell him to close the door. I pull away. I, of course, just mean to scare him. I look in the rearview mirror and see him running behind us as fast as he can. His face is contorted in fear, panic, and sorrow. His eyes are wide and his mouth is twisted in anguish. Tears are running down his face and he is screaming for us to stop. His face in the rearview mirror shatters me. I've never seen anything like it. His face . . .

I'll never forget his face twisted in terror like that. I can't even type this without tears running down my cheeks.

. . . I slam on the brakes and run back to him and swoop him up in my arms and hug him and tell him I'll never leave him. Never. He hugs me back and says, "I'll be good now."

Study 6

My daughter and I are watching great machines tear down the apple orchard across the street. The trees are easily knocked over by the remorseless metal and pushed over into a pile. We watch in silence. There can be no other response. It's not our land. It is owned by another. They will build just a few big houses. How can I complain? Was not an orchard removed for my house long ago? We've walked in that orchard many times. It harbored deer, pheasants, many songbirds, and occasionally something rarer and more transient like a weasel or a hawk. There were snakes and toads, but we loved mostly the insects. Butterflies swung over the irrigation ditches with abandon. It's just a manmade orchard. Still, mostly it was an inviting, pleasant place. Shady and quiet. Unnatural, but capturing many of the good things about wild places. *Life* was present there. It was a favorite place for me and my daughter to walk and observe the world. The old apple trees gave a sense of security. For some reason I thought of Tolkien's shire when I walked there. I am surprised how quickly the apple trees are uprooted and removed. They seemed so permanent just yesterday.

Later.

Not many of the houses have sold. The economy collapsed just after several of them had been completed, and many stand unfinished in silence. Raw dirt, piled up here and there, is still standing waiting for some action. Naked earth where the trees once graced the landscape.

So you see. I have been the victim of violence, and I have participated in violence both as actor and spectator. And I don't understand it. It puzzles me. Why is it so? Why is it written into the deep fabric of the universe?

What does Christ's atonement mean?

Back to the woman giving a lesson in my ward who said that when we met Jesus in the next life he would take us in his arms and our sorrows would melt away. I can picture this meeting in a painting for children. But I admit that I rage against such a depiction. It may bring comfort to other people, but it does not bring comfort to me despite my faith in Jesus's gospel. A simple hug to mend all wounds? Is my life nothing more than a boo-boo to be smoothed away with a kiss and covered with a Band-Aid?

When I meet him.

I hope he lets me feel his wounds—I want to push my finger into the holes made by the nails and feel, and assure myself, that they go all the way down to the very bottom of existence. And I hope he reciprocates that intimate touch and reaches up with his hand and puts his fingers on my mouth presses down to feel where the teeth and bone are missing. Not to heal them. But to somehow just acknowledge them. And I hope he takes my broken nose into his hands and reads the anguish written in the lines of my face and makes something good out of the violence—the violence that I have received and given. And I hope he can explain to me why our stark universe demands so much pain from both him and from me and from people that I love. For it seems odd to me still that we live in a universe that demands that its own God must suffer violence—deep, unimaginable violence—not just through the horrors of the cross, a mode of execution that many have suffered, but that he took upon himself violence of the most existential kind. A suffering the remembrance of which keeps him from finishing the sentence describing the pain in a revelation given to Joseph Smith:

> Which suffering caused myself, even God, the greatest of all, to tremble because of pain, and to bleed at every pore, and to suffer both body and spirit—and would that I might not drink the bitter cup, and shrink—Nevertheless, glory be to the Father, and I partook and finished my preparations unto the children of men. (Doctrine & Convents 19:18-19)

Why did the universe, or perhaps at least some aspect of the universe, demand such costs? Why does it demand its payment in violence? In torture? In horror of a kind I don't understand? Why is this the price? No wonder grace and mercy lie at the heart of the gospel, when violence exacts such a toll and seems to undergird our universe in relentless and unfathomable ways.

Such that even God suffers—

Notes

1. David Bauscher, trans., *The Original Aramaic New Testament in Plain English with Psalms & Proverbs*, http://biblehub.com/aramaic-plain-english/psalms/33.htm.

2. "Leslie Morgan Steiner: 'Crazy Love,'" The Diane Rehm Show, April 14, 2009, http://thedianerehmshow.org/shows/2009-04-14/leslie-morgan-steiner-crazy-love.

10

My Madness

> On all sides, madness fascinates man. The fantastic images it
> generates are not fleeting appearances that quickly disappear
> from the surface of things. By a strange paradox, what is born
> from the strangest delirium was already hidden, like a secret,
> like an inaccessible truth, in the bowels of the earth.
>
> —Michel Foucault[1]

I SAT IN THE BED FACING THE TWO SMILING DEMONS—leaders of the great
Satan/Wal-Mart Organization that ran the hospital. They were trying
to convince me that I should let them adopt a clone of my five-year-old
daughter Emily. She had been created by new genetic techniques developed by their powerful company, and they insisted, "Her place will be
great in the new world order." Over the last few days, however, they had
lied to me so often I knew it was a sham. Despair seemed to overwhelm
me at the thought of the strange global changes that had recently taken
place under this evil organization's machinations. But I was resolute. I
would never let them have the copy of my daughter.

For a week, I went crazy—completely and utterly insane. I still wrestle
with which word to use to describe my condition: *crazy? insane? mad?*
They all seem too general and indistinct. However, *schizophrenia, demen-
tia,* and *psychotic disorder,* while more specific, all seem too clinical and
lack existential force. Because I hope to give you the view from inside
my mind, I have decided to go with the first group. They describe better
what I felt happened. I went crazy. I was insane. Madness.

A few minutes ago, I was looking at MRI brain scans taken during my illness. As I scrolled rapidly through thin sections of my brain, a shiver ran down my spine as I realized I was looking at the small organ that in some ways defined who I was. Everything that I think of as defining "me"—my memories, what I've learned, my personality—is sequestered in the physical brain captured in these images. Somewhere in that fleshy blob was a memory of walking under the stars with my father along orchard canals when I was twelve years old; over there might be my goal to run a marathon; to the left might be my knowledge of functional analysis from a graduate math class; the processes that defined my love for my wife and children were written somewhere within the mass represented on the screen. Even though we believe in a spirit, its dependence on our brain for making our way in this physical reality is absolute. Just think of the destruction of identity that comes with Alzheimer's.

Prior to my experience, I imagined that going insane merely involved seeing and hearing things that were not there, so I was surprised to find not only that my sensual experience had been rearranged and re-created, but also that my entire belief structure about the world was rewritten. In addition to seeing people who were not really there, they were also placed in a coherent system of thought and belief that, while similar to my normal toolkit for dealing with the world, was decidedly different. Not only did I see and hear things that did not jibe with the rest of the world I had known, but the way the world worked changed. I was handed a completely new calculus for looking at the world that rejustified, reinterpreted, and made new sense of the things my mind presented to me. I became paranoid. I believed in magic. I embraced a new set of natural laws for the universe. And most strangely, God disappeared. These laws and rules were strikingly different from the usual text with which I had previously structured the world, but to me they were just as coherent as the laws of physics with which I am normally so comfortable.

Philosopher Colin McGinn points out that this is the kind of rewriting of our belief systems that occurs when we are dreaming.[2] In a dream we don't question our ability to fly; we just do it (albeit perhaps with a bit of surprise). However, unlike when I am in a dream state, in this madness I did not believe everything presented to my mind completely uncritically. Moreover, some things occurred that required complex thought, analysis, interpretation, decisions, contemplation—aspects of rational thought that are very unlike our consciousness in dreams. My madness seemed a weird mixture of hallucination and interacting with the real world. But it was a consistent world that seemed oddly coherent from the first-person perspective. At those times when something occurred that did not conform to my understanding of the way the world worked, my mind created explanations to cover the anomalies. Unlike a dream, in which the laws of the universe, our relation to past beliefs, desires, and our understanding of the world can simply be set aside, my mind was constantly providing explanations and reinterpretations of my experience to ensure that it coherently fit together in some way. Because of the strange sensual inputs, there were bizarre twists of logic and interpretation; but unlike in dreaming, my brain was trying to put things back together in a sensible fashion. A consistent reality seemed an important value to my brain.

While interpreting the experience has been a challenge, the direct cause of my insanity was not in question. It was caused by *Burkholderia pseudomallei*, a malicious bacterial species that causes melioidosis, usually a respiratory disease not uncommon in Southeast Asia. I picked up the infection during a recent visit to Vietnam. The physicians in Utah, largely unfamiliar with melioidosis in general, were especially unprepared to deal with the rarer form of the disease manifesting as a brain infection.

It started with headaches so severe I thought my skull must be ripping apart. Doctors diagnosed it as viral meningitis, started me on antivirals, and sent me home with instructions to take ibuprofen for the pain. Nevertheless, the pain went on and on, with the doctors, over repeated visits, insisting that treating viral meningitis takes time and I needed to be patient. The pain was unbearable, and despite priesthood blessings, prayer, and the constant care of my wife, Lori, nothing seemed to relieve it.

On April 7, 2002, almost a month after my first diagnosis, something strange started happening. In addition to the pain, I began to have strange visual perceptions. Anytime I closed my eyes or was in the dark, I would see rolling waves of vivid colors, swirling surfaces of reds and greens, weaving spectral nets waving like a flag in the wind, which suddenly became a slow tornado of multicolored patterns flowing wildly through my visual field.

That night, as I lay down to sleep, my headache seemed better than it had been for a long time. Rather than intense pain, things had mellowed to a dull background ache. I noticed that the bed was covered with a beautiful pattern of soft light green that glowed brightly through the dark room.

Unexpectedly, people began to arrive. Strangers. I did not know who they were or why they were there. Several young women and an older man walked around my bedroom, browsing through our odds and ends as they would at a small shop. Although they did not appear dangerous, I was slightly afraid of them and wondered what they were doing in our home. My reaction seems odd. Normally, I would have actively tried to confront intruders, but now I just watched them from my bed, timid and afraid. They looked real—not in the least dreamlike. Moreover, although solid, they had the ability to pass through things like outlandish ghosts. They did not appear to be interested in me, however, and seemed to wander aimlessly, chatting casually with each other. Occasionally, through a subtle motion of a hand or head, the wanderers caused a starburst of white dust to rain down on me and cover the already-glowing bedspread. I could not understand how they did any of this, but it was unsettling.

When the visitors got to the far end of the room, I jumped up and turned on the bedroom light. The people scattered. They did not simply disappear like the dark shadows created by ordinary objects, but I could see them physically flee as they zoomed away like roaches scampering to hide from the sudden light. Lori told me to turn off the lights. She was exhausted from caring for me and just wanted to get some sleep. I tried to explain, but she said I was dreaming and to come back to bed.

I turned out the lights, but in only a few minutes the people returned. They again seemed to wander about the room like nonchalant tourists in a museum. Sometimes one would look at me and the others would warn him or her not to do that, as if it were a breach of etiquette. It never occurred to me that they were not physically there or not real. My natural skepticism had been suspended. I accepted all this activity as patently real.

The people vanished for a moment, so I jumped out of bed to gaze out of our second-story bedroom window into our backyard below, trying to get some sense of what was going on. My grassy backyard had been plowed, leaving a system of crooked brown furrows where my lawn had once stood. People were migrating through my yard; I could see small groups of people marching slowly in the same direction as if gathering for a special event. A few seemed to be wearing military uniforms and might have been driving the people somewhere. I was not sure, but it scared me.

The visitors came back, so this time I tried talking to them, asking them to please leave my family and me alone. That changed everything. Rather than being casually strolling sightseers, unconcerned with my presence, they immediately focused their attention on me. *Please go. I just want to get some sleep*, I explained. A few left, but a group of about five teenage girls told me they would go after they were allowed to do inappropriate things to me. I said no. They became insistent and started reaching for me. They angrily accused me of breaking a promise I had implicitly made or somehow otherwise implied by my acknowledging their presence. I had broken some code of acceptable behavior. By talking to them, I was now bound in a contract that allowed them to do whatever they wanted. All five of them started trying to reach for me from different angles.

I reached out to block one of the girls and pushed her back. She instantly withered up and died. The other girls looked on in shock. "You killed her!" one said. They backed away angrily. "I didn't mean to!" I said, trying to explain. "I just meant to push her away." They seemed annoyed, rather than being horrified as normal people would react at seeing a murder. Death, I inferred, was a common theme in the lives of these visitors. They backed up and left, but I felt they were not far away, watching me. I felt guilty. I did not mean to kill her. Was I guilty of murder?

These girls continued to harass me until finally I tried to restrain one of them. She got away, and it turned out I was actually choking Lori. She was now scared and begged me to go to sleep. I had been out of bed several times during the night, and she had walked me back to bed, becoming increasingly frightened. I was clearly delusional, but now I was becoming dangerous.

I will not try to describe the full events of that first night of madness; the horror, the despair, and the frustration were real and unrelenting. These events were interspersed with a number of weird interactions with the people of that world. As dawn began to break, a person informed me that I had joined their cause and I was now part of a powerful Satan and Wal-Mart conglomerate, the "SWO." The person told me that great benefits were mine but that I was bound for life. My wife had even joined a mutilation fad and had cut her eyeball in half horizontally. She was placidly spinning the lower half.

Seeing I was clearly out of my mind, Lori put on an old movie and I settled into watching it while she tried to contact our doctors. The people still wandering around now took the form of workers provided by SWO to take care of domestic needs. One of them came and sat next to me to watch the movie. I was a little annoyed because he was supposed to be working and he was just sitting there watching TV. He wore a kind of chief's outfit that included buttons and a cap, and had distinct manner-isms including things like yawns or occasionally readjusting the blanket in which he had wrapped himself. He would occasionally even direct a smile my way. I had to tell my mother to be careful because she almost sat on him.

In addition to appearing real, these apparitions were amazingly con-sistent. If I went into the kitchen to get a drink, the people on the couch were still there when I got back. When I looked out into my backyard, the ground was plowed and the fences that ringed our suburban backyard were all down, as I had seen from the window last night.

My wife realized that I was in deep trouble, so she drove me to the hospital. I was in a state of amazement: the hospital was brimming with large, colorful insects! I am a biologist, and this did not cause me the fear I suppose most people would feel. Mostly I was delighted! I thought the idea of filling the hospital with insects was an inspired approach to cleanliness because they could eat harmful bacteria. I also thought the insects might be used to help keep up a healthy pool of bacteria that were susceptible to antibiotics and keeping down the level of antibiotic resis-tance in the hospital. I also surmised that the insects had been genetically engineered by the SWO for this purpose.

Finally, an intern decided I was quite in need of admittance, noting in my record: "At the time of admission, the patient was oriented to person and to place only. Furthermore, the Patient was having vivid hallucinations at the time of admission."

After a long wait, they finally wheeled me into my room. I was so tired. My head was again aching with debilitating pain, and I had not slept in forty-eight hours. Last night's adventures were still fresh in my mind when I retired to my bed. I felt safe in the hospital. Oddly, though, I discovered that not only was my room full of insects and other various creatures, but my bed was too. I had my first sense of consternation. Filling the room with insects was one thing, but my bed too? That was going a little too far. I told one of the nurses that I appreciated what they were trying to do with the insects but that having them in my bed was going too far. She told me that if I turned on the light they would go away. I tried that and it appeared to work, so I got back into bed.

Like the previous night at home, my first night in the hospital was terrible. People were walking in and out of my room, some reminding me I had murdered that woman at home. At one point during the night, the room began to fill with water; at another time, monkeys invaded the

The evil rulers of the Satan/Wal-Mart Organization

room begging for asylum from the SWO. It was another long, busy night with little sleep and grossly disturbing dreams when I did sleep. Despite my wild hallucinations, I could still distinguish between sleep dreaming and my waking states.

The next day, my wife brought me two hand-drawn pictures my five-year-old daughter Emily had made to cheer me up. She hung the pictures on a bulletin board facing my bed. In the middle of the night, it slowly began to dawn on me that the two beings depicted by my daughter were the heads of the SWO—not drawings of the leaders of the SWO, mind you, but the actual rulers of the SWO themselves. I started talking to them and they answered back. In so doing, I began a conversation with my daughter's drawings that was to last the rest of the week.

As dawn broke on the second day, I imagined I saw my wife approaching through a window that lined a hallway, but I knew that this approaching woman was not really Lori. I rushed out to the nurse's station and told her to call my wife because a copy of my wife was coming and it was not really her. "Please get on the phone and talk to her so that when this impostor arrives you will believe me." The copy of my wife arrived and I pretended to play along; but thinking better of it, I told her that I knew she was a copy. (I could tell Lori from this fake because the copy of my wife repeatedly used foul language, something Lori would never do.) My impostor wife seemed very angry and gave me an evil look mixed with hurt. It occurred to me that this copy of my wife actually loved me. She could not help her evil nature; it was just part of her cloning. Just then, Lori came around the corner. The impostor ran away; I could see her scampering all the way down the hall.

Lori had come to be with me for an MRI. Throughout the hospital were groups of people scampering in and out of hiding. I saw a couple of my children among them and noticed with surprise that they were all wearing army fatigues. When I asked my wife what our kids were doing here, she insisted they were still at home. I then realized that copies had been made of all my children. Evil copies. Just like the copy of my wife I had just met, these copies had all the memories and feelings of my kids at home but had somehow been made evil. Sadly, they did not even know they were copies. They thought they were my real kids. The crimes of the SWO began to grow and grow. When would this end? Who could control an organization that could wield such powers over life and death? I despaired.

I was loaded into the MRI machine and told to "hang on for the ride" by the technician—and what a ride it was! I thought the large machine was bolted to the floor, but when I climbed inside, much to my delight, I found it was mounted on a set of wheels. We started bouncing down a dirt road in the MRI toward the nearby Provo River, which flowed about a mile from the hospital. We rolled along at a good clip, and through a small periscope that allowed me to peer outside, I could see a whole wagon train of MRI machines. Suddenly, again to my amazement, we started flying. We flew upstream to where the Provo River rushes from the outlet of Deer Creek Reservoir Dam; then, entering the river, we floated down the river in peace and delight. I could see other MRI machines bouncing along with us as we rode the rapids or smoothly bobbed along in the calm places. It really was a great ride. What a hospital!

All these adventures were intermixed with conversations with doctors, my wife, friends, nurses, and others. I remember their presence and interaction with my world. My conversations from their perspective were bizarre at best. For example, at another point I was brought in for an additional MRI. About midway through, they let me out for a short break before they put me in for the second half of the procedure. The technician was explaining the second part of the procedure and suddenly said, "You deserve to die for killing that woman. I am going to make sure it happens. Get back in the machine." I was frozen in fear. His conversation alternated between a mundane explanation about why we needed to complete the second half of the MRI and swearing at me, telling me that he was going to kill me. The vehemence of his denouncements of my crimes was startling. He told me he would personally make sure I did not come out of the machine alive. Naturally, I refused to get back in the machine. While he was talking to some others about my refusal, I bolted back to my room. I knew they would be looking for me, so I returned very cautiously, peeking around corners, hiding whenever a crowd approached me.

I have snatches of memory about many strange sights and events, but these were not just perceptual hallucinations. In my madness, I not only saw and heard things arising only from my imaginative facilities, but I *believed* things about the world that were informed by cognitive delusions. I believed that the hospital was run by the SWO and that my children had all been copied in a strange new kind of cloning. These were not just new images but new cognitive beliefs about the world.

It was these beliefs that made the experience of my madness so hellish. I agonized over the question about what I was to do with the evil versions of my kids. Was I still responsible for them? Was I their father? What was the ethical thing to do? I often ran into my kids in the hospital. They were always dressed in fatigues, always engaged in some sort of military training exercise. Once I saw them in the courtyard of the hospital practicing kung fu moves that included fantastic leaps off buildings and gargantuan jumps onto the roof of the hospital.

Later that night—several hours after this experience with my soaring children—I watched the evening news with my wife. My mind conjured a news story (with both audio and visual hallucinations) on the new military training at the hospital that showed the same things that I had seen in the courtyard earlier. Most surprising is that the file footage shown on TV was filmed from the perspective of the ground rather than from the seventh floor where I had watched it originally, showing the news footage from a different angle than I had seen it earlier that day.

This is something that continues to amaze me about this experience: the consistency of the world in which I lived. Things that happened, no matter how strange or bizarre, continued to be a part of the reality and were often referred to later, like the woman I "killed" back home. The narrative in which I found myself was internally consistent and self-referential, interacting smoothly with the reality I was handed (albeit a distorted one). Moreover, there was a narrative structure to my madness. There seemed to be a plotline exerting itself as I interacted with the people and demons of my imagination.

Emily was perhaps my greatest worry. I saw her often around the hospital. She was never involved in the war games my older children were engaged in whenever I saw them around the hospital. On one occasion, I saw Emily with one of the evil leaders. I thought they were going to try to keep her because I was not caring for her. What could I do? My wife did not believe she even existed. I was so sick I was incapacitated most of the time, and these horrible creatures were taking away my daughter—or at least a copy of her. She was so young and innocent that I did not believe she had been corrupted like the older children. I could not let her go with these powerful and evil entities.

I tried praying while I was in this state, and I don't really know how to put it except that God was gone for me. I wanted to pray, but there was a hopelessness about it that seemed very real and impenetrable. Satan/Wal-Mart ruled here completely. This was especially strange because prayer has always been a part of my life. How could that be taken away? In contrast, as these events unfolded, Lori had distinct impressions of receiving help from beyond the veil and felt the direct influence of many people praying for me. To me, however, this spiritual aspect of my life vanished.

After I spent about five days in the hospital, a new doctor finally joined us. He believed that my illness had a bacterial origin and began IV antibiotics targeting this bacteria rather than the former diagnosis of viral meningitis, which had been based on the lack of bacterial activity in my spinal fluid.

My delusions and continued wrestling with this demonic world continued for two days after I started antibiotic treatments. On the morning of the third day, every time I ran into one of my alternate children, I asked them to meet me at 8:00 that night. I told Lori that I had set up the meeting and that our cloned children would come to the hospital room at 8:00 that night. She insisted that the kids were home; but I knew that, even though my copied children had been made evil, they still loved us and would be there at my request. My wife bet me that the children would not show up at 8:00. I was sure they would. It occurred to me that if they did not come, then Lori might be right and these children were not real. I believe that this possibility was the first intimation that I was returning to reality.

At 8:00 I fully expected my kids to knock on the door. In fact, I was sure I heard them talking outside the door a couple of times. However, they did not come. At 8:15 I was a little concerned. At 8:30 I still thought, "They might just be held up," but a new hope was bubbling up. What if

Lori is right? Maybe I did not have to worry about my evil kids bunking with my real kids and our trying to raise them all together. Maybe there were not two Emilys and I did not have to give one up! Maybe I had not killed someone! At 8:45 I felt happier than I had in days—like a dream in which you lose all that is most precious to you, but you awake and find it all restored. I remember looking at the clock and thinking over and over, *Lori is right! Lori is right! There are not two sets of kids.* All the ethical problems that surrounded me were gone. I felt like rejoicing.

From that time on, I no longer saw strange people, doors, animals, insects, landscapes, malevolent copies of all those I loved, or events that no one else could see. Even so, I am struck by the memory of how real they were. The memories laid down from this time do not seem like the memories of a dream. They are as real and as vivid as any memory I have. I can recognize them only by the incongruity with the rest of reality, as I know it. Their richness of color and detail are as clear as those of any other memory I have.

I have been asked how my madness compares with dreaming. There were several similarities. Like a dream, there seemed to be a narrative structure to my madness. There was an ongoing story that I seemed to be embedded in: I had killed a woman, an act that obligated me to membership in the SWO; my family had been cloned and were being trained by this organization for their diabolical purposes and had been purposely made evil; the leaders of the SWO wanted to adopt the clone of my little girl and were constantly pestering me to allow them to have her; and everywhere I went, people in the hospital were playing a game with complex rules that I could not understand. The narrative structure seems to have informed everything I thought and did at this time and provided a matrix for the images with which I was confronted. Like a dream, I would also suddenly "know" very complex things without the imposition of intervening facts and information.

However, in some respects, the madness was decidedly not dream-like. There seemed to be more details in my visual hallucinations than in dream images. The memories of my interactions seem more real than memories of dreams and are embedded in a perceptual context that was conditioned on real perceptions. For example, I can remember my colleagues visiting me with my cloned son standing next to them crying. In my memory there is no difference between the qualitative aspects of my son's presence and those of my colleagues' presence. Both seemed as real as any percept I would see when my brain is behaving normally.

My madness seemed also more consistent than dreams. For example, I had the hallucination of my cloned children practicing kung fu moves seven stories below me, and then six hours later watching file footage on TV of their practice seen from the ground.

During this time of madness, I also reasoned much more deeply than I normally do in dreams. My obsession with the ethical dilemma of whether I had a responsibility to raise the cloned children because they believed they were my real children weighed heavily upon me. I deliberated, argued, and reasoned about this question in ways that I never do in dreams.

Unlike in dreams, I also tried to explain why certain features of the world were the way they were. Why was I the only one that could see certain things? Why could my wife not see our cloned children? The "answer" was that I had a genetic defect that allowed me to see what others could not. (I also reasoned that the SWO had glasses that would allow others to see these invisible people, but the SWO passed them out only to their confederates.) Why was the hospital filled with insects? To control bacterial infections. These explanations seemed to make consistent things that otherwise would not fit neatly together.

It fascinates me to consider those things that remained of my normal consciousness during the illness and those things that were lost. I retained a sense of ethics, love, and emotional attachments as well as my scientific understanding of genetics, antibiotic resistance, and other scientific facts. Some of the powers of reason remained. But I was paranoid: I assigned causes to things that did not exist; I believed that conditions held that did not, which I appeared to pull from thin air, like the existence of the SWO.

However, one thing that amazes me more than anything else is how powerfully the brain was able to construct a consistent world—a world filled with images, people, and beliefs that had no bearing on reality. It was able to integrate this constructed world with elements of the real world and produce a coherent presentation to the conscious self. Having seen the creative elements of the brain display such an impressive array of abilities, I cannot help wondering how much of our current reality is likewise a construct. How pliable are our minds? These nagging questions have taken away a bit of security about why I believe the things I do. If not only the percepts presented to my mind can be manufactured by the imaginative faculties of the brain but also my beliefs and desires can be rewritten, how can I ever be sure that what I believe about the world reflects an objective reality? That is an old and almost hackneyed question, but one that takes on new meaning now that I have seen the brain in action at its creative best.

I have avoided some questions and even now find difficulty in writing them—mostly because I have not come to any answers that satisfy me. How did I find myself in a place without God? What does this experience imply about the connection between the spirit and the body? How could the very things I believed be changed? I don't know what to say. I was teaching a priesthood class a while after returning to cognitive normalcy, and one of the brothers commented that God never abandons us. I could not let it pass because I *had* been abandoned. So completely, so utterly, that looking back, no other words fit. There were no "footprints in the sand." I was not being carried. God disappeared for me and only demons remained. This has left me shaken because, as the questioner in my quorum meeting suggested, this was not supposed to be an experience I *could* have. I still do not know how to fit it in.

But then, a few days after I came back from my madness, I ordained my son to the office of priest in the LDS priesthood. Standing there in my hospital robe, supported by my good bishop, brothers, and friends, I felt that same spiritual connection I have always known. I felt the presence of God and the flow of the priesthood. But seeing how completely, how frighteningly, my brain can construct and deconstruct realities, there are questions that I still don't know what to do with.

Notes

1. Michel Foucault, *Madness and Civilization: A History of Insanity in the Age of Reason* (New York: Random House, 1967), 23.
2. Colin McGinn, *Mindscapes* (Cambridge, MA: Harvard University Press, 2004).

11

Noah's Lament

NOAH STARED AT JAPHETH IN HORROR. His voice shook a little, "What do you mean an opossum escaped at our last stop?!" Noah was angry. *"YOU KNOW ALL THE MARSUPIALS ARE SUPPOSED TO GET DROPPED OFF IN AUSTRALIA!"*[1] It was another blunder in a long series of blunders. Sailing around the earth, dropping off the animals in their appropriate habitat had been difficult work, and Japheth only dimly understood why it had to be done, but a marsupial in North America was going to get him in trouble.

Japheth had usually been reliable. He could be counted on to get the animals dispersed into their proper location, but lately he seemed to be slipping up with greater frequency. His brother Ham and his family were carting the rabbit-like pikas to the tops of the Rocky Mountains (curse those adorable little beasts that can't cross lower elevations, making it so that every individual population had to be placed on a separate mountain). Meanwhile, Shem was stocking the individual, unique species of pupfish into each of the individual springs in the Great Basin Desert, which meant that Noah was left on the ark making sure that what was left of the twenty million species of animals and plants were being properly taken care of. Aquarium maintenance alone was nearly killing him. With the flood, of course, all saltwater aquatic species had to be brought on the ark because they could not survive the osmotic gradient that the flood induced with its infusion of freshwater, nor could the freshwater species survive in the salty water, so *all* the species of fish and aquatic animals (corals had been particularly challenging) had to be taken aboard the ark—no small feat. The saltwater tanks were now empty (Noah looked longingly at the

187

massive whale shark tank—he missed those gentle beasts), and having sailed around dumping those marine creatures back into the ocean, back into their appropriate habitats, he was feeling quite satisfied. But the family was still scrambling to disperse the freshwater fish. They were working on western North America and at the moment carrying the barrels of high-altitude cutthroat trout high into the Rockies. This was being arranged by one of Ham's sons in conjunction with Ham's pika work since both needed networks of high elevation to disperse.

But what to do with Japheth? He just didn't seem to be grasping the overall vision of the work. He was always complaining, "Why can't we just open the door and let them all go?"

Noah had tried to explain when it came to a head in the Galapagos Islands.

"Look, Japheth! See the beaks on these finches? Each species' beak is used for something different—some eat insects and some seeds of varying sizes. We can't just put them all on the same island, because they'd compete for food and eventually go extinct, so each island in this chain has to have its own unique set of finches, but remember they have to be sets that are compatible. See?"

"Yeah, yeah," said Japheth, "I know, and they all have to look like they *come from* the species on the nearest mainland. They have to be more closely related to the South American finches than the Asian finches."

"Right." Noah gave a strained smile. "How else can the good Lord try his people in the last days? And trust me, they are really going to need trying—if we don't get these species distributions *right* and manage to get things looking like they've *evolved* in a geographic context."

Japheth sighed, "I understand the reasons why things have to look like they evolved. It's just . . . well . . . I'm tired. You know, getting all the honeycreepers sorted the same way in Hawaii about did me in, but those thousand species of fruit fly? Come *on*, Dad. It took years to get those pesky flies into their respective habitats, and frankly I'm burned out."

Noah understood. His wife was even starting to tire. She seemed indefatigable in the beginning. But even little things were starting to wear her out, like sorting out the monkeys with prehensile tails (which could be used to hold on to a branch) so that they could be dropped off in South America from those without such tails that were to be dropped off in Africa. All this was starting to put her over the edge.

Just yesterday she had exploded, "Why do we need seven thousand passenger pigeons on the ark! Their racket is driving me crazy."

Noah had started to explain, "You know they won't breed unless they are surrounded by thousands of their compatriots . . ."

"I KNOW. I KNOW," She fumed. "I'm just so tired of them flapping around so . . ."

Noah had tried to calm her. "Just think how much people in the last days will appreciate these wondrous creatures. I mean they'll love these classy birds. . . . We do it for them, not for ourselves; just imagine a world without passenger pigeons!"

Noah shook these unpleasant memories away and returned to the problem at hand.

"Look, Japheth," Noah sighed. "Remember when you were a young father dropping off separate species of blind cave crayfish in the Ural Mountains?"

"Yes . . ."

"Remember how discouraged you were when I told you that nearly every cave system in the world had to have a different species of cave crawfish and cave crickets and so forth placed in it?"

"Yeah, pops. And it had to match the species that lived in the streams nearby aboveground! And there are so many caves on this planet. I thought I was going to die."

"What did I tell you?"

"One cave at a time, you said. Don't think about the caves you haven't done, you said, just do the caves one at a time and it'll get done."

"Yeah."

"Did it get done eventually?

"I *know*, Dad. I'm just tired. I'll try harder. I really am sorry for letting the opossum out."

"Don't worry. We'll make do. I'm sure the people of the last days will be able to make up a story about why there is just one marsupial on these two continents joined by a narrow land bridge. Just don't let this sort of thing happen again, okay?"

"Okay."

That night Noah called a family council.

"Okay, gang, I know we're all tired. We've replanted every habitat from here to there," he said, waving his hands this way and that. (Why the good Lord made most plants such that they drowned so easily was a bone Noah himself planned to pick with the Lord in the next life—it would have been so much easier if he and his family had not had to re-plant every single habitat from the tundra to the rain forest, but then, the seeds had not taken *that* much room on the ark.) "But we are almost done. We've got the lemurs, lizards, and unique birds to drop off in Madagascar and the dodos and other endemics on the Mauritius Islands, but after that it's smooth sailing and we'll head to Mt. Ararat for a nice long rest."

Note

1. All place-names have been translated from the Adamic tongue to modern twenty-first-century English.

12

Crossing Boundaries and Sacred Spaces

> And [Jacob] took them, and sent them over the brook, and sent over that he had. And [he] was left alone; and there wrestled a man with him until the breaking of the day. And when he saw that he prevailed not against him, he touched the hollow of his thigh; and the hollow of Jacob's thigh was out of joint, as he wrestled with him. And he said, "Let me go, for the day breaketh." And he said, "I will not let thee go, except thou bless me." And he said unto him, "What is thy name?" And he said, "Jacob." And he said, "Thy name shall be called no more Jacob, but Israel: for as a prince hast thou power with God and with men, and hast prevailed." And Jacob asked him, and said, "Tell me, I pray thee, thy name." And he said, "Wherefore is it that thou dost ask after my name?" And he blessed him there. And Jacob called the name of the place Peniel: "for I have seen God face to face, and my life is preserved."
>
> —Genesis 32:23–30

I.

I'm at home looking out over my backyard. Thinking. Remembering. I am transported back in time to a few weeks ago.

Every year an old friend and I undertake an adventure. Steve Hawks and I are middle-aged now, past our prime and youth when our adventures were bolder and more carefree. I can remember when we then, full of laughter, took his new pickup and rubbed its shiny sides against aspens for luck while searching out some secreted beaver dam in which to toss a fly. Now we fuss and fret. We worry endlessly about our kids and their kids and temper our exuberance with caution, having faced too many sorrows and misfortunes since. We are stressed and plagued with the press of the day to day, and we both in demeanor have that worn edge achieved by a cheese grater applied to a block of granite.

But once a year we become eighteen again. We plan a day of adventure and fashion ourselves into grand explorers and take to the environs of our youth.

His wife drops us off on a dirt road. In pictures she took we cut a pair of comical figures. Camelbaks, pants, and trekking poles make us look like a pair of amateur bird-watchers more suited to a stroll along a paved parkway than two bold men (in our minds at least) out for rugged adventure. In one picture, one of us points to the desert. It is a hint that today we are not taking to common trails.

We are making for a deep valley. On Google Earth it runs like a scar from a plateau that skirts the La Sal Mountains to the Moab Valley. There are no roads or trails that access that valley, but dim memories of my friend and the secret knowledge, rumor, and arrogance that tiptoes through Moab natives make us think that there is a hidden slot canyon that runs to some willow-lined Shangri-La. We will try to find it. To do so we will cross many boundaries, roads, geological formations, and transitions in soil and vegetation. In anticipation of our exploration, my mind wanders. Boundaries. They surround us as we walk. They define the paths we take and steer us toward and away from certain features of the landscape.

Boundaries, or ecotones as they are called by ecologists, are often marked by physical transitions, sometimes abrupt, as in water to land or rock to earth. Sometimes they are more gradual, as in chemical gradients in soil or elevational changes as you move up a mountain. There are lots of examples, like forest to grasslands or coral reef to open sea. There are also landscape-level changes like that from desert to Sahel. In Hawaii there is a transition zone from rain forest near the Kilauea Volcano crater to the Kaʻū Desert, where it rains very infrequently. This transition zone is only a few hundred yards wide. Ecological boundaries are always boundaries *for something*. Something specific. For a snake, a freeway may be an impassable boundary that for a bird is treated as nothing at all. But whatever organism it is, it always involves the perceptual awareness of *someone* marking the border. Borders can have very well-defined areas; consider the trout locked into a stream from which it cannot move or bears that have ambiguous territories, marked by their awareness of the presence and signs of other bears.

Ecological systems are also complex, and their complexity grows as new layers fold into and blossom from other layers. Life expands in evolutionary time to fill new niches and in so doing creates new niches or places of flourishing. For example, as plants emerged from the oceans onto a barren world, they created a new level of complexity of habitats that were soon exploited by insects, which in turn created more complexity allowing vertebrates—then birds, then mammals, then us—to enter into these complex dances while natural selection explored these spaces of possible life-types in creative ways. These new niches in turn allowed more complexity to arise and more niches to unfold into the world.

This is creation.

Boundaries are created in this process, and they are always both temporal and spatial in nature. These things come to mind as my friend and I prepare to launch ourselves into the landscape, a patchwork of such boundaries.

We abandon the road and take to navigating through, around, and between the Navajo sandstone fins that slice through the high-canyon desert, making our way to the valley. We are careful not to damage the cryptogamic soil as we wend our way through the frozen dunes fashioned from Late Triassic river delta deposits. We wander for a couple of hours, weaving between this rock formation and that until at last we find ourselves on the precipice of a great cliff. Thousands of feet below us we see the wide stream of the creek bed lined with ancient cottonwoods. Our objective.

A wind blows hard and cool as we step cautiously away from the edge. There is no obvious way down there. We see several slot canyons entering the wide ravine below, but everything looks as if it ends too far up from the valley floor. We sit down and eat an apple. We realize that if we hike about a quarter of a mile forward, we will be on a higher rill from which we may see more of the valley. So we climb up that steep red rock and see hope. There to our left (I cannot give ordinal directions, as we are without either GPS or compass—being from Moab we are gifted with a sixth sense) is a slot canyon that may work. It is a slice in the rock like the narrow gouge of a saw-cut in a pine plank (on Google Earth you cannot even see it from above—it looks like a small groove in the landscape). Actually there are two canyons side by side. Either one looks like it will get us into the desired valley.

"We should have brought field glasses," Hawks says.

I nod. I think it will work. To get to the place where the narrow canyon begins requires another half-mile scramble, but we find it and start down. It is steep, and soon we are in deep shadow as we scramble over the debris and push our way through patches of sometimes-thick holly. The grade grows steeper. We decide on some stopping rules. One danger in these canyons is you risk scrambling down something you can't get back up, and then after, coming to a drop you cannot get down. You are stuck between drops. Then you get rescued or die. We decide that if we reach something we are not sure we can get back up, we stop.

We are crossing into a new ecological zone as we enter into the canyon. I think about the deep time that has structured this new assemblage of plants and animals. And how this canyon marks out something new. I recall that ecological boundaries always have historical contingency. They exist because certain features have unfolded in the way that they have in time because of physical processes or additional ecological complexity. This historical contingency also means that each feature is like a snowflake—unique in ways that are not duplicated. They exist for a time, emerging on the stage of Earth life for a moment (perhaps a geological moment), never to be duplicated exactly or repeated. This canyon is such a moment—marked out of deep time.

We've gone a long ways down. Thousands of feet of rock rise above us. Although it is midday, it is dusky and dark. We've been scrambling down a while when we reach our first decision point. Continue or go back. A large boulder has fallen into the crack we are lumbering down. It is wedged in the slot. There is a small hole that will take us under it and a rocky scramble above. I crawl forward over the boulder, edge along a sandy shelf, and find myself rockbound. It's only about a twelve-foot drop, but I can tell if we go down here we can't get back up. The sandstone is crumbly, and we may have transitioned to Kayenta Formation, much less stable. I try to make my way along a ledge that looks like a possible descent. But I don't see one. Hawks wants to look, and I back up to where he is and he edges forward. He thinks it looks like he can get down, but I argue that we can't get back up; it's too loose. I am the more fainthearted and skittish and talk him out of trying. We both foolishly threw our trekking poles down there thinking it would be easy before deciding it likely wasn't. We back away and look at the little hole that leads under the boulder. Could we fit through that? Not likely.

Hawks is unwilling to give up and is looking more closely at the little hole we might be able to climb in. I back up, and behind a fallen slab about the size of a pancaked SUV leaning against the wall of rock, I find a passage. I tell Hawks, and he looks and we agree it is worth a try. He goes first (again, being the less timid) and wiggles his way through on his belly. He yells that it ends at a drop-off about seven feet high. I hear grunting and huffing and puffing. ". . . If I can just twist around . . . I can go feet first." More grunting, then an exclamation, "I've done it!" I then belly through this birth canal and emerge scratched up but smiling. We continue. The canyon is very narrow now. We cannot face forward in some places without each shoulder touching the wall. Two more places require us to chimney to get down similar seven-foot drops, but they are coming more often and getting trickier to negotiate.

Down one, Hawks says, "I'm going to go see what's ahead." I wait above our most significant drop yet. He's very quiet, and I worry a little at his silence. Then his voice returns, "We're stopped. Do you want to come see? Or just believe me and I'll come up. There is a big drop ahead." I want to see. Not that I doubted him, but I want to stare the beast that defeats us in the eye. It's a matter of desert pride. I climb and chimney down. He points down canyon and I pass him in a wide space and stare down at what looks to be a fifty-foot drop. "If someone put a gun to our heads, I think we could get down," I say. He says, "I think so too." But neither of us is really suggesting that we go on. It's just an observation. We likely could not get back up.

We also note that our eighteen-year-old-kid-and-spouse-free selves would have continued on. How strange that as we reach this boundary, this stopping place, I am forced to confront temporal boundaries that seem to intersect with these physical boundaries. The barrier before us is not *just* a physical boundary, but one created by who we have become since our youth. The cliff itself marks a combination of transitions in our life—like growing older, gaining "grown-up" responsibilities, and becoming a new self, marked by temporally conditioned boundary markers such as marriage and having children—and the geological history of the canyon. It is not either thing alone that stops us from going on down the canyon, but the united coming together and mingling of our personal history and the history of the canyon.

The way back is much harder than we thought. Getting back up some of the things we got down is much more difficult than anticipated.

This seven-foot climb up to the hole turns out to be particularly difficult. Hawks puts up a knee, slaps his thigh, and says, "Step on my leg; then when you get up, you can pull me up." I don't. I'm pretty sure my kind of weight would separate his knee like the joint of boiled chicken being boned for soup. (Well, I'm stretching. More likely it would just leave him with numerous knee operations and a lifelong limp.) Or maybe he'd be fine. But I refuse. I grab some handholds, and with major grunting, pulling, and some fine rockwork for a lumbering middle-aged man, I get up to the hole. I try to pull him up. It's hopeless, so he does the same as I had done. Our stopping rules proved wise. There is no way we would have made it up the fifty-footer if we had gotten pinched off between drops—a mere seven feet almost leaves us stuck. Embarrassing but true.

Finally, after some hard scramble, with constant back-and-forth mutterings between us of "I don't remember this . . . Do you remember this?" we wend our way back up the slot. We finally reach a nice rock shelf and stop for sandwiches. It's been about two hours since we entered the rift. As we eat, I'm struck with a sense of insignificance. The boulder we climbed over might have been stuck there since Europeans first arrived in North America, or it could have been lodged there yesterday. I cannot tell. There next to us is an old twisted pinion whose branches are yet full of living green and flourishing exuberance, as wide in trunk girth as any I've ever seen. We speculate it might be two hundred years old. Maybe six hundred. I wonder how time passes for a thing that was likely already ancient when I was born.

And the canyon itself. There is a presence here. I cannot describe it. I've tried to write it, but it won't come, so I yield. It is not a sense of watchfulness, because I feel I don't matter here. I feel small. Nothing. I sense I am but a fleeting thing, like the fly that lands on my hand, takes a taste with its proboscis, then disappears. Around me are old, old ancient things. They seem present and godlike. It would not surprise me that once people fell to their knees before it. But now I just feel like a minor thread in a grander tale. This seems like a sacred place suddenly. An old holiness.

After a time. We make it out and find a jeep trail. That sense of the sacred seems to dissipate. We are back in secular time. The path joins a well-marked dirt road that we follow. We reach the top of a slickrock knoll and sit for another apple. As we sit there, a shiny yellow jeep drives past. A shirtless man in a cowboy hat, his head out the driver's side window as he negotiates the rock, sees us. We wave, two characters grinning like hobbits on a stroll. Silly looking if the pictures we took from that knoll with the La Sals in the background target our aspect in any way aright. He does not wave back, but gives a slight reluctant nod as if we spoil his manly pursuits. He roars past and we hear his engine a long time after. Finally, the sound of the wind returns and we rise and start our walk back to the main road.

Hawks and I have aged. Our joints are complaining, and we both comment that we will likely be sore in the morning. How did we reach middle age? It was only yesterday we were eighteen. Heck, in my head I'm still eighteen. It's only the rest of me that protests its age. Unexpectedly, I remember a poem from Tennyson that brings out a smile and causes me to straighten my back a bit and step forward with a little more verve.

A fitting capstone remembered only in part then, but here repeated:

> *Though much is taken, much abides; and though*
> *We are not now that strength which in old days*
> *Moved earth and heaven, that which we are, we are—*
> *One equal temper of heroic hearts,*
> *Made weak by time and fate, but strong in will*
> *To strive, to seek, to find, and not to yield.*[1]

II.

Boundaries, the natural and the metaphorical structure so much of our world and our life. I've thought about this while adventuring in the wild, and I've also written about it philosophically.[2] I'm not a professional philosopher, mind you, but once in a while I like to safety-pin on a philosopher's cape and don a paper-cutout mask and whoosh around the room jumping off the low furniture. Occasionally, real philosophers will pat me on the head, and say, "Isn't he cute!" and let me play around their feet. As I ruminate on boundaries, I suddenly wonder: Are there boundaries and ecotones in *sacred* spaces, in the transitions between sacred spaces— those markers that disclose and define a sacred space? I think so.

Consider Çatalhöyük, a large Neolithic ritual center in the Anatolia region of Turkey occupied from 7500 to 5700 BC. Found in the ruins of these structures were platforms and panels decorated with etched bulls and bull-horned pedestals. Presumably rituals took place there. Animal or human blood was found on some of the altars. What's more interesting to me, however, is that the entrance into the sacred space required a formal transition from the outside to the inside. Archaeologists Lewis-Williams and Pearce describe entrance into this ritual center:

> Access between rooms was afforded not by full-length doors but by small porthole-like openings through which people were obligated to crawl. . . . Entry into a complex of rooms thus entailed, first, descent into a dimly lit area; secondly, having descended, people had to crawl or bend low in order to move from one walled space to another and thus deeper into the structure.[3]

In other words, people had to transition from the secular, ordinary world of day-to-day life to the world of ritual. Sacred spaces had to be entered formally. This holds for later civilizations from ancient Israel to Egypt and beyond. Most ancient ritual centers unearthed by archaeologists all over the world—even those that predate civilization and domestic crops, like Göbekli Tepe from the twelfth century BC—seem to provide openings and borders that allowed a prescribed transition into sacred space. As Latter-day Saints, we too do this when we enter our sacred temples. We sometimes begin this transition before arriving at the temple by fasting or praying about something in particular. We change from our regular clothes to church clothes. This is just the first step. As Hugh Nibley has eloquently described, we go through a process of passing through guardians who are set to ensure we have the proper credentials to enter the sacred space, and we transition further by entering an area specifically set aside to put on white clothes that will be worn during our "work" within the temple.[4] All of these activities are undertaken in preparation to enter sacred space. We encounter still more transitions throughout the temple ceremony itself. These transition places form border areas, an ecotone of sorts, as I talked about in part 1.

I don't think we can think about sacred space without thinking about sacred time. Like the space-time manifold Einstein has argued we live in, I'm quite certain that even though sacred space and sacred time can be decoupled conceptually, the lived experience of sacred space requires, at least, a temporal dimension. Abraham Heschel, the Jewish philosopher, touches on this in his description of the temporal boundary that frames the Sabbath:

When all work is brought to a standstill the candles are lit. Just as creation began with the word, "Let there be light!" so does the celebration of creation begin with the kindling of lights. It is the woman who ushers in the joy and sets up the most exquisite symbol, light, to dominate the atmosphere of the home.

And the world becomes a place of rest.[5]

The temporal passage from regular time to sacred time embodies both natural events (such as the setting of the sun) and human actions (like setting aside work and lighting the candles) that mark, signify, and symbolize the transition of boundaries. Also at play are human memory, tradition, and recognition that a boundary is being crossed. The "now" being created is different from, and holier than, that of a moment ago. The transition is often a social act, with others present (perhaps God as the only other "other").

Of course, space and time are not so easily separable, and any discussion of time usually returns us back to a discussion of space. Besides formal, set-aside sacred spaces that we must transition to, such as the temple in Salt Lake City or Turkey's Çatalhöyük, there are sacred spaces that emerge out of the complex relationship between the spatial location, its history, human memory, or the complex relationships of sociality. To get a sense for what I'm trying to explain, consider this personal experience of mine where circumstance, history, and memory combined to transport my social experience into a sacred realm:

As a young man serving in the army, I was touring Israel with a tour group from Germany, where I was stationed. About half of us were LDS, including my army chaplain and his family. He brought them there, in part, in order to baptize his son in the Jordan River. At some point on the trip (I don't remember where we were along the river—I just rode the bus and got on and off when they told me), we piled out and I watched as my chaplain, dressed in white, waded into the muddy water with his son. Nothing about the place seemed remarkable. It reminded me nothing so much as the little dry-land rivers we used to fish in near Evanston, Wyoming, when I was a kid—desolate and wind-riven. Something like tamarisk grew along the banks in patches of mud. It seemed an unpleasant place. Dirty and mucky.

There was a bit of exasperation in the group, as some seemed impatient and eager to move on to our next stop. Maybe I was one of them. But suddenly, as our LDS army chaplain raised his hand to the square, Primary paintings of John the Baptist and Jesus standing in the same river that I now stood beside popped into my mind. The place changed quite dramatically. I was there on the banks of the River Jordan, watching the same thing that was done anciently. The river was no longer a muddy creek. It was shifting to a new place under my very feet. The boy came out of the water. It felt holy. And then a dove cooed. I looked up and saw a pair of doves sitting high in some trees overhanging the river. No one that knows the ecosystems of the Holy Land would be surprised by doves along the Jordan River. But at that moment, in that place, a sense of its sacredness filled me up.

"And the Holy Ghost descended in a bodily shape like a dove upon him" (Luke 3:22).

I could not speak. I tried to say something about the doves but could not open my mouth. I pointed them out to someone, but he was not interested. I, however, was breathless. What took place in that instant between standing beside a common muddy river and suddenly standing in a holy place? It took a combination of place, memory, and recognition. The holiness stretched from horizon to horizon, as if for me the entire world had been made holy by this one place. A place contextualized by the events, people and memories coming together in complex, emergent ways. Like an ecology, several layers added to the depth and meaning.

III.

Sacred space always involves a transition from the secular into that location deemed holy. This transition is not something we often talk or think about directly, and something seems missing in the very telling. And yet, trying to understand moments and places of transition seems to be an important part of defining and interacting with our sacred spaces. Like an ecotone, these present us with an area of in-between-ness that is unique and contingent upon its standing as a boundary between spaces.

Even now, as I finish polishing this essay, I look out over my backyard and let the memories of my hike with Hawks, the baptism at the River Jordan, and other sacred spaces fade as I transition from memory to an awareness of the present. I notice the lawn needs mowing, that the badminton net is sagging, that the sun is making its way along a downhill slope to the horizon. I rise. The memories are sticky, and I do not reenter the mundane world easily. Transitions take time. But by the time I pull the rope to tauten the net line, I'm looking around to see if anyone wants to play a game, reorienting myself to new concerns.

Notes

1. Alfred Lord Tennyson, *Ulysses*, http://www.eecs.harvard.edu/~keith/poems/Ulysses.html.

2. See Steven L. Peck, "Whose boundary? An Individual Species Perspectival Approach to Borders," *Biological Theory* 4/3 (2009): 274-79.

3. David Lewis-Williams and David Pearce, *Inside the Neolithic Mind: Consciousness, Cosmos and the Realm of the Gods* (New York: Thames & Hudson, 2005), 105.

4. See, for example, the essays collected in Hugh Nibley, *Eloquent Witness: Nibley on Himself, Others, and the Temple* (Salt Lake City: Deseret Book and FARMS, 2008).

5. Abraham Joshua Heschel, *The Sabbath* (New York: Farrar, Straus and Giroux, 1951), 66.

Appendix

Selected Published Works of Steven L. Peck

Selected Peer-Reviewed Papers

"Resuscitation and Resurrection: The Ethics of Cloning Cheetahs, Mammoths, and Neanderthals." *Life Sciences, Society and Policy* 10/3 (2014), doi:10.1186/2195-7819-10-3. Coauthored by Sariah Cottrell and Jamie L. Jensen.

"Life as Emergent Agential Systems: Tendencies without Teleology in an Open Universe." *Zygon: Journal of Religion and Science* 48/4 (2013): 984–1000.

"Digital Ecologies as Tractarian Systems." *Philosophy Study* 3/1 (2013): 64–69.

"Why Nature Matters." *Dialogue: A Journal of Mormon Thought* 44/2 (2011): 1–5.

"Death and the Ecological Crisis." *Agriculture and Human Values* 27/1 (2010): 105–9.

"Crawling Out of the Primordial Soup: A Step toward the Emergence of an LDS Theology Compatible with Organic Evolution." *Dialogue: A Journal of Mormon Thought* 43/1 (2010): 1–36.

"Whose Boundary? An Individual Species Perspectival Approach to Borders." *Biological Theory* 4/3 (2009): 274–79.

"My Madness." *Dialogue: A Journal of Mormon Thought* 41/2 (2008): 57–70.

"An Ecologist's View of LDS Culture and the Current Environmental Crisis." In George B. Handley, Terry B. Ball, and Steven L. Peck, eds. *Sacred Stewardship and the Creation: LDS Perspectives on the Environment*. Provo, UT: Religious Studies Center, Brigham Young University, 2006.

Sacred Stewardship: LDS Perspectives on the Environment. Provo, UT: Religious Studies Center, Brigham Young University, 2006. Coauthored by George B. Handley and Terry B. Ball.

"The Current Philosophy of Consciousness Landscape: Where Does LDS Thought Fit?" *Dialogue: A Journal of Mormon Thought* 38/1 (2005): 36-64.

"Randomness, Contingency, and Faith: Is There a Science of Subjectivity?" *Zygon: Journal of Religion and Science* 38/1 (2003): 5-24. (Also included in Sara Fletcher Harding and Nancy Morvillo, eds. *Religion and Science: Critical Concepts in Religion Studies.* Volume 4. London: Routledge, 2010.)

"Two Soldiers Gathered in His Name." *Ensign.* March 1997, 66-67.

"Water, Mud and Insects." *The Friend.* May 1995, 28-29.

Fiction

Novels

Rifts of Rime. Cedar Fort Press, 2012.

A Short Stay in Hell. Strange Violin Editions, 2012.

The Scholar of Moab. Torrey House Press, 2011. Finalist for the Hoffer Montaigne Medal and Association for Mormon Letters Best Novel of 2011.

The Gift of the King's Jeweler. Covenant Communications, 2003.

Short Stories

"Tales from Pleasant Grove," *Every Day Fiction*, 2015, http://everydayfiction .com/.

"Down Courthouse Wash," *Perihelion*, 2015, http://www.perihelionsf.com/.

Wandering Realities: Mormonish Short Fiction. Zarahemla Books, 2015.

"Démodé." *Nature Physics* 10/1 (2014): 80, doi:10.1038/nphys2860.

"Plague Ship." Published in the anthology *Space Eldritch II: The Haunted Stars* (2013).

"How the Mother of Vampiro Rojo de Santanás Died at the Hand of the Ethicless Thing." *Silverthought Press Online*, 2013.

"The Silence of the River." *Quantum Realities: A Journal of Speculative Fiction* 2/2 (2013): 48-70.

"Emergence." *Encounters Magazine* 2/6 (2013): 58-74.

"Dragonfly Miscalculations." *The Journal of Unlikely Entomology* 3 (May 2012).

"Should I Tell Her?" *Daily Science Fiction*, 2012, http://dailysciencefiction.com/.

"A Strange Report from the Church Archives." *Irreantum*, 2011, http://irreantum.mormonletters.org/winners.aspx. Second-place contest winner.

"Let the Mountains Tremble for Adoniha Has Fallen." In *Monsters and Mormons*. Edited by Wm. Morris and Theric Jepson. El Cerrito, CA: Peculiar Pages, 2011.

"The Flaw in the Lord Harrington Scenario." *HMS Beagle*, 2001 (online science journal by Elsevier).

Poetry

Incorrect Astronomy. Hemet, CA: Aldrich Press, 2013. This work is a collection of poetry.

"What the Ant Knows & Walks the Ape Warder." *Silver Blade*, issue 14, 2012, http://silverblade.silverpen.org/content/.

"Four Poems." In *Fire in the Pasture: Twenty-First-Century Mormon Poets*. Edited by Tyler Chadwick. El Cerrito, CA: Peculiar Pages, 2011.

"The Five Known Sutras of Mechanical Man. *Tales of the Talisman* 6/2 (2010): 50. Nominated for the Rhysling Award.

"Winter Gifts." *Victorian Violet Press Poetry Journal* 5 (2010).

"Sage." *Red Rock Review* 22 (Spring 2008): 87.

"Ant Lion." *Glyphs III* (2007): 141–43.

"Reflections of Stellar Ecology." *BYU Studies* 33/4 (1993): 742.

"Advice on Correct Astronomy." *BYU Studies* 35/1 (1995): 40.

"Winton Night Walks." *Dialogue: A Journal of Mormon Thought* 21/2 (1988): 155.

Fiction Awards

2015 Best Short Story Published in 2014. Association for Mormon Letters Short Fiction Award for "Two-Dog Dose," published in *Dialogue: A Journal of Mormon Thought* 47/1 (2014).

2012 Four Centuries of Mormon Stories Contest. First place for "Avek, Who Is Distributed."

2012 Four Centuries of Mormon Stories Contest. Second place for "When the Bishop Started Killing Dogs."

2012 Irreantum Literary Fiction Contest. Second place for "A Strange Report from the Church Archives."

2012 Best Novel published in 2011. Association for Mormon Letters. Finalist for the Hoffer Montaigne Medal for *The Scholar of Moab*, Torrey House Press.

2011 Nominated for the Science Fiction Poetry Association's Rhysling Award for "The Five Known Sutras of Mechanical Man."

2010 Sunstone Eugene England Memorial Essay Contest. Second Place.

2010 Honorable mention in the 2010 Brookie and D. K. Brown Fiction Contest for "The Problem."

2010 *Warp and Weave* Science Fiction Short Story. First place for "Stratton Yellows."

Blogs

By Common Consent, writing under SteveP, http://bycommonconsent.com/.
The Mormon Organon, http://sciencebysteve.net/.

STEVEN L. PECK is an associate professor of biology at Brigham Young University, where he teaches courses including "The History and Philosophy of Biology" and "Bioethics." His research in theoretical mathematical ecology and insect populations has been recognized by the National Academy of Sciences and the United Nations for helping to fight insect-borne illness. His published works include over forty scientific articles in prominent publications like *American Naturalist*, *Newsweek*, and *Zygon*; fictional works like *The Scholar of Moab* and *A Short Stay in Hell*; and a number of poems and short stories.

A
Living Faith
Book

LIVING FAITH books are for readers who cherish the life of the mind and the things of the Spirit. Each title is a unique example of faith in search of understanding, the voice of a scholar who has cultivated a believing heart while engaged in the disciplines of the Academy.

Other LIVING FAITH books include:

Adam S. Miller, *Letters to a Young Mormon*

Samuel M. Brown, *First Principles and Ordinances: The Fourth Article of Faith in Light of the Temple*